My Dear Li

My Dear Li

Correspondence 1937–1946

Werner and Elisabeth Heisenberg

EDITED BY

ANNA MARIA HIRSCH-HEISENBERG

AND TRANSLATED BY

IRENE HEISENBERG

Yale UNIVERSITY PRESS/NEW HAVEN & LONDON

Published with assistance from the Mary Cady Tew Memorial Fund.

The translation of this work was supported by a grant from the Goethe-Institut, which is funded by the German Ministry of Foreign Affairs.

Yale University Press books may be purchased in quantity for educational, business, or promotional use. For information, please e-mail sales.press@yale.edu (U.S. office) or sales@yaleup.co.uk (U.K. office).

Designed by Mary Valencia
Set in Fournier type by Westchester Publishing Services
Printed in the United States of America.

All photographs courtesy Heisenberg family archives.

Library of Congress Control Number: 2016931969
ISBN 978-0-300-19693-1 (cloth : alk. paper)

A catalogue record for this book is available from the British Library.

This paper meets the requirements of ANSI/NISO Z39.48-1992 (Permanence of Paper).

10 9 8 7 6 5 4 3 2 1

For my siblings,
Wolfgang, Jochen, Martin, Barbara, Christine, and Verena

CONTENTS

TRANSLATOR'S NOTE

AN INTIMATE TEXT such as these letters must meet a high standard of authenticity to be as credible and persuasive in translation as it is in the original. I thank Maria Hirsch for her wise stewardship of this correspondence and, ultimately, for the decision to publish it. No other document about or by Werner Heisenberg is as immediate. Even his autobiography is couched in tentative language—"I may have said"—as he is mindful of the fact that memory is not infallible and therefore not equal to the truth.

To transmit this characteristic precision and thus carefully render his words was my foremost goal not only for his voice but equally for Elisabeth's. Heisenberg's frequent qualifiers in a sentence, seemingly unimportant, or his style of routinely placing the logical emphasis at the beginning were essentially maintained, as was the informal use of semicolons. Although the letters were written spontaneously, often hastily, they consistently show the disciplined, reflective minds and undisguised hearts of two extraordinary people.

Reading the letters on the west side of the Atlantic, with its very different historic experience of wartime Nazi Germany, may require an open and discerning mind, as it is a significant change of perspective. The full consequences of Heisenberg's choice to remain in his country under Hitler are visible in the many details that are so faithfully exchanged between the couple. These range from factual descriptions of the war to profound reflections to the minutiae of family life. One may come away from reading these letters in genuine awe of Heisenberg's steadfast determination that science, truth, and love must survive as central values throughout—and beyond—the long period of Germany's dark perversion. In Elisabeth he had found, intuitively, a most suitable partner who shared his core beliefs decidedly, bravely, and lovingly.

I want to thank Yale University Press and in particular Joseph Calamia for his skillful guidance. I am grateful also to the Goethe-Institut and Stephen S. Wilson for his contributions to the translation. Without the valuable insights and generous assistance of my husband, Jochen, this work could not have been completed. We both appreciate the meticulous editing through which Robin DuBlanc brings this seventy-year-old correspondence into the present.

Irene Heisenberg
Durham, New Hampshire,
May 2015

WHEN MY MOTHER DIED in 1998, I inherited two carefully wrapped bundles of letters: my father's to her and hers to him. At my mother's wish, the letters came to me as the eldest daughter. Around this time the debate about my father's role in World War II was rekindled, partly prompted by Michael Frayn's play *Copenhagen;* thus I decided to take a closer look at the letters my father had written from 1937 to 1946. Perhaps they might shed some light on his wartime experiences as well as what he thought and felt about the aberrations and catastrophes of that time.

Immediately and increasingly captivated, I began to transcribe the letters. It soon became clear to me that they would not reveal direct answers to the political questions that are so readily discussed today—such as any statement about the Jewish Question or about Hitler and National Socialism; those topics were taboo. But in their immediacy, the letters show what enabled my father to survive this merciless time. First and foremost, this was Elisabeth: his wife, our mother. Her great love and mental vitality—added to her increasing proficiency in managing domestic issues—gave him, time and again, the strength to remain true to his intentions. In every one of his letters, one can sense this close, strength-giving relationship. Thus I decided to read and transcribe my mother's letters also. I became increasingly impressed by the interplay between the couple, by their unconditional love, their motivation to share their lives, no matter the adversity, and to pull through together. Each complemented and completed the other: the youthful vivacity of Elisabeth (fourteen years younger than her husband) energized my father even as his mature judgment and life experience provided her with the support she needed to develop her own strength. Their correspondence is an impressive testimonial of conjugal love and loyalty.

Initially, I transcribed the letters envisioning their audience as my siblings, children, and grandchildren. I had often felt in family conversations that overly simplified clichéd ideas derived from books, articles, films, and the political trends of the day were pushing the reality of my father's life and experiences further and further into the background. There is no other medium that reproduces experienced reality as authentically as letters do. Even written or recounted memories are always already somewhat removed from the reality. Moreover, contemporary witnesses, able to report on the war years from personal experience, are becoming rarer, so that firsthand knowledge about that time is decreasing.

Thus, the question of publication for a wider audience naturally arose, and after consultation with my siblings and friends, I decided upon it. There were three factors, each quite different and each crucial, that led to my decision.

First, the letters constitute an important historical testimony both in terms of what they report and of what they do not address. Particularly in the later years of the war, it is markedly evident that all statements that could be construed as a criticism of the prevailing conditions had to be carefully avoided. For example, whenever there is any breaking military news, Elisabeth writes: "Oh, my dear, dear heart! If only one could talk with you." Anything written was in danger of falling into the wrong hands. Only once is Werner indiscreet, carried away after an important meeting with minister of the Reich Albert Speer and senior representatives of the military in June 1942, when he reports to his wife about the "festivities at court." In his next letter, he immediately inquires with concern whether the letter had arrived safely.

More frequent and tangible are the letters' depictions of an everyday life increasingly consumed by the struggle to obtain daily necessities as the war proceeds. Nothing remains routine: shopping turns into a lottery, travel into a dangerous adventure, and the nights into nightmares. In addition, the proliferation of government decrees and regulations increasingly constricts people's individual activities. Is it any wonder that mental strength at such a time was directed toward simply surviving to the next day, leaving no room for broader political concerns?

My second reason for publication is that the correspondence provides an important contribution to the recurring questions relating to Werner Heisenberg: why did he not emigrate, like so many others? Did he want to build the atomic bomb for Hitler? Did he try to?

During his travels in 1939 (and even after the war), it was repeatedly suggested to him that he should come to America. He knew that working and living conditions there would be far more favorable than in Germany. Moreover, he liked America and believed that Germany would lose the war. But emigration would have seemed like desertion to him. A comfortable life for himself was not his priority. He felt responsible for his staff and his colleagues, and he saw it as his mandate to help preserve science in his country in "the time afterward," when a new order would be established in Europe. He did not allow himself to be swayed from that objective, however hard it sometimes was for him.

He was not happy in his professional duties as a professor in Leipzig and as scientific director of the "Uranium Project" in Berlin. He complained time and time again in his letters about the "futility" of his work. However, he had good reasons not to turn down the Uranium Project, which was offered to him by the Army Ordnance Office [Heereswaffenamt], because that way he retained control of the ongoing atomic research and was able to protect himself and his staff from being sent to the front. He had no idea of the dangers this position brought with it, however. In 1941 he had come to recognize that the building of an atomic bomb, although theoretically possible, was not a realistic undertaking for Germany during wartime. He was able to convince the Army Command [Heeresleitung] that there was insufficient time to build such a weapon to decide the war, but that it would be completely sensible to continue research into the peaceful use of atomic energy for the postwar period. Thus he was able to remain true to his goals of doing something for "the time afterward," retaining control of atomic research, and protecting his staff from military service.

My father could never afford to drop his guard; he needed not only to abstain from active resistance but to demonstrate his loyalty to his country, especially abroad. The effort weighed heavily on him, often bringing him to the brink of exhaustion. Witness his letters, in which he repeatedly expresses that he is unable to do that which he was essentially made for: undertake the "undisturbed inquiry into nature." As a substitute for this, he uses his free moments to escape into his "private philosophy," resulting in "Reality and Its Order" (*Ordnung der Wirklichkeit*), in which he counters the destruction of his time. (This manuscript, not intended for publication, was published [in German] only after his death as part of his complete works.)

The building of an atomic bomb was out of the question for him. After the war also, he actively voiced his opposition to arming the German Armed Forces [Bundeswehr] with atomic weapons. After the dropping of the bomb on Hiroshima, he wrote to his wife that his "British and American colleagues . . . have my sympathy, because their names are now tied to this atrocity."

My third reason, not the least of the three, for publishing my parents' correspondence is to showcase its testimony to the strength of a marital partnership. Theirs was not a relationship in which each partner insists on his or her own need, but instead a mutually loving bond in which each helps the other weather the storms of life. The portraits the letters give of the house in the mountains, far from the centers of political power, and the flourishing of the family act as a counterpoint to the disintegration of the period and also as a guarantee that there will be a "time afterward," a time when hope can be renewed. "We will have no choice but to pass through this purgatory," writes Werner in a letter to his wife, but both he and Elisabeth draw strength from their union. As he writes to her in his last letter before their wedding: "I have the firm conviction that we are a good match for each other and that we are better able to do justice to our place in the world by being together."

It was, of course, essential to condense the correspondence considerably; otherwise, it would have gone beyond the scope of a readable book. The cuts were not as difficult as I had initially feared because such a correspondence, by necessity, will contain many repetitions, unimportant references (regarding scheduling and other organizational issues, for example), and allusions to people and telephone conversations no longer of interest to today's reader. However, I have made an effort to retain all that is historically relevant as well as descriptions of the writers' experiences, reflections, and thoughts, all the while attempting to avoid jarring gaps. Only when it came to descriptions of life in the nursery have I sometimes made energetic cuts. All omissions are indicated by ellipses. The unabridged text of the letters and the diary entries is available for viewing at the Heisenberg Archive of the Max-Planck-Gesellschaft in Berlin. Two letters appear here that were not included in the German edition: one from Werner's travels to England (written from Manchester in March 1938), and one from America (written July 24, 1939).

Placing the letters in a chronologically coherent sequence was anything but easy: a great number of them, particularly from my mother, are missing, and their dating is often incomplete and imprecise, particularly regarding the year. Moreover, letters often crossed in transit, thwarting a straightforward chronological ordering: for example, a letter from each might have been written on the same day, yet an answer only came days later. I often had to complete the precise dating of the letters myself or deduce them from the content. Those additions are given in square brackets.

The letters are ordered by year, and each year is preceded by a short introduction to the most important events that took place then. Occasionally, explanatory comments are inserted. Overall, though, I have tried to let the letters speak for themselves. An exception is the year 1945. For a better understanding of the events associated with the end of the war for the family, I have introduced into the correspondence my father's diary entries for the last fourteen days before his arrest in Urfeld. These entries are published here for the first time.

I would like to thank my siblings for their support. I am grateful to the Residenz Verlag and my editor Dr. Sippl for her expert help.

Anna Maria Hirsch
Feldafing,
June 2011

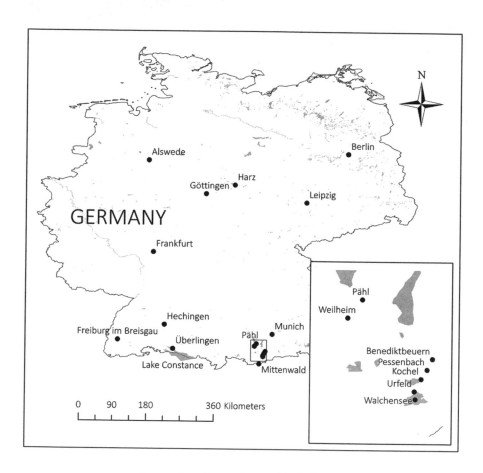

German locations referenced in the letters

The Correspondence

1937

WERNER HEISENBERG *is thirty-five years old when he meets the twenty-two-year-old Elisabeth Schumacher in January 1937. Since 1927 he has been an established professor of theoretical physics at Leipzig University, and in 1933 he was awarded the Nobel Prize for Physics. He owns a house on Bozener Weg. Yet in several respects all is not well with him: the political situation and the beginning exodus of German scientists are weighing on him. He personally is confronted with considerable hostility and accused of being a "White Jew" in the* Völkischer Beobachter *(the "Nazi" newspaper of the National Socialist German Workers' Party) because, steadfastly, he presents Einstein's theory of relativity ("Jewish physics") in his lectures. His chances of being appointed as the successor to Arnold Sommerfeld, professor of theoretical physics at the University of Munich, are successfully torpedoed by the "German physicists." (Philipp Lenard and Johannes Stark, Nobel Laureates, proclaimed that only experimental physics was "Aryan physics.") In his private life, too, he has disappointments: he has to bury the hope of being united with the sister of his best friend, Carl Friedrich von Weizsäcker. It is not surprising that his physical health also suffers at this time.*

What always restores his comfort and zest for life is playing music with others, and it is at one such musical evening at the Bückings, a family of publishers in Leipzig, that he meets Elisabeth Schumacher. Having broken off her study of art history in Freiburg im Breisgau, she has only recently arrived in Leipzig to begin an apprenticeship in the Bücking publishing house. She is the fourth of five children of Hermann Schumacher, the respected professor of economics at the University of Berlin; Hermann Jr., Edith, and Fritz are several years older than she, and Ernst, a late arrival, is nine years younger. The father, almost seventy years old at the time, is a stern and hot-tempered family patriarch who tolerates no contradiction, thus making life difficult for his wife and children. Elisabeth's own excitable impulsivity mirrors her father's; the two clashed over her decision to give up the university career he wanted for her.

On that evening, January 28, 1937, Elisabeth makes the acquaintance of Werner Heisenberg, who is playing piano trios with the violinist Erwin Jacobi and the host. Family lore has it that Werner won Elisabeth's heart with Beethoven's "Largo con espressione" from the piano trio Op 1., No. 2. In any case, something akin to a flash of lightning must have passed between the two, as only fourteen days later, Werner writes to his mother:

Yesterday—assuming your approval—I became engaged. The friendship with Elisabeth is scarcely fourteen days old and arose out of an, at first, seemingly casual conversation at a social gathering, in which a close affinity of opinions on matters of central importance emerged between the two of us. This mutual understanding, in which one, as it were, only needed to continue a conversation begun a long time ago, soon went so deep that it seemed natural to me to ask Elisabeth whether she would like to be with me forever.

Father Schumacher could certainly not raise any objections to such a son-in-law. However, he asserts his authority one more time by insisting that the wedding should take place only after the elder brother, Hermann, already engaged, had celebrated his wedding, and that the married couple should be chauffeured to the station after the wedding, even though the groom had wished to leave in his own car.

Werner and Elisabeth's wedding is set for April 29, and the weeks leading up to it—as the following letters from the period of their engagement show—were filled with preparations for their married life in Leipzig.

Werner to Elisabeth

Leipzig, March 15
Dear Elisabeth!

It is strange to think that this is the first letter I am writing to you. For it actually seems to me as though, for many years already, we have been close

and acquainted, and the present state of being alone is only a painful interruption in an ever-beautiful, already almost accustomed shared life. I am
indebted to you for bringing me so much peace and security and am looking
forward with my every thought to the time when, together, we can enjoy the
daily changes between the serious and the beautiful. Thank you for
everything!

The ride from Steglitz to Leipzig was not very pleasant in rainy and
stormy weather: I arrived home on the stroke of 12, and was at first no good
for work. In the meantime, however, I have written three pages of the essay
for *Die Antike* and have a pretty clear picture of what it should look like later
on; but I am not happy with my German today, the wording comes out
unsuitable and clumsy; but things can be corrected.

I received a really nice letter of congratulations from Pauli, which I will
show you soon.—

When I collected the music for Saturday, I talked briefly with Mrs.
Mittelstädt and Mrs. Bücking, who could barely contain themselves with
congratulations; we will certainly be celebrated vigorously when we show up
for music together. But of course, at the end of the day, all that is part of it
and does no harm.

What might you be doing this evening? I want to get in an hour of
piano practice, and then catch up on sleep, and I hope that you too are fully
compensating for the shorter periods of sleep over the last few weeks. To
your dear parents: many thanks for these past few days. All my love to you,
I am close to you in my thoughts. Yours, Werner.

Elisabeth to Werner

March 15

My love—

Did you arrive home safely? And now you are already quite buried
in your work—for sure! How glad I am that you stayed on until yesterday,
so that we also had the evening and the morning together!

The day has become long since you left, although a lot has been packed
into it. The nicest thing first: it is this letter from Maria W. [Westphal], which

I am enclosing for you, because it will certainly please you, and because her essence comes across in it as so bright and joyous. I was a little sad, because in my exuberance I gave it to Papa to read and also to Edith, but met with almost no response. That is the same old misery here, which I always had from when I was a child. They never understand what brings me the greatest joy in life, and what I love about people. And I am not someone who can enjoy happiness all on my own. How good it is to have you, that you are there, and that I can make you a gift of everything and all that I have.

Now you may have to write to Rolf [van der Leyden] to tell him that we already have music. Poor soul! But otherwise it will be really all too much, I think.

Also, we have already dealt with the church office. You do not have to do anything else about that. It seems to be going without any problems. We have also been to the civil registration office. There is just a little work for you to do, namely, please fill in this form and have your signature witnessed at the Leipzig civil registration office. Then send your papers along too so that we can do everything for you.

Good night, love! You are so terribly dear to me, and I find myself almost stranded here without you. I will be with you again in five days. Li.

Werner to Elisabeth

[Leipzig], Tuesday after midnight [March 16?]
My dear Li!

I was so happy about your letter that I'm sending you another short greeting, although I am pretty tired. The letter from Maria Westphal is very fine and shows me quite clearly the nature of your mutual appreciation; I'm looking forward very much to getting to know your closest friend, and the music she is playing in our church will be a good way to do that.—I will cancel Rolf, who will understand.

Tomorrow I will fill in the form. You should receive it as soon as possible. In the meantime, my work is progressing fairly well; I hope to finish the essay the day after tomorrow, so that we will have the two days at the end of the week just for us. Perhaps I will be able to play the whole first movement of the Schumann piano concerto for you then; I have studied diligently.

Now be happy, despite the separation; I am looking forward an awful lot to our time together. Yours, Werner.

Elisabeth to Werner

March 16

Dearest—

Just now, as I returned home from Irmgard, I found your letter. Thank you for writing to me immediately. True, I have actually not been quite conscious of the fact that these are the first letters we are writing to each other, so much do we already belong together. But today, now, I'm sensing the meagreness of letter writing a bit because my heart is so full, and only such a very small part of it can reach you. And when that is with you, it will have become something quite independent, when in reality it belongs right in the middle of a whole mountain of thoughts and feelings.

Today is a magnificent spring day here; the storm has swept the sky clean and the birds are singing in deep, full voices already. And so I always trick myself a little, when I sense the spring, and think it will make the weeks shorter and May will come sooner!

I am very curious about your essay, and I am glad that you already have it so well prepared in your mind. Will I be able to understand it?—There is still an indescribable bustle in the house. . . . But when things have become a little quieter here at home, I too will do some work on physics and try to read Zimmer. I am looking forward to it. . . .

This evening I have to be on aunt-visitation—a whole evening! But I will simply think of you the whole time, and then my good cheer will not run out. And you, please, interrupt your work sometimes to go out into the garden and look at how big the tulips have become already which will be in bloom on our wedding day!

All my love to you! I am always totally with you in my heart. Li.

Happily engaged in March 1937: Elisabeth Schumacher and Werner Heisenberg

Werner to Elisabeth

[Leipzig], March 17
My dear Li!

I have a bad conscience today because the form is not yet filled in; when I looked up from my work at the clock, I had just missed the opening hours at the town hall. But I will go to the town hall first thing in the morning. However, today, I am practically done with the essay, and tomorrow I want to just make a few corrections to it. So please forgive my dawdling.

Your letter arrived already very early this morning; thank you for the love that so clearly comes through in your letter.

When I read your letter and think of you, I see how badly I am behaving, in concentrating my thoughts on a piece of work now which is not all that necessary, instead of staying with all my thoughts on everything we share, this great gift to both of us. But as soon as you are here again, I want to forget everything that is not only about us. I believe it would be good in general if, during this summer, physics were pushed into a dark corner, to be picked up again later, for first I have more to learn from you than from all the treatises in the world.

When you come on Sunday, there will be more flowers in bloom in the garden already than last time, and the tulips will have grown considerably bigger. I am looking forward so much to our time together! Yours, Werner.

Elisabeth to Werner

Wednesday, late evening [March 17?]
Dearest—

What a full day of work! With my sleeves rolled up, and clad in a big blue apron, I rushed around the house all day long—I cleaned, I washed, and I accomplished an awful lot. And in the midst of all this labor, your letter came like a sparkling ray of sunshine. Do you even know how I cherish you? Never forget it, not for a moment.

I am so glad that work is progressing so well. But, you know, Werner, when you are at times unable to write because of so much work, do not think that I might be sad. I know, of course, that you are with me in your heart all the same, right? I am hardly a capricious, unreasonable female! But for me, any day on which I cannot tell you things does not feel quite right. And I can, can't I, tell you each amusing remark and every little foolishness?

This evening, Ernst played the violin a little and I was pleased how clean and simple it was. You must play music with him sometime. There is altogether so much more light in our house than earlier, so much more life and joy. And I am so enormously grateful to fate, that now I can make up for so much of the pain I caused my parents in earlier years. I have often had a terrible fear that the time would come when it might be too late. And so often I felt I had to lay whole kingdoms at Mutti's feet because she is someone for whom life is always somewhat too burdensome. And then I would think: later, when something has become of me, I will return, and I will have no more barbs and I can spoil her to my heart's content. And now, suddenly, everything has fallen into my hands and I can make her happy. And so I am ever more showered by good fortune! And even when it is often also painful that I cannot be with you, I am grateful for this time, precisely for this reason.

Edith has just come home, so I must close, since she wants to go to sleep; she has moved down to me again so that we can chat a little sometimes before nodding off.

Good night, dearest. Only two more days, and then I am coming to you again! I am looking forward to it so terribly much. Li.

Werner to Elisabeth

[Leipzig], Thursday afternoon [March 18?]
Dear good Elisabeth!

It is nice that you write to me so often; thus I am practically always with you and involved in whatever you encounter.

You can see from the many papers that, in the meantime, I have been to the civil registration office. The clerk, who apparently had counted on a slow day, was clearly irritated by the disturbance I caused. When I produced your form, he immediately stressed: "Forms from Berlin are out of the question for us." After some gentle persuasion, he then issued a form from Saxony, which one hopes will serve the same purpose. According to him, you also need my birth certificate and my parents' marriage certificate. I am enclosing both; hopefully you will not have any more problems.

My essay is ready and is now being typed; I can now show it to you the day after tomorrow. When are you actually coming? Write and tell me when I can pick you up. (As soon as possible!)

The final rehearsal for the St. Matthew Passion is on Thursday evening. I have reserved two tickets for us, and I am looking forward to share this most serious side of art with you also.

In the meantime, I have planted the lilac bush from Munich in the garden. . . . A few hepatica and cowslips are now in flower in the large flower-bed. There are also quite a few of the small blue ones that also grow in your garden already up; only the crocuses are a little late. There is something calming and heartening in observing nature, day by day, as it slowly ventures out with new life and changes old and ugly disarray, almost effortlessly, into something orderly and alive.

But now this letter must get to the post office for registered mail. So good-bye until we meet again, fortunately in less than forty-eight hours! Yours, Werner.

Elisabeth to Werner

Thursday, March 18
Dearest—
Today you only get a short little letter, for I am so tired, I can scarcely think anymore. . . .

I am so very glad that you have finished the essay so quickly. You must have been mighty busy! And, you know, dearest, I am very glad that you had this work, for then the days pass much more quickly and smoothly. It's good that way. If you wish to take some time off from physics in the summer, dearest, that would naturally be for me a little like being in paradise. And you can be quite sure that I will never be upset later on, when you spend long periods of time on nothing else but physics. It needs you, too—I know that. And I am good on my own, when I know that you love me.

Look, now I can already say I will be with you again the day after tomorrow! Li.

Werner to Elisabeth

[Leipzig], Thursday evening [April 1?]
My dear good Li!

It is nice that I can come to you again after the various activities of the
day to share and consult with you. On the face of it, nothing much has
happened since I returned home; but I need to tell you mainly what the
doctor found out about poor physical me. It was deemed overall completely
in order, nothing wrong with the major organs; but the glandular system is
not yet fully recovered from the illness five years ago. The liver is not quite
functioning properly, the pancreas also sometimes seems to go on strike a
little and, as a result, the red blood cells count is only 84 percent of what it
should be if they behaved decently. This is the cause of my frequent malaise.
The doctor thinks that I should have it looked at more closely to see what the
matter is; to this end I have to go on an extremely boring basic diet for three
days before I can have a blood test, etc. to determine the extent of this
deficiency. He deemed it not really worrisome, and definitely not a hindrance
to marriage. [Physical suitability for marriage was a legal prerequisite.] It
may just mean that I might have to follow a very specific dietary regimen for
a long time for everything to be in order again. Besides, my personal opinion
is, that when I am really doing well in my soul, which will be the case in four
weeks, then the boring glands too will catch on to the changed situation.
Incidentally, the next checkup will be early on Monday.

But how is your knee? Write and tell me soon what other doctors have to
say about it.—By the way, for the above reasons, I will unfortunately not be
able to leave Leipzig before Sunday evening. You know that I would like it if
you came here. But if it is better for you to stay in Berlin, then stay; we will
see each other again on Friday afternoon at the latest.

I was so pleased with the days in Berlin, most of all with our walks. We
will have to make much room for this outdoor life later on in our activity
schedule.

Now see to it that your knee will be better again soon, and be cheerful.
Yours, Werner.

Elisabeth to Werner

April 1

Dear Werner—

What happened today? What did the doctor say? All my thoughts are with you, and I am having great difficulty getting used to this state of not really being near you. And now they will not even let me come to you on Saturday. In addition, today my leg was put in a large stiff bandage, and extreme rest has been advised, so that any chance of coming to you yet is lost.

Now I want to report exactly what they found today. Gocht himself was away, and will only be back next week. His assistant gave me a thorough examination and had me X-rayed. The result is not yet available. He said that there were several indications that the meniscus has a tear. . . .

And now my leg has been very thickly bandaged and I am creeping about like an old woman. The idea is that the hematoma that is still in the joint should disappear. I have to go back in eight days. I will then be seen by Gocht himself. Things do not look very rosy. Well—this whole thing cannot do us much harm, and perhaps nature on its own will prevail, and everything will heal much more quickly than all the doctors think, who easily and sometimes too readily make you much more sick than you actually are. So do not be dismayed if you too have been afflicted now. Things will surely improve as soon as we are married, right, dearest?

This morning I worked on something quite amusing and very peculiar. Namely, I have a large box in the attic filled to the rim with old letters, diaries, school-related papers, and the like. I wanted to tackle all of it because it is impossible to simply just keep everything. The diaries held me captive for a long time; they immediately reawakened a long-forgotten past. But it is odd that it now appears so unfamiliar, while at the time it was lived with such eagerness and such fervor. And it almost felt as though one were entering a cemetery, where lots of people are buried, whom you knew and were connected to, and yet you are glad that these times are gone. So I threw all these diaries into the fire. All of it amounted merely to a groping and searching; the real life is only now beginning. . . . Good night, dearest. I now want to be where you are! Li.

Werner to Elisabeth

[Leipzig], Friday evening [April 2?]
Dear little Li!

How nice that you wrote to me in so much detail! But your letter does cause me some concern. What is to become of your knee after this? Please write to me as soon as you know the result of the X-ray. And for how long will your leg be bandaged? Will you be able to go to the party on the eve of Werner M's [Marwede] wedding or to Hermann's wedding? . . .

If the meniscus really has to come out—and I am actually very sad if a doctor were to poke around in your body with a scalpel—it would be best if it could happen in the summer, in the two months when we cannot be together anyway. Naturally, I do not want to postpone the wedding for so long under any circumstance, unless you yourself want to.

I myself am not doing so well today, probably because I was unhappy about the result of the tests yesterday and, in particular, as a consequence of that, having to wait eight days until I can see you again. . . .

My preparations for the academic teaching this term are slow. Things are just as they always were for me: at any one time I can only do one thing properly and with enthusiasm. And since I now wish to be with you and to marry you, nothing will come of other work, but that is hardly important.

Please write and tell me the result of the X-ray.—Ever since we were last together, I am with you more than before in my thoughts; somehow I already look on everything I do as though I am doing it for you. Yours, Werner.

Elisabeth to Werner

Friday after midnight [Saturday], April 3
My love—

Today was my class get-together. You would not have believed it! At 6 o'clock they had already arrived, and only just five minutes ago they left: everything to the last crumb was eaten; everyone is talking at once and as loudly as possible; frank and without sentimental disguise everyone says what they are thinking; and the most unbelievable stories are dug up again! It was just like it used to be earlier; one does not even notice that everyone now has found their own circle, so vibrant has our bond remained. For a moment I had to collect myself just now to realize that I am not back five years, that one has become a true adult in the meantime. It was really incredibly nice; and the girls have all turned into really special people, everyone in her own way very capable.

I was so relieved about your letter today. You know, the main thing is that the organs are not really unhealthy. Everything else is bound to improve greatly later on. Of this I am certain.

Dearest, we will have such a wonderful time!

So we will not see each other this weekend! Why don't you at least come in the morning on Friday if you can, so that we also get some quiet time to ourselves?

By the way, I had a very unpleasant talk today with Papa (about the time of the wedding, etc.). Dear, there is really nothing I can do when he gets something in his head. Everyone wants the same as we do, Mutti, Edith— but when the reply to everything one says is "Those are no arguments," then it's impossible to talk to each other. I'm afraid we have to give in. And I would appreciate if you could consent to it for Mutti's sake, for she is very distressed that these differences continue even now, and would give every-thing to make it as right and beautiful for us as humanly possible. She is finding it particularly painful now how deep the rift is between Papa and us; and since she belongs to Papa and also sides with him against us, she feels so clearly how she has already lost us and is losing us more and more. And she is so terribly tormented about this.

But now I am so tired that I must sleep. Good night, dearest. Li.

Good morning! What an incredible day this is! The birds are singing jubilantly, the air is totally saturated with sunshine, and the wind is fragrant, sweet, and forceful! Beloved, spring is coming!

Elisabeth to Werner

Saturday evening, April 3
My love—

Edith is so awfully eager to see the new colored film with me. So the letter will be short. In reality, the whole evening should belong to you, since there is so much I could tell you. But everyone has been pleading a lot for me to go with them.

Were you very surprised by the express letter, which did not contain anything urgent at all? I had such a dreadful thought that otherwise you would receive no letter from me today, not a single word. I did not know what else to do about it.

Love, I do not find the results of the test all that bad. I am quite sure that eventually everything will function much better than in this unnatural time right now. And do not be all that concerned about my knee. . . . I will most certainly come to the party on the eve of Werner's wedding and go to Hermann's wedding. I will simply walk without the bandage then and be real careful. It will be manageable. All will work out just fine.

I was very industrious today and wrote endless numbers of thank-you letters. Quite proud of myself!

Love, I am so glad and happy about us. Stay cheerful too, and always remember that four weeks from today, we will already belong to each other completely, and no one will ever come between us. Really, you are so awfully dear to me. Yours, Li.

Werner to Elisabeth

[Leipzig], Sunday evening [April 4?]
Dear little Li!

Last night I began to feel all sad because I had not heard anything from you, but then your express letter came after all, just when I started my piano practice. And this morning yet another letter arrived, thank you so much for everything, I am so happy when you write to me. It is good that you are less worried about our health than I have been these past few days. Do not strain your knee unnecessarily, perhaps then everything will get better on its own. . . .

The afternoon of your class get-together must have been very jolly; from your letter I could picture so vividly how all the girls were talking at the same time.

Do not be too dismayed about the conversation with your father: we both recognize now that not a lot more can be done about the wedding celebration; it will simply be formal because of the inn, stiff because of the tuxedo, and tiring because of the large number of people. But if it is set for late in the day, it will only involve us for a shorter time, and thereafter we will make our very own celebration so beautiful, all alone with the woods, the stars, and the lake, and the firm intention to build our life together, giving it meaning that does not require a lot of external formality. But I am not really averse to these formalities, which in earlier times were a genuine expression of the life that the best people led. If we bow down to them now, then we show our respect to this world, though it is bygone, hoping that we can take part in building a new world that is just as valid as the earlier one.

. . . Be cheerful, my thoughts are constantly with you.

Yours, Werner.

Elisabeth to Werner

Sunday, April 4, afternoon

My love—

What are you doing this Sunday? Are you working all day? Are you playing music? That would be nice! . . . The lectures begin tomorrow! What are you lecturing on, actually? Do it really well, otherwise everyone will think: "It seems that getting a wife is not the best thing for him!" They must not be allowed to think that!

Write and tell me exactly what the doctor says to you at the second checkup. Hopefully the result will be better than it seemed at first!

Actually, I am not in a very good mood today. But that this Sunday without you would be a bit dreary, I should have already known—and I did. You know, it just is not easy for me to be at home here. Papa is so dissatisfied with everything. They don't know anymore how to be grateful to fate, poor people! They appear as if in a prison that they have built for themselves.

But why I am not quite at ease today may be mostly due to the brace on my knee that is making things worse. The foot is totally swollen from the compression, and the knee has become all stiff. The doctors always succeed in making one really sick! I no longer quite trust them all. I have now removed the brace and do hope to get to see Gocht on Tuesday so that, finally, the proper treatment can be started. But the circumstances around it are so appalling. Suddenly one is treated like an invalid and becomes the object of sincerest sympathy, which I simply cannot stand. Then, I am not allowed to do anything, I receive wise counsel from everybody, and I have to lie on the sofa all the time—oh, you—it is easy to go crazy! I believe I am also not very amicable at the moment.

The film last night was simply exasperating. Seeing the colors was interesting enough, some of them were even quite pretty, but in my opinion, the problem is in no way really solved at all. The colors are much too bright, and in color photography it is not yet possible to capture different distances with the same focus. This means that only the main subject of the picture is focused and clearly recognizable and all other outlines and colors become distorted. And people will yet have to become way more discriminating in order to produce something really artistic, beautiful, and good with these ever more perfect technical tools. This film was dreadful to the point that I actually got heartsick. I always get so enraged when I see the nonsense with which people satisfy their fantasies. And I am afraid the producers will not comprehend that they now have an even greater responsibility with their films, because such a film in color has an effect that is so much more arousing and seductive. . . .

Good night, Werner! I am looking forward so terribly much to the time in four weeks, dearest! . . . Yours, Li.

Werner to Elisabeth

[Leipzig], Monday evening [April 5?]
My dear Li!

I am so awfully sorry that your knee is causing you so much trouble; your letter sounds very sad and it is so important to me that you are fine. Gocht's assistant doctor seems to be one big ass. . . . My doctor also is still following several leads, without yet knowing for sure what the matter is. Early this morning, he did a blood test, and then this afternoon determined that it did not fit with his other findings, so I had to devour enormous amounts of glucose and tomorrow he will study my blood work again; he seems to consider me some kind of chemistry laboratory. I am often reminded of the doctor in Pfitzner's *Das Christ-Elflein,* who throughout the opera has to repeat just one single phrase, over and over: "This is a complete mystery to me." But something is bound to show results.

But now on to the more enjoyable part, namely, the preparations for April 29. The baptism certificate was nowhere to be found, unfortunately, but I have determined through Mama that the baptism took place on December 28, 1901 (or perhaps one day earlier or later). . . .

Good night now and do not be sad. Yours, Werner.

Elisabeth to Werner

Sunday evening, very late in bed [April 4]

Werner, when I took your letter to the mailbox just now, it was so beautiful outside that I recovered all my joy. It was raining, but it was an exquisite rain, so beneficial, warm, and bountiful. It was a misty spray that soaked deep into all my clothes and surely just as much into the soil, and it filled the air so that it hung like a fog under the street lamps. And it had a fragrance of damp soil and decayed leaves—You, I would have liked to go with you through this rain! The first spring rain of the year! When I came back to the house, I sat down at the piano and sang. Now everything is well again, everything back to life. My love!

Elisabeth to Werner

Monday evening [April 5]

Today I began the day with a letter from you. Mutti brought it upstairs to me because I was so lazy. It made me really glad! And it actually helps me quite a bit, improving my behavior here at home, especially when it comes to my parents. Thank you, love!

Today I cooked all morning!! In white apron and with cooking spoon in hand, I created totally delicious things. You will be pleased! Except, of course, if you are only allowed to eat ultra-boring stuff—well, we will not let it affect our happiness! I expect to find out tomorrow what the doctor thinks of you. Don't be too upset if it is not what you hope for. All will be well, I know it for certain! My knee too cannot make me sad for very long, either. I always know that everything will turn out right somehow, will not be an issue of concern, as soon as we are together. In general, I think of life becoming infinitely easier to untangle, everything will then be so simple, and all sources from which life is generated may become available. Such bliss sometimes just overcomes me now. My love! Please be happy too! And listen to the birds sometimes; they sing particularly beautifully this spring. Their jubilance often fills the air completely.

Now I must practice our song for Hermann's wedding. Are you also playing music tonight? I am thinking so much about you, dearest. Yours, Li.

Elisabeth to Werner

April 6

My love. Did the doctor come to a conclusion today? I am very curious; I am not quite sure how much confidence he can inspire! Hopefully, every-thing will go as well for you as it did for me! So listen: I went to see Gocht today. He looked at my knee very briefly and said: "Well, no wonder it is painful. There's a large hematoma in there and now the whole knee is full of water. You will have to continue wearing the brace. We will bandage it differently so that your foot does not swell up again." Nothing at all from the meniscus. Isn't that terrific, love! Then I asked for how long I needed to wear

the brace. "Six weeks" was the answer. I was totally shocked and said:
"Well, dear professor, I'm willing to wear four braces for three weeks and
even to stay in bed for fourteen days should it be required, but six weeks—
that is impossible!" My vehemence softened him, and he said later on it might
be enough to just bandage it. And that is not a big deal! I see that as a great
result. All concerns are suddenly blown away! I am so pleased. A hematoma
is nothing horrible. You won't believe how cheerful I am again.

Dearest, do not be cross that I wrote you such a sad or disgruntled letter
on Sunday. You know—and it was always like this earlier too—you need
unbelievable inner strength here at home, if you want to drown out the
stifling atmosphere. . . . I could only stand last summer here at home because
I had furnished myself a little room right at the top—that is to say, there
was nothing in it other than primitive old furniture with wobbly joints, an
old iron stove, and then ancient wallpaper with yellow and purple (!!)
flowers; but a large window always filled the whole room with light, sunshine, and the scent of blossoms. There I lodged, and basically lived on the
windowsill with all kinds of good books. It allowed me to find my way
back to everything that was important and of value to me, and there I was
dreaming a lot.

Love, I often think how strange it is that suddenly everything is on solid
ground, all dreams have become reality. How few people have such good
fortune!

By the way, I received a letter from Wolfgang Rüdel yesterday. He sent
along to me many other passages, but they all do not strike me as quite right.
Very beautiful is Psalm 103, verses 15–18, perhaps more beautiful yet, Psalm
36:10: "For with You is the fountain of life; in Your light we see the light."
That is perhaps the most beautiful passage I found. And it combines in it so
much about you and me, and us together.—The longer I think about this
word, the more beautiful it appears to me. It might well be so profound that it
is fitting for the beginning of our life. What do you think? . . .

Good night, love. Think of me sometimes and be happy, right?
Yours, Li.

Werner to Elisabeth

[Leipzig], April 7
My dear Li!

Many thanks for the wonderful news that your knee should soon be better again; the three weeks in a bandage will not be so bad, once we know that there will be no more problems. I hasten to also share my own relief: after all the tests, the doctor has determined that we are dealing only with chronic intestinal enteritis with unpleasant side effects; all other fears were unfounded, thank God. I must now be on a regimen for three weeks, which is a nuisance in some respects, but then he hopes to have everything back in order. So at the wedding, we will both be fully cured.

I have written to Wolfgang. Your suggestion is fine with me.—The music was great yesterday; but now I am so dead tired that I need to go to bed straightaway. So, the day after tomorrow, we can talk about everything else in person; thank you again for the good news! Yours, Werner.

Werner to Elisabeth

[Leipzig], Monday evening [April 12?]
My dear Elisabeth!

. . . Did you arrive home safely, and did you, like I, regret a little, that we just made the train? Afterward I wandered around for a while as though in a dream and did not quite take it in that you were suddenly no longer there; now I will just have to wait until Saturday. . . .

Not much will come of my work before May. My thoughts are always circling around joining our lives, that common goal in front of us, and it becomes really difficult to wait for the 29th. The truth is I already cannot quite cope without you, although I always remind myself that I have been able to manage for many years and so, according to conventional wisdom, it ought to be possible still. The present mindset is reminiscent of the typical nights before a major tour in the mountains, when you toss and turn in bed in joyful anticipation of the coming morning and with just a little trepidation, lest not all should go well. And only at the moment when you pick up the ice axe in front of the hut do you know that all will go smoothly. How beautiful everything will be, once we are together in the dark by our lake.

I am sorry that I objected to the singing yesterday; you know, I am always afraid of showing something animated to people, because they will mostly become irritated. But I hurt your feelings with it a little and have a bad conscience. So please don't be upset anymore. If the weather is nice on Saturday, let's go out together. You are very dear to me. Yours, Werner.

Elisabeth to Werner

[Berlin], April 12

My love—

That the train had to be late! And just think, when I arrived here, the garden gate was closed, and the rusty old thing would not budge at all to open. First I tried gently, then with brute force so that the key broke, then I rang the doorbell incessantly, but there was not a soul in the house, and finally I scrambled over the fence with my wooden leg. In the meantime, it was half past 1!! But early this morning, I was on time for the cooking class, which made me feel very superior, morally speaking.

Love, I am so incredibly happy about our every time together. I am so aware how we always move forward in our relationship, how it moves us along, one great step each time. And now one can see ever more clearly and with certainty how likely it is that we will reach all that one possibly can reach. And, you know, the times when I am filled with fear that you might be disappointed with me will be rarer and rarer. People have always objected to my intensity; but I know that you only have to take this into your hand for me to become quite tame again. When I am doubtful, it is never about you but stems from the fact that I do not have very much self-esteem. But if you love me properly, then I will get it too.—

Love, I have so completely understood everything you have told me. And I was very glad that you did. I think I am only able to help by loving you so much that you soon believe it in the deepest reaches of your own heart, right? Oh, you, it will not be very long now before everything will be better! . . .

I am mighty tired today because I was out all day. Good night, love. And stay very close to me all these days now, right? I care about you very, very much. Li.

Werner to Elisabeth

[Leipzig], Tuesday evening [April 13?]
Dear little Li!

You wrote me a particularly nice letter today, and I, monster that I am, have only five minutes between two meetings in which to reply. . . . It is so good that you are coming here on Saturday. As it is, I am not reasonably engaged in work anymore, only when you are here for good will it improve. The thing is, there is some exciting news in physics; I believe that when you are here for good, and when I am feeling completely well, my work will also get back on track as before.—So, in a hurry, many, many greetings! Yours, Werner.

Elisabeth to Werner

April 13, very late and very tired
My love—

I was really incredibly happy today with your letter. Oh, you, once we have left the chauffeur at the station and then drive on alone into the totally silent wood at dusk, over the peak where we once watched the sunset—my love, then we will have our whole life ahead of us, and I believe it will be good.

Today I have done some pretty exhausting work: I have such a messy pile of letters. I began to tackle it and thinned it out as much as humanly possible. And all those years, from when I was almost grown up, arose in front of me. My head is quite numb after so much looking back. But love, I saw how difficult it is to point children to the right path, to help, to understand. We must always support each other a lot, so that we do not let the lived life and reality slip through our hands. . . .

Love, our children must have it better than I did! Will we be able to achieve that? Oh, how relieved I will be once we are together for good! I am counting the hours and I am glad when it gets dark. Then that means one less day. I am up to my neck in preparations and it is unbelievable fun. Except that at home I am not too kind, I'm afraid.

And you know I stopped being angry with you a long time ago about not being allowed to sing in the train. Such things pass quickly for me. And really, when I understand how things are and why, then I have nothing left to be upset about. Do not worry anymore about it, my love.— I am terribly fortunate and full of expectation, and I love you very much. Yours, Li.

Werner to Elisabeth

[Leipzig], April 15
Dear sweet Li!
You really do help me a lot with your letters. I am sometimes a little worn out now; being alone is not making it any better, so that it is really good when I can feel you quite close to me through your letters. Fourteen days from now, we will already be outside by the lake or in the forest, or in our room high up in the turret, from where one probably can look far out over the lake.—When might you be coming? It would be lovely if it could be tomorrow already, but it is not very clear from your letter. I am fairly free from midday tomorrow until Monday; we are free to do whatever we like. . . .

That we will be together forever, starting in fourteen days—I cannot quite wrap my mind around it; but if it were not to be, I could not do anything at all with my life anymore. In the beginning I will not do much thinking and simply be happy, realizing, gradually, that you are always with me. But later we will want to be conscious of creating a shared life, mindful that honesty is paramount, that life's essence should always be clearly noticeable behind the love, or the music, or the work.

How wonderful that your knee is getting better; do take it easy now, so that in fourteen days everything will be all fine. My inner self seems also to improve slowly, but it may still take some time until it is completely restored; the trip to the Main River is bound to help the most.

So now, on to seeing you again very soon—hopefully tomorrow, or at the latest the day after. Yours, Werner.

Elisabeth to Werner

Monday night very late, April 20
My love—

. . . I have started once more to do an awful lot today. And all of it is for us; every detail that I can cross off my list is making me feel a little bit closer. Oh, you, how happy am I about everything. . . .

You know what—I have a sneak proposal for you to consider. It really hit me today that Mutti does not know your—our—house at all, has no idea how and where I will be living later on. And I sometimes imagine: what if all this were happening to me—to my daughter. Of course I would

The house at Bozener Weg 14

be different, but the thought of not having any idea about the "home" that one's own child is going to have made me wonder whether Mutti should come with me to visit you on Friday. Then we could all travel together to Berlin on Saturday. You know, we will soon have everything going our way—I would love to do this for Mutti. It is just that she has terrible inhibitions about coming along as the mother-in-law like this, but she will get over that. Don't you think this is a good idea? But tell me frankly what you think, right?

In the meantime, the chests here are filling up with treasures and gifts. I am finding it good fun. Love, the days are now going by quickly. It is not much longer. Oh, you, how I love you! Yours, Li.

Werner to Elisabeth

[Leipzig)], Tuesday evening [April 20?]
Dear sweet Li!

Everything you wrote me in your letter was perfectly alright with me; I would have been sorry if we had somehow wounded your parents, even if nothing about our way appeared misguided to me. Now we must leave everything else to the future, which begins in just over eight days for us.—I am still a little leery about the actual wedding festivities; but afterward we are free to take the reins of the carriage firmly into our hands and steer our own life appropriately. . . . You had a very good idea, bringing your mother here with you on Friday. I had that in mind myself earlier, but then wanted to postpone it until after the wedding, to have the house fully furnished first. I would really enjoy your mother's visit very much; perhaps it will be easier here, outside of your circle, to get closer to her. . . . Wouldn't you just like to stay here all weekend with your mother? Either way would be fine with me.

It is wonderful that you are happily excited about the future. Then surely everything will be well. Yours, Werner.

Elisabeth to Werner

April 21
My love—

If you only knew how we are slaving away here! And everyone is giving
us lots of unsuitable things that I will have to exchange. But today we received
from Aunt Gi Pütter eight volumes of Beethoven piano music for four hands.
They all come originally from my grandfather, but are in mint condition. But
I think I will never have enough courage to play them with you!

Yesterday I went to see Gocht. He was actually very satisfied and said
that it would soon be fully healed. I should, gradually, make the bandage
smaller! . . .

Oh, you, only one more week to go! Only then life begins for real: you
cannot believe how much I hunger for peace and belonging! If only I can,
actually, be the wife you need! But in reality I am full of confidence.

Good night, you! I will see whether I can come on Friday. I do not yet
know whether with or without Mutti. Little brother Ernst is doing better.

And you, I hope you are well too? I love you terribly much. Yours, Li.

Werner to Elisabeth

[Leipzig], April 26
Dear good Li!

I was very happy with the two days in Berlin; I felt that I had become a
little closer, at least, to your mother.—I am no longer too worried about the
wedding festivities, and then everything will be glorious. In two days, all of
us will already assemble at your house.

The drive home yesterday, however, was unusually horrible. I stalled in
Potsdam because the carburetor gave out. I did not have the tools to repair it,
so I had to call in some mechanics and could only continue on after 7 o'clock.
The roads were awfully slick, and rain came pouring down. I almost had a
collision near Michendorf; a car in front of me had run over a deer, I had to
brake sharply and got into a slight skid; the poor deer also made me feel
sorry for a long time. In the Düben Heath, the carburetor began to misfire

The wedding takes place in Berlin on April 29, 1937

again and to hiss, and large amounts of gasoline were leaking out underneath; repair was inconceivable in that rain. So as not to lose too much gasoline, I drove on full throttle, which soon became almost impossible due to fog. After Düben, the weather eventually changed to a virtual cloud burst, so that at least I had little reason to fear a carburetor fire. Near Leipzig, I had to brake sharply once, which stalled the engine. It took me a quarter of an hour to get it going again. Thus it was already almost 10 o'clock when I arrived home, exhausted. Hopefully, the day after tomorrow will be a more enjoyable drive.

I do not want to report only such "stuff" today, but I do want to tell you that I have the firm conviction that we are a good match for each other and that we are better able to do justice to our place in the world by being together.

Good-bye until the day after tomorrow. Yours, Werner.

1937–38

In the first two years *of marriage Werner and Elisabeth are rarely apart and thus have few occasions to write letters to each other. Werner spends several days skiing with Elisabeth's brother Ernst over New Year 1937, while Elisabeth is at home expecting their first child. The twins Wolfgang and Maria are born in early January 1938. In March Werner is away for somewhat longer, on a lecture tour to England, while Elisabeth goes with the children to her parents in Berlin.*

The young couple attempts to counter the nightmarishly troubled times prevalent in Germany with a quiet, domestic happiness. Elisabeth—young and apolitical— is devoted wholeheartedly to her new roles of wife and mother. Her elder sister, Edith, engaged to the journalist Erich Kuby, finds herself much more involved in the spirit of the times. Nevertheless, the Heisenbergs' peaceful domestic scene is not spared politics: Werner has to continue his fight for his reputation, and his hope of being appointed Sommerfeld's successor in Munich remains unfulfilled.

Werner to Elisabeth

[Harz], in the evening, December 29
Dear Li!

It was good that you have sent me out into the snow. The fresh wind clears the head from thoughts of senseless politics, and skiing is good for lazy legs in every way. The ascent of Schierke was more strenuous than I thought. Since it was not possible to make out either maps or signposts in the dark, it was difficult to find the way. But a night march between completely snow-covered fir trees is exhilarating and stimulates cheerful conversation. Thus Ernst was not all that tired when we arrived. Early this morning, we awoke from a golden blue light that permeated our room. The sun was rising in a bright blue sky and sparkled through the windows with their thick frost patterns. Below us was a thick cloud covering, pierced only by a few other peaks near the summit. We then made use of the morning with an energetic excursion: Brocken-Oderbrück-Achtermannshöhe and back. We were on our skis for almost five hours nonstop; Ernst, quite intrepid, held up fabulously; he is still a bit inexperienced in downhill but indefatigable in level skiing and uphill. . . . In the afternoon I wrote and worked; Ernst studied some books of family history. Meanwhile, the sky has clouded over, an intense storm is rattling around the house, and tomorrow there likely will be more snow.

I found it really difficult to leave our Christmas room behind. How you have managed to transform our house into a comfortable, inviting home. But next year you will have to come along in the snow again, regardless. Sleep really well and do not overdo things with the visitors! Thank you so much for everything you have done for me. Yours, Werner!

Elisabeth to Werner

[December 30]
My love!—
I have just taken Edith to the station and felt very cozily entitled to be just alone for myself. I kept walking for a while longer through the white snow-dusted streets of Marienhöhe and got to thinking about how little of what one has experienced and learned one can talk to another person about, and how much less still the other person understands what you mean. Everyone has a wall built around them and only you are able to come to me inside mine; and at the present time one is building the wall thicker and taller and never going outside of it. . . .

Last night we let the candles on the Christmas tree burn out. It was so beautiful, how it gradually became more and more enveloped in darkness; at first, everything on it glittered and sparkled, and eventually it became all black and serious. . . .

And this morning your letter arrived, my love. I could almost feel the cold, the freshness, and the joy. How nice that you had sun right on the first day! Next time I will come along too! And it looks as if you were really lucky that there is so much snow! I am sure you did not need me to prompt you all the time about skipping politics; but unlike you, I do not have the wind blowing about my ears, so that one keeps thinking about how, and even if at all, something is about to change.—People are now making out of New Year's Eve something ever more depraved; probably very telling—a sad signal. I am thinking you cannot celebrate it quietly enough, and a giant bonfire should be lit both in gratitude and as a sacrificial offering. Later, once we have our cabin in the mountains, we will make that happen, right?

. . . Now farewell, my love. Thank you for everything! Yours, Li.

Werner to Elisabeth

[Harz], New Year's Eve, shortly before midnight
My dear sweet Li,

I was so happy just now to talk briefly with you; now I know that you do not feel too lonely, and you know that I am with you in my thoughts. How much beauty the past year has brought me through you! And yet everything up to now strikes me as a mere beginning, only to be followed by even more beauty and togetherness; together we are now able to really shape our lives. I am looking forward so very much to the next period and can only hope that you too will always be well in everything you will have to withstand.

Hopefully you are halfway content with this New Year's Eve even without me. I myself am spending it in a very senseless environment. Below us, in the ballroom, a half-drunken mob of odd people, some giddy and some sad, is going wild; there might also be a few nice ones among them. Outside, the snowstorm is howling around the house, such that Ernst and I have had to give up on our planned walk. Instead, we have spent the evening somewhat serenely by reading aloud in the room upstairs; the tale of "Sisto e Sesto" [by Swiss author Heinrich Federer] has made a big impression on both of us again. Tomorrow it will be *Der Schimmelreiter* [by Theodor Storm], which you so kindly sent me; thank you for that and even more for your two letters, which lessen my missing the Christmas room at home.

By the way, Ernst is doing quite well; just that he petered out toward evening, then slept solidly for twelve hours and was very cheerful again today. Now he is lying in bed and trying to sleep through the roar from below.

So now it is almost 12, and I wish you and the two of us in every respect a happy and beautiful New Year, dear Li! Yours, Werner.

Elisabeth to Werner

January 1
My love!

I had not expected at all that you would call (not being quite a twentieth-century person!) and so I was very surprised. It made me extremely happy. Thank you, my love!—Shortly after 11 o'clock, I took Mama to the [bus or train] stop and your letter to the mailbox. It was still snowing and windy; one had to stride quite forcefully to get ahead. At home, all alone (Martha was out), I crawled happily into bed, opened all the windows to let in the exquisite snowy air and the sounds of New Year's Eve. It had stopped snowing so that people were going out into the street. Louder and louder a swell of noises and fireworks arose through the snowy silence and then suddenly all the bells began to ring out, filling the whole air with sound. I just love that! With a thousand thoughts about the past year and the year to come and with my whole heart filled with gratitude and joy, I entered the New Year. If you had a similar experience—love, how happy that would make me. In spite of everything—we have so many reasons to feel lucky! You need not worry about me. I just know that all will go well and I have not even the slightest trace of fear or concern. On the contrary! . . .

Get a good rest, and love me a little. Yours, Li.

Elisabeth to Werner

January 2

My love!

Thank you a thousand times for your loving, poignant letter. For me too, it is as though everything up to now has only been a beginning, and that so much more, even better, should come out of this last year. But when I dream about it, I often flinch; and I hesitate to look toward the future with hope. It is full of horrible apparitions. I cannot believe that there will not be a high price to pay, considering the way people are living now: arrogantly dismissive, in a frenzied intoxication, mocking God. And then all of us will be in for it, regardless. So I am trying to take hold of the present as much as I possibly can and to be happy with the current riches. And these are good enough to be happy from the bottom of our hearts, right?

This is the last letter I will write to you; others would probably not arrive anymore, I suspect.—It is so good that you are returning soon! One tends to become a little strange all by oneself. . . . All my love and best wishes. Yours, Li.

Elisabeth with the twins,
Wolfgang and Maria, born in
January 1938

Elisabeth to Werner

Berlin, March 21
My love!

It is actually quite nice to be home once again, especially when one can regard everything from "an elevated standpoint" now. The dreary atmosphere at the house does not disturb me anymore; I belong somewhere else and no longer need to defend what is important to me. That is a good state to be in, and I realize so clearly again how rich you have made me—my love!—I only feel sorry for Ernstl [little Ernst]; if only one could create a kinder and more robust world for him! Here Mutti is, unfortunately, very downcast; she is much nicer when she is with us, so incomparably more serene. But she has also had a lot going on and is tired and drained. Now, when things quiet down, she must spend a lot of time with the children. They are like rays of sunshine in the big dark house. . . .

So I loaded Papa and Ernstl into the car from 4 to 6 and drove out to Nikolskoje. It was glorious. And I wished you over here with all my might to see this tender spring, the sun's sparkle on the blue water, the warm, soothing air. How was your journey? The crossing? Was it very windy? I am mighty anxious to get the first news from you.

Actually, I am glad that you are getting out again and can talk to people about your matters. It often saddens me that because of me you have so little time to work; but I think that quieter times will also come again, when you will be able to concentrate fully; and I will not be jealous! Also, I will do my best to create a range of interests for myself again; then it will not be as difficult for me, when you fall in love with your physics, as it is now, when I live completely through you. . . .

Tomorrow you will hear more from me. Good night, my love! It is glorious with the children. When the boy is happy, he looks exactly like you! All my love and best wishes! Yours, Li.

Werner to Elisabeth

Cambridge, March 23

Dear Li!

I do not know whether I will manage a reasonable letter before Manchester, I have barely a minute of free time here. Last night, I had to give a lecture, today I have another one at 3 o'clock and I still have to prepare that. I also have to deal with various people just about now, at 10 o'clock, at the institute; afterward I have been invited out for lunch. Despite this busy schedule, it is very nice here, I am being spoiled everywhere and do enjoy the carefree demeanor that people here have. Incidentally, the British are not as appalled by the Austria affair as I had thought. Most of those I met were more on the side of Chamberlain than of Eden and would not be averse to a friendship with Germany, if we became more reasonable about the church issue and similar things.—How are you and the little ones? I am eagerly awaiting a letter from you and am looking forward to it. I will write to you properly in Manchester. Take good care of yourself! Yours, Werner.

Elisabeth to Werner

March 23

My love!

Now you are already in Manchester. I'm very curious to hear how it was in Cambridge. I could imagine that—aside from physics—you are experiencing in England what I have found again on a smaller scale here in Berlin: we are rediscovering how big and wide the world is, and how much diversity it encompasses. Here is a meeting place for the whole world, you can feel it. And I always find it so very exciting to see how this giant clockwork of a city runs; how the people with their own worlds are only small components; how people are mastering technology, and yet, at the same time, technology has so much power over people—you learn that here so very directly. It is very nice to be here for a short time, especially after such a period of confinement. The only thing is, I would love to have you here to confer with you on all that is so much on my mind these days.

Today we have still had good weather. For the children this does wonders. . . . I am now in Mutti's sitting room and on either side there is a baby basket, from which I hear the wonderfully peaceful breathing of the sleeping children. Without the two of them I would hardly feel so comfortable here. Now you always find peace and your center again, as soon as you come to the children. . . .

I am done for now. I am very tired and my head cannot deal with more. Also, it is the children's turn now. My love—I love you so terribly much! You know that, don't you? Yours, Li.

Werner to Elisabeth

Manchester, Saturday morning [March]
Dear good Li!
Your letter—only the first one I received because the mail does take longer than I thought—made me very happy. It is wonderful that everything is going so well for you and the little ones; I would like to hear so much more about you all: how much the two of them weigh now, whether the boy is calm and sleeping well, what and how much they drink, and lots of other things, too many to list. I am very much looking forward to seeing them again, grown bigger and more filled in.

I have been here in Manchester since the day before yesterday and have been engaged with physics and physicists almost nonstop. Last night all of us were invited to the Blacketts, and that evening was the most animated yet of my trip. The Blacketts were in Göttingen in 1925 and belonged to the closest circle in Göttingen at that time. So the conversation wandered automatically back to this incredibly free time, when none of us had any money, everyone put up with the most basic material circumstances, but every sunny day they all would lie on the grass somewhere behind the Hainberg with a volume of Hölderlin's poetry or a physics book. It is nice to know that for Blackett, such a true Englishman, his whole life was basically also shaped by this period.

I was also impressed with the way they talked about politics and the current Germany. The English have a much greater understanding of the propriety, or at least the necessity, of German foreign policy than I would have thought. At the same time, they are arming themselves very quickly and are anticipating a world war soon. But not even this possibility prevents them from speaking about present-day Germany with the greatest respect. Incidentally, I no longer believe that Eden will play a major role again; but it may well be that the segment of the people I am meeting here think differently than the general public. . . .

Now rest up, along with the little ones. I will probably return to Leipzig on Monday—perhaps already in the morning. Good-bye! Yours, Werner.

Werner to Elisabeth

Manchester, March
My dear Li!
. . . In the last couple of days I was somewhat unhappy; from all sides I get criticized for not writing enough. But I simply do not know how I could do it. I hardly ever get to bed before 12:30, get up around 8 and talk almost without interruption all day long with physicists. It is important to me to get completely into physics now; the preparation for the lectures also takes time, since Tuesday I have had daily lectures from 3 to 4 in the afternoons. Physicists from Liverpool, Edinburgh, Leeds, Birmingham, and Bristol have come here, and naturally they do not just come to hear my lecture but also to discuss their problems with me. So I do not get to anything else; but I did write to you, a total of four times, I believe. I am terribly tired and am looking forward to getting home soon, but I did learn a lot.

If I do not write anything else or send you a telegram, I will arrive Monday morning at 7:58. You do not have to come to the train station! Sleep a long time after making the trip to Leipzig, and I will take a taxi. I am really looking forward to seeing you all, the feedings, the weighing, the bathing, and everything else that goes along with that.

Bohr wrote to me and invited me to come on April 5 and to help him inaugurate his new enlarged institute. Of course I have to decline, much as I would like to see him. . . .

Yours, Werner.

Elisabeth to Werner

March 24

My love!

How terribly rushed you are, poor you! Hopefully things will be somewhat better in Manchester! Take a page from us: Ernstl, Miss Oertel, and I went to Sanssouci today. . . . The view from the castle over the park was just lovely. The trees were covered with a hint of green, the sky pale blue, and the sun poured a festive glow over the whole of nature. It was as if heaven and earth were rejoicing.—Then I invited the two of them to coffee in the Historic Mill, which also turned into a very jolly get-together. . . .

Mutti is like a shade plant here. I find myself always checking her eyes to see if she has been crying. This is very sad. Also, despite the best of intentions, I have clashed with Papa. But it was not bad. He just said, very condescendingly, that what you had written about politics and what I had told him could not possibly be a true impression—you can imagine how that annoyed me and you will understand that I did not take it silently. But it was harmless and is already forgotten, but without the children—that much I know—I could not stand it here for long.

Miss Oertel, by the way, is proving her mettle. She is hard working and attentive with the children. She has taken the little ones very close to her heart and is delightful with them. We also are getting along better and better. She is such an upbeat person, with her heart in the right place. We have a lot of fun together. And I am glad to become better acquainted with someone who was not quite so plausible as a nanny at first glance. One is becoming more cautious in judgment now, and probably also a little more generous.

I am enjoying this time without household chores very much. I think I have more talent with the children than for domestic housekeeping. And in this regard I am feeling so surefooted that I will be very reluctant, later on, to let the children out of my own hands. I believe you can raise children better with much love than with sternness and severity. But the future will be the judge.

Make time for yourself sometimes and try to stay clear of any overly conventional engagements—even though it may be difficult for you! Be quite unyielding about it!

I am always with you in my thoughts, my love! Yours, Li.

Werner to Elisabeth

[Manchester], Monday morning [March?]
Dear little Li!

Yesterday was a good day; I received two letters from you at the same time. . . . I am now planning to leave London on Sunday morning and arrive in Leipzig at 8 o'clock on Monday morning. If this changes, I will, of course, write. Then you could perhaps drive to Leipzig on Sunday (but very carefully!). I can well imagine that you find Berlin so full of life. It is where all the important links from your earlier time connect you to the larger outside world and you only have to pick up one of these links. I too have barely any real connection with Leipzig, but when we come to Munich, this would certainly be different.

My stay here in England has been enormously instructive as well, especially in terms of politics. It may well be that the British speak to me about National Socialism more politely than they do otherwise. But it seems almost fashionable to complain about the Treaty of Versailles and to accept Hitler's foreign policy. A true consensus is hampered mostly by the domestic policy. Events such as the imprisonment of Niemöller are referred to as "incipient Bolshevism"—the British have an immense fear of Bolshevism—and further events *à la Stalin* are anticipated. One Englishman recently said: England gave up the war in Abyssinia because otherwise Mussolini would have been toppled and Bolshevism would have broken out in Italy. It is also characteristic that England has apparently stood behind Franco for some time and is preventing France from giving aid to his opponents. (This is generally asserted here.) Overall, it seems to me that the political opinion here is very different from that which one hears described as the "British" opinion in Germany. But perhaps my sources of information here are too one-sided. On Saturday night I will talk in London with the German representative of the Academic Exchange Service; I am curious to hear his views on politics; otherwise, I have not met any other Germans here (which is a bonus for my language skills).—To the three of you all my best wishes, and good-bye until next Monday in Leipzig. I am looking forward very much to coming home. Yours, Werner.

Elisabeth to Werner

Sunday, March 27
My love!

It is a mystery to me that by Saturday you only had received one single letter from me. I had written three letters to Cambridge and, starting on Wednesday, one each day to Manchester. Probably the mail is held up at the border for real. Your letter took less than twenty-four hours! In some of them I wrote in great detail about the children. They are both doing well. . . .

Today we had some great amusement: we placed the two children closely together, side by side, in the laundry basket with their little faces turned toward each other. This had no effect on the boy whatsoever. He was hungry and crying. But she looked at her screaming brother with very interested eyes and must have found it very comical, for she suddenly started to laugh, not really loudly, but she looked really amused and kept on laughing until we picked the boy up. It was really quite delightful.

Hermann came here for noontime dinner. I experience all the awful tension, the strain and the constant friction, between him and my parents that I used to have myself. Thank God that I am now away from that field of combat! . . . I hope everything goes well for you, my love! Yours, Li.

Elisabeth to Werner

May 1
My love!

How glad I am that Nietschke was here! So: Everything that worried us about the boy, his fidgeting, the sweating, the frequent crying, the bloating, all this is due to the fact that he already has a rather pronounced case of rickets. She also has it, but not as severely. N. was *very* indignant about the doctor, who should have long ago prescribed Vigantol, because for twins born in winter it is a given, without preventive measures. And for the boy, it is already quite advanced. He has prescribed a very powerful medication, which will alleviate the worst symptoms immediately (a mixture of bromine and calcium). I cannot tell you how glad I am. The boy's restlessness in the past few days has been truly terrible. During these recent nights we have been carrying him around for hours to try to make him go to sleep a little. Also, the spasms, while drinking, were really bad. N. said that these are not entirely without danger and could turn into proper convulsions under certain circumstances. But with this medication, these spasms should disappear within eight days.—He showed me how soft the bones on top of the head are already; if you press on them you can easily leave deep imprints. . . . N. said that the valerian is useless because this is not a nervous phenomenon but a real disease. Neither does he approve of any homeopathic medicines. N. made a very extraordinary impression again. Too bad that you did not speak to him yourself.

So I'm setting out tomorrow. . . . This will likely be the last letter I write to you; I don't think others would still reach you.

All, all my love! Yours, Li.

1939

AS A KIND *of consolation for the dwindling hope of being offered the chair in Munich, Werner begins in spring to look for a house in the Bavarian mountains that might serve as a summer vacation home and as a refuge for the family in case of war. His mother, who lives in Munich, is better able to inspect available properties; thus it is she who comes across the house of the artist Lovis Corinth in Urfeld on the Walchensee, which had been standing empty for some time. It meets Werner and Elisabeth's specifications: it is by a lake, has a view of the mountains, is surrounded by a lovely wooded area, and is spacious enough for a growing family. For the family is growing: Elisabeth is expecting their third child (Jochen, who is born in May). The purchase agreement for the Urfeld house is completed in April 1939, and from then on, Mother Heisenberg is busy preparing house and garden so that the young family can move in that summer.*

First, however, in view of the increasing anticipation of war, Werner travels to America for several weeks. As he writes in his autobiography, Physics and Beyond [Der Teil und das Ganze]: *"I had many friends in America and felt the need to see them before the war started—who knew if we would ever meet again? And I also realized that, if I was to help in Germany's reconstruction after the collapse, I would badly need their help" (quoted from the translation by Arnold J. Pomerans).*

This is the first time since their marriage that the couple has been separated for an extended period, and both strive to share their lives as before, at least through letters. Elisabeth reports on the development of the children and her concerns about finding a new nanny, since Maria Oertel, a young acquaintance of the Jacobis, who had assisted her since the birth of the twins, wishes to return to the Jacobis and take a job as director of a nursery school. Werner, for his part, relates his travel impressions in a country that is not yet touched by the military unrest on the other side of the ocean, and tells of his encounters with old and new friends. Neither Werner nor Elisabeth refers to his real reason for the journey; one gets the sense that there is an agreement, spoken or unspoken, not to address political issues in their letters. But their worry about an impending war comes through from time to time.

Elisabeth to Werner

[Leipzig], June 15
My love!

I am already in bed and it is late. But I feel I must say good night to you, even if I do not know when and where this greeting will reach you. But I will write often now, as though you were with me and could hear me and talk to me, because, actually, I talk with you all day long—so close are you to me even when you are far away.—

Jochen is asleep next to me in the basket, a small symbol of the manly protection I so need. He is quite well, only he cries quite a lot, rather more than the twins, it seems to me. Perhaps he is not getting enough to eat! Although he drank 645 grams today, and he did gain weight, too.

It was nice that I could speak with you again. I thank you for the call. . . .

Oh, you—surely you must experience your time abroad so differently this time, knowing that there is one place in the world where all hearts are beating for you and a circle has been drawn with you at its center, now and forevermore. Even my solitude is different, because the children always remind me that I am not alone, that you belong to me.

Good night, dearest! Yours, Li.

Werner to Elisabeth

Thursday evening [June 15]
Dear Li!

Now the first day of this travel is coming to an end already, and I notice that on such a day a lot was happening. Your telegram at first gave me a startle. But afterward I was doubly glad about the telephone call.

The trip under a cloudless sky was really nice; near Goslar, we had the whole north side of the Harz Mountains and the Brocken in front of us for a long time; that awoke many a memory: of our flight to Frankfurt and of the ski trips with Ernst, and of earlier excursions. . . . —A while ago we crossed the border. Now we are traversing a dunelike wooded area, and one can tell that we are soon approaching the sea. I am looking forward to it.—

But now I also have to answer your questions: My addresses are: from June 22–26, New York, c/o Karl Heisenberg, Wooster Street 69/71. From June 27–July 1, Purdue University, Physics Dept., La Fayette, [Indiana]. From July 23–August 2, New York.— . . .

Meanwhile, we have reached Utrecht. In Hoek or Rotterdam I want to try to post this letter. My very, very best to you and the little ones! Yours, Werner.

Elisabeth to Werner

[Leipzig], June 17
Dearest—

It was a stormy day today; I am quite exhausted from it. But your letter made me infinitely happy. . . . In the morning I went to town and learned, to my regret, that, strangely, airmail only operates in one direction, and my letters to you can only go by a mail boat. And those go so rarely. I had them give me the schedule, and I promise never to let a ship leave without a letter to you. Just don't be sad if you only hear from us so rarely. Now this letter can only leave on the 20th.——I could cry about it. How I wish for all this to be in your hands!

When I returned home, I found Miss Oertel completely beside herself. Ursel [Ursula] Frels had helped with the children and dropped Maria from her lap.

. . . Miss Oertel was all distraught from the shock. Besides, she had bad news from Stockholm and has to go there, possibly on Thursday, after all. With long debates on all this, we passed our noontime dinner, and when I came to Jochen, he was crying, but not worse than usual. When I picked him up, I noticed that he did not calm down but rather cried more; and on the

changing table he also kept crying the whole time, did not make his pre-
feeding motions, but was whimpering pitifully. Once I had unwrapped him,
I found the cause right away. A circa four-centimeter piece of his colon had
protruded through his groin, hard as rock, and the boy screamed at every
touch. I got a deadly scare, called for Miss Oertel and rushed to the telephone
at once. While I talked with Dünzelmann, Miss Oertel had succeeded in
pushing the colon back in, except for a little piece. D. advised to keep the
head lower in bed. He himself would come by. After a long time, the little
man calmed down. Then he also drank a little. Now he is quite active again.
But one has to watch like crazy that the hernia does not become strangulated
again as it must have this time, or else the boy would not have had such pain.
Now it is all behind us. . . .

My love—goodnight. Yours, Li.

Werner to Elisabeth

Liverpool, June 17, afternoon
My dear Elisabeth!
Meanwhile, I have already moved on a little westward. I am sitting in the
offices of the Cunard line, not far from the ship and am using the three hours
before departure time to write. Since my arrival in London yesterday morning, I have been talking about physics almost nonstop, and have learned a
great deal. The only interruption to this scientific activity was a brief meeting
with your brother Fritz. He was particularly appealing this time around: he
was very lively, engaged in all kinds of problems and issues, and we got along
very well. He seemed, despite all the difficulties, optimistic and in good
spirits. In the evening, I was at the Blacketts' and also spent the night there.
Blackett had been quite ill (a strep infection) but looked pretty good again. In
his institute, I saw many nice and new pictures of cosmic ray showers. . . . I
have seen the ship only from the outside thus far; only at 4:30 are we allowed
to enter it.

With the many rapid events of the trip, I have so far not quite been
conscious of the fact that I am going far away. When I was aware once in
a while, I would look at the pictures of you all and imagine that at home

probably all is going well. That is my hope, whenever I think of you, and I am tremendously looking forward to your first news.

All of you stay healthy and cheerful! I am with you in my thoughts often. Yours, Werner.

Elisabeth to Werner

[Leipzig], June 18
My love!—
Now you are already quite far out at sea. How might you be faring? Hopefully you are not seasick! Today, on Sunday, I missed you very, very much. Nobody was here to start the day with Bach and no one to keep me away from my daily chores. So Sunday went on just like any other day; only that I spent more time with the children, and that was very nice. . . .

Good night, my most beloved! Yours, Li.

Elisabeth to Werner

[Leipzig], June 19, noon
Well, Miss Oertel received a telegram saying she had to get to Stockholm for an appointment on Thursday. Now we are packing like mad to take the children to Berlin tomorrow morning. On July 4 my mother will bring them back to me. I am not very happy in my heart that I should give them away, but there is no other way. They are so cute now. And I will then be so very alone. Jochen may have to comfort me. Miss Oertel is not coming back at all. But she thought it necessary to make it clear to me again today just how I had exploited her and how much Anneliese [the new nanny] hates it here—how unlucky Anneliese felt that Miss Oertel had resigned before her. Well—I had my own thoughts about that.

Then she also said that the Walchensee was a terrible imposition for Anneliese and she was not at all looking forward to it. Well—you can imagine that, right now, I am not sad about her departure. I listened to everything quietly, but will increase Anneliese's pay on the 1st to 5 marks. That seems right to me. In reality, I am really somewhat sad—you hold out your hand to people time and again, and then they are like this and are content if they offend and sadden you. But it is just the old truth, very rarely are people unselfishly and honestly committed to you.

Now I have to go into town to buy the children shoes and coats for the city. They should look decent when they travel. And in Berlin, they will be shown off to everyone, so they will have to be looking their best. And the letter must also go out, for it is to go with the *Normandy,* the first ship to take mail since you left. So you will receive news only in Chicago. I am sad about it myself.

Elisabeth to Werner

June 20, at night in bed
My love!

I received your letter yesterday. A thousand thanks, love! I am so glad that you got along so well with Fritz.

. . . All is quiet now after an unbelievable commotion. This is what happened: on Monday Miss Oertel received the telegram from Sweden: "Please come!" So we organized everything for this sudden departure, I dressed the children ready for the journey—we packed up and sewed and ironed until late at night. And this morning it went on; I rushed into town again, got money, ticket, and all sorts of forgotten things. And then— imagine!—a telegram arrives: "Not necessary to come." I was sorry for her because she was really unhappy about this commotion. But now I have sent the children to Berlin anyway. My parents are so looking forward to it. . . .

As I was coming out of the station, I met Jacobi, who had missed us. He invited me to the Europa House for a coffee, and since I was feeling lazy and not duty-bound, I accepted the invitation. . . . Something he said troubled my mind all evening. When I mentioned, somewhat sadly, that I rarely get to go to concerts any more, he said harshly: "You have decided to be richly blessed with children—you cannot have everything!" Is it really so? Is it always only one thing *or* another? But I certainly do not expect to become a plain little wife. And what harm does it do, if you simply devote a few years entirely to that domestic life? Do you then need to unlearn how to fly, to forget about learning!? I certainly do not want to, and we must always help each other so that we do not forget and unlearn, right? Sometimes I, actually, am afraid of becoming completely submerged in everyday life, but then I tell myself that the life that envelops me is surely as instructive and productive as a whole closet full of books—even more so.

But I must close, I am always dozing off! Yours, Li.

Elisabeth to Werner

[Leipzig], June 22
Love—

The letter has to go out today, so that it still can get onto the *Bremen*. Are you there yet in that foreign, large country of America, for which my heart always harbors certain anger, because I have always only found that it spoils the people from Europe and steals their hearts from them.— . . . Just now, Anneliese is putting a plate full of the most delicious cherries from her own garden in front of me. They are so big and wonderful, unlike any I have seen before; during the past two days, I have been constantly thieving cherries right from the tree—unfortunately the blackbirds and thrushes do likewise. . . .

Also: a letter arrived from Mrs. Bohr. Very nice. But she writes of an accident that Bohr had in which his face was badly smashed; he fell off his bicycle—she writes—in a collision with another bicycle. She reports that he is up again, just still very tired and worn out.

Otherwise, nothing else has come. I am going out into the garden now to pick gooseberries. We are in the midst of canning. So that in winter you can eat eighteen gooseberry tortes!

I am reading Storm a lot now. His stories are quite evocative of summer and of fragrant flowers and thus are fitting so well into the current season. Also into my own quiet and solitude, for they still speak of the solidly established, calm, only inwardly impassioned time of the last century. Some of it reminds me of Stifter, who is even greater yet. But I can now understand that your father liked him so much. He has a kinship with Schubert too; and so it is only natural and perfect and good, when I now sometimes will take out the

Schubert, evenings, and sing a little. Only, what is really missing is the accompaniment. . . .

Love, I am so looking forward to your cable! All my love and best wishes to you! Do you know that you are my life? Yours, Li.

Werner to Elisabeth

Mauretania, [June 18]
Dear Li!

Yesterday before our departure I wrote you at length one more time. Now I will start a kind of journal which, however, can be sent off only after our arrival in New York.

The departure in Liverpool was very festive and one could clearly tell how popular the name *Mauretania* is in England. Countless people were standing at the pier and in the harbor streets, around the ship a multitude of small vessels, and at the moment of departure a deafening tooting and whistling of all the larger boats rang out.—The weather upon departure was changeable, quite chilly, and only rarely sunshine. In the dusk, I walked the deck for a long time with Mr. v. Wartburg. I like talking with him about serious issues. . . .

Monday night

Now another day of the sea voyage has gone by. The weather, as predicted last night, has already, during the night, changed over into rain and fog. From midnight on, one could hear the low drone of the foghorn every minute and a half, a sound that surrounds the ship with a somewhat eerie atmosphere. Fortunately, around noon, it turned a little brighter; the sea is completely calm now. We spent the afternoon playing in the sun on deck. But now the foghorn is starting up again.—Later on, in the afternoon, they played a movie on board, which I attended after overcoming some reservations. I get annoyed every time about the smooth and boring faces in which even the faintest hint of character is carefully avoided. But the piece dealt, if you stripped it from its outward presentation, with the ancient battle of the devil against God, in which the former, in the disguise of telephones and business telegrams, was practically making a personal appearance; God had, of course, morphed into the appearance of a *"sweet girl."* What a shame, that he will appear to so many people today only in this way.—

Tuesday night

For the first time it has been totally clear for some hours already. The sea is still rather turbulent from the bad weather at noon, but the air is calm, in the northwest a few broad bands of clouds are at the horizon, wearing a red fringe from the sunset. The water playfully reflects these clouds in light blue and yellowish-red colors.—I am now sometimes aware of how far I am already removed from you and I am in danger of becoming a bit homesick. It is a good thing that I have at least the pictures of the little ones with me. Only from Jochen I do not have such a reminder, and when I return, he will probably look quite different from what I am imagining.

Wednesday night

Unfortunately, a glance at the map that registers our daily position at noon tells us that we are still more than two thousand kilometers from New York. An arrival tomorrow is out of the question; even on Friday it is hardly likely. So we may only get there on Saturday morning. This will shorten my time at Uncle Karl's considerably, and may even make my stay at Princeton impossible. . . .

Friday noon

Today the sky is almost cloudless and the sea is as quiet as even the Walchensee can only be in the calmest weather. The first sailboats are appearing, a few birds are circling the ship, and with each hour one can sense the coast approaching. Maybe very late tonight Long Island will come into sight. Tomorrow morning, at 8:30, we are supposed to be in New York. Since the mail will leave the ship before our arrival, I will herewith end the journal; I am very much looking forward to everything new over there. And I hope to hear from you soon. All the best to you four! Yours, Werner.

Elisabeth to Werner

Thursday, June 22, evening
My love!

. . . I had a nice visit this evening: Erwin [Heisenberg] invited himself to supper and we sat comfortably in the garden for almost two hours, talking about this and that. It was relaxed and nice; only when the conversation turned to the future, I was overcome again by all the fear and terror and I could not shake them all evening. Will a war really start in the autumn? This conversation stood in a grotesque contrast to the evening's peace. As the twilight deepened, the larkspur began to glow, which made me think a lot about the flowers of Hildegard Kress. But I have to stop for today, I am so very tired. Yours, Li.

Elisabeth to Werner

June 24, evening
Love—

Anneliese brought me your cable just now, when Mrs. van der Waerden was here for tea and we were talking about you and the first telegram. How good it is that you now have solid ground under your feet again! I am excited about your next letter. Thank you for the news.

Today I played music all evening long—nothing but Schubert. And I experienced the bliss of playing music myself once again—the bliss that makes you forget time and your surroundings. I felt like I used to earlier, when, after an afternoon full of music and with glowing cheeks and still far away, I would come to the table and my parents would not quite know what was wrong with me. I used to feel so royally happy. Love, I do not understand myself. Why does it only happen when I know that you are not here? It is so absurd! And I know if I stopped being shy, then it would be so much better, for you, for me, for us; because then I would be so much more sure, happier, and more independent. I know all this, and yet, when I know that you hear it, I do not dare make egregious mistakes, playing the same thing wrong time and again, dropping out of key or doing similarly bad things; then everything must be correct, and immediately inhibition sets in, gone are the enthusiasm and courage. How silly, how ridiculously silly of me. But I know, as of yet, no remedy. You would not believe how happy I was to bring these tones and superb harmonies to life through my own hands. I could scarcely hear enough of the song "O Du Entrissene mir" [Oh, you, stolen from me] and I practiced it carefully, so that I could accompany myself quite fluently. It really is one of the most beautiful songs I know. Now that I can play it securely, I also sing it quite nicely. I am terribly excited when we will sing at the Walchensee with the windows open and with only the rustling of the beech trees and the bird songs as a soft accompaniment.—

Good night, love. Dream about the Walchensee, that we will be together again and that, so God will, true peace will embrace us. "*Sei mir geküsst*" [take my kisses], dearest you! Yours, Li.

Werner to Elisabeth

New York, June 25, Sunday evening
My dear good Li!
Actually, I am very tired already, but my journal from the steamer will only reach you with some delay; so I still want to write today, before I continue on to Chicago. . . . The approach to the harbor of New York is a very powerful experience each time. The big buildings of Manhattan were visible for some time only as silhouettes in the somewhat hazy atmosphere. The whole city then appears like a huge fairy-tale castle. At the pier, I soon spotted Uncle Karl and Otto Bauermeister. I was sincerely happy to see them both again. . . .

Today I spent the Sunday with Otto in Flushing. We used the afternoon for a visit to the World Exhibition. How many incredibly different people there are here! Whites, blacks, all kinds of mixes, ugly mugs, and also wonderfully strong, fresh faces—everything mixed together. That this mixture can amount to a nation seems like a miracle, when you think of what we denote with the word *Volk*. The World Exhibition itself is interesting, but actually not in a way that would make one glad. Everywhere just technology and propaganda. The best, still, is in an area where technology is at the frontier of its capabilities: at the newest train locomotives, automobiles, etc. Italy and Russia too have erected two big buildings; Germany is not represented. Italy is showing much artisan craft work, technology too (airplanes, etc.). At the Russians' [exhibit], the best was the large sculptures. The interior of [the Russian] building partially filled with the cheapest and most mindless propaganda. Interesting, what the different nations are taking pride in: at the Russians', e.g., the statue of a woman, accustomed to driving a tractor; of a miner; pictures of famous pilots. A nation like America, by contrast, describes itself as "The World's Most Famous Playground," "The Happiest City"—etc. Overall, though, the exhibition is showing a world completely devoid of meaning, even though externally glittery.— . . .

I find it awful that I have not heard from you and everybody in such a long time. Of course, it is not possible, but I miss it very much. I am having so many new experiences and no one really with whom to process it properly. The people here are just thinking quite differently than where we come from, particularly the young ones. An eighteen-year-old cousin of Mary [Bauer-meister] is living here at the house too, and is often visited by a rather nice *boyfriend* as well. The totally automatic assumption is that life is about "having a good time." If they were to realize that for me this looks a little different, they would think I am crazy, or not telling the truth. But, of course, I am not letting on. One thing is very nice here: everything is seemingly working smoothly on its own, without effort.—By the way, so far, I have not encountered anti-German sentiments; all the Americans have treated me very nicely.—I hope to hear from you very soon! To you and the little ones all my best! Yours, Werner. . . .

Elisabeth to Werner

Tuesday, June 27
My love!
The thought that today you are finally receiving a letter from me makes me all happy. It feels as though, after a long day of work, we are still taking our walk to the mailbox together. Oh, my love—just keep on loving me diligently—you would not believe how sad I would become otherwise.

. . . Jochen is coming along practically perfectly. . . . He looks so well and so contented often; and he will look at you, and then a smile will slide across his little face. He is the dearest little fellow, and I am so very happy about him. You will be mighty amazed when you see him again. Good night, dearest! Yours, Li.

Elisabeth to Werner

June 28, 6 a.m.
Dearest—

Now I am at a complete loss. The young miss I hired [as a nanny] has just sent me an express letter saying that she has now become engaged and wants to get married in the fall, so she could not come. What to do, says Zeus!? I feel totally out of luck. All the others were already told the position is filled.

Elisabeth to Werner

June 29, evening

Well, last night I was too tired to write anymore, simply fell into bed. Almost all day long I had been moving heaven and earth. My decision was soon made. In July I will manage on my own; the washerwoman can help Annelies[e], and Annelies[e] can lend me a hand with the children. It will work quite well. And then I will keep on looking without rushing it. . . .

But how are things with you? Do you also miss us at times? Or is America swallowing you hook, line, and sinker? It has only been fourteen days since you left, and it already seems like an eternity to me. Another six weeks. Oh, my dearest, then it will be glorious. And then the Walchensee! I am looking forward to it, all excited. Good night! Yours, Li.

Werner to Elisabeth

Chicago, Tuesday morning [June 27]
My dear Li!

Above all else, I want to send you many good wishes for your birthday. I find it awful that I cannot set up your birthday table myself; I hope you have your mother visit and celebrate with you and the three little ones. How might you all be doing, I wonder? I have not heard a thing from you all, but that is also hardly possible; yet it creates a feeling of uncertainty when you are without any news for a fortnight. . . .

The trip from New York to here was lovely. For the first few hours you drive along the Hudson River, in many ways reminiscent of the Rhine. It is wider, but also confined on both sides by small mountain ranges. The shores are settled very sparsely; once in a while there is a hamlet of wooden houses up high. On the river itself there are steamboats and paddleboats, and on the shores you can see half-naked folk who want to escape from the heat into the waters. During the night, we once came through a forest, glittering with millions of fireflies, it looked like in a fairy tale.—This morning, I first got lost driving in Chicago but then, eventually, got to where I wanted to go. Unfortunately, my suitcase is not here yet, so I cannot yet change clothes. But it is indescribably hot; the sky is overcast and the air all humid; I hope there will be rain this afternoon. . . .

Thursday night [June 29]

. . . I am happy to see so many old acquaintances again. It is strange in a way, to return after ten years to a faraway place on earth where one once was very familiar. Not much has changed; the people have all aged a little—I myself probably as well. But they are all very nice to me. The day before yesterday, I was invited to the house in which I had lived for half a year. The piano stood in the same place, and I had to, of course, play it.—I also met Bonhoeffer today. He is soon going back home and will bring you greetings and catch you up. . . .

Werner to Elisabeth

[Chicago-Lafayette], Friday evening [June 30]
Dear, good Li!

Now the conference here is over; today I have also given my talk and now I am exhausted from all the many discussions. Overall, I have learned many new things and am very happy that I have participated. But tonight, it would be nice if I could sit comfortably with you and tell you everything.

Instead, I am alone in a rather boring hotel room, am so tired that I can barely think anymore, and would probably not be able to go to sleep anyhow on account of the heat. I seek solace in pictures from Leipzig, partly in my head, partly from my pocket. . . .

I am staying here in the guesthouse of the university, the whole area of the campus looks a little like the Kaiser Wilhelm Institute in Berlin and the Harnack House. On a little stroll (once again in awful heat) I found out that already within about half an hour one leaves the city behind completely. On the other side of the campus there begin the cow fields; next to a large farm building the university cows are grazing, behind it is the airport, and then a little further on the woods. I think I will find it very pleasant here these next three weeks.

Evening

Meanwhile, there was a party at the "head of department's," who plays the violin and viola quite well. Naturally: Kegelstatt Trio and Vivaldi. He lives on a hill on the other side of the river; the river is called Wabash, is a bit more than the Saale, and goes right through town. The town itself is barely the size of Göttingen; there are, of course, no old houses, just modern stone buildings in the English style, and then many, mostly wooden, homes. One has the impression of a certain wealth; the university in particular seems to be very well off. . . .

At 7:30 a.m. is my first, somewhat official lecture, so I have to quickly close now. To the four of you my very, very best, I am thinking of you so much, and maybe you can sense that a little too. Yours, Werner.

Elisabeth to Werner

July 2, midnight
Love—

It is now already midnight again. Not good! Today it was just my writing that kept me busy for so long. It was a quiet day. The third Sunday. Now five more Sundays to go, then you will be here again. Today I took advantage of having free time, and I read and played music—actually all day long: Storm and Schubert. My senses were completely filled by these two. As for Schubert, I am mainly engrossed in the Müller-Lieder. And Storm—I find it marvelous: this diversity of fateful lives that he can depict so warmly and vividly. Behind everything that is merely specific to the times he depicts, there is always a piece of the great Law of Life emerging, so that the sum total becomes one big mosaic. I enjoy reading it very much—and yet am crying like a child.

Here we have really crazy weather. Humid, and then severe thunderstorms, hail, and cloudbursts.

The children will be coming tomorrow. I am out of my mind with joy. Since Miss Oertel has left, I am even more excited, because now they are really mine, all mine!

So much for today, all my love and best wishes to you! Yours, Li.

Elisabeth to Werner

Monday, July 3

Love—

Now the children are back—they have grown much. Maria did not pay much attention to me; but the boy flung his arms around my neck and beamed. The house was immediately familiar again to them. They were dead tired, and we put them to bed right away. The boy was incredibly joyous, and his laughter, as always, gave me such great pleasure. Maria had been rather overly active on the train, so that she was more tired than he was.—

But in midmorning I had another big scare, and it made me tired all evening. Jochen had a strangulated hernia again, like before, but it just would not go back in. Finally, I called the surgeon, Dr. Hörhagen. He wanted me to come in with the little guy. How children cry when they are in severe pain—it's terrible. So I ran quickly to get the car. When I returned, everybody was on tiptoes—Jochen had gone to sleep. Pale and exhausted, he lay on Mrs. Frels's arm. We packed diapers and baby jackets and shirts in a suitcase—you can imagine how I felt. Then we set off. Jochen was sleeping.

When we arrived and the doctor had unwrapped him, the hernia was back in.—I could have cried with joy—and Dr. Hörhagen stroked his hair, lovingly, and said, "Well—it would be such a pity about this nice little guy!" For a young child, an operation like this can be quite life threatening. Dr. H. gave me precise instructions about what to do, and also the address of the best surgeon in Munich, in case it should happen at the Walchensee. He said that he should be operated on in a year; and it is better if it can be avoided before. I am now well informed and will be calmer about it next time. But I was proud that I had done all the right things on my own.—But that I was somewhat exhausted after everything, you will understand. So I need to sleep now. Tomorrow I will be a quarter of a century old already!

Werner to Elisabeth

La Fayette, July 4
My dear "Birthday Girl"!

Today you have to celebrate without me; but the little ones will be coming with your mother to congratulate you—they are like somewhat of a greeting from me—then you are getting a few little things, of which I don't quite know if you will like them, and lastly, I sent a telegram just now. That will not get to you, though, until rather late. For our time differs from yours by six hours, so that now you are already into early evening. . . .

I was so very happy about your letter. I can imagine the garden so well and miss it that here there are no roses. Your conversation with Jacobi also is very clear to me; he is quite right that one cannot have everything. But if we do not want the things we are doing to remain superficial, then it seems to me we will always have to arrange our whole life such that we renounce most options voluntarily. I do not view this as a calamity. I am also firmly convinced that later on, when the times for an intellectual life become more favorable, we will participate in it much more than so far. What impresses itself particularly strongly on me here is how much these possibilities are dependent on the whole surrounding atmosphere. Here there are very dynamic people; especially the young ones engage in intellectual matters more than where we are.

Wednesday night [July 5]

... Yesterday, your birthday, had a very nice ending for us here. Toward evening, we drove far out into a hilly area that extends from here towards the south, covered with woods. We stayed outside at an amazing waterfall amid rocks until almost midnight. A little fire was lit, and slowly memories came back about a time long ago; inevitably, it so happened that I was in charge of the fire by myself, and I placed, almost without thinking, piece after piece of wood into the fire, following the long-standing procedures, till it was all symmetrical and round and burning perfectly even. Above the fire, a magnificent clear starry sky was stretched out, looking only slightly different from ours at home. Later on, the moon came up and changed the whole scene again; in the moonlight the woods looked homey and familiar; as I was watching the fire, and also smelled the smoke in my clothes, it felt as if a very deep chord had been struck that had not sounded anymore in a long time.

Thursday evening [July 6]

The letter must go, and in five minutes I am expected at the institute. Today I gave my lecture, played tennis, and had many discussions. I have the feeling that I get younger here and more mobile. I also rarely read the newspaper. America has a strange effect, on me too. But I am happy as well that I will soon come home again. In four weeks I will be leaving. So, in a hurry, a thousand heartfelt greetings! Yours, Werner.

Elisabeth to Werner

July 4

The last half hour of this day is to be for you alone, my love! Tonight, I really miss you very, very much, although my parents made everything so very nice for me, and although your cable arrived, bringing me your greetings. Thank you, my dear. I was so delighted—also with the nice things from you: the handbag, which I find very nice, the lovely tile, the book, and the wonderful lace tablecloth, which certainly will look splendid on the round table in the living room. The bag is my very favorite; but the tablecloth is also wonderful. My parents too were very generous with gifts. Papa had a really nice idea. He got hold of a painting by Corinth, which shows the exact view from our house. If we like it, he would like to present it to us in the original size, or thirty-four and a quarter inches wide, twenty-seven and a half inches high. . . .

We had a radiantly beautiful day. Everything was nice and harmonious, except the evening. . . . My father was determined to take the twins back to Berlin so that I might concentrate just on Jochen. But I resisted that plan. I do not want to do without the children any longer. And then we were all tired, especially me, I suppose, since Jochen is now always very restless, and afterward things stopped being pleasant. And he means so well. He is basically a poor, lonely man; he loves the children with great devotion and affection. And they love him too. But—there is no solid bridge from him to me. Nothing can be done about it. And when I am with him for a while, I get doubly struck with homesickness for you, because I only feel *really* at home with you, really glad and happy. . . .

Elisabeth to Werner

[July 5]
My love—
Today all your beautiful presents were inaugurated. The handbag proves to be fabulous because a huge amount can disappear into it, which is very important! . . . I'm also studying the book by Haarer diligently. It is very good for me, because I am right now not doing so very well with the children. You know, because of Jochen they have inevitably become some-what remote from me in recent weeks—perhaps even months—and Miss Oertel had backed that up. Now we need first to become attuned to each other again; with Maria in particular it is difficult for me, and I do not know whether my mother being stern is quite right. In any case, I now seek advice in the book on many things. If only I will get someone for the children. I am often scared to death.— . . .

We have glorious weather here. The children are running around all day dressed only in short pants. I also let Jochen be all naked, kicking his legs—it is so warm. He has become a blissful little guy—looking splendid, and with a delightful smile; he will soon be laughing jubilantly. . . . The letter has to go now. Take good care of yourself, my love! All my love. Yours, Li.

Werner to Elisabeth

La Fayette, Friday, July 7, evening
My dear Li! . . .

Saturday afternoon [July 8]

I do not quite manage yet in these incredibly high temperatures. I am wilted and not motivated for any kind of work. I am wearing as little as is possible and decent; however, five minutes of piano practice are enough to make you sweat like two hours' worth of basic training in the military. It really is very good that, in a month, I will arrive back with you all. What the little ones will look like? I always look at their pictures and am aware that they may have changed completely in the meantime. I wonder if the two big ones are already talking some? I am terribly curious.

Sunday night [July 9]

Last night we ended up making music. Leclair, Handel, Brahms [horn trio]. Same thing tonight: I am accompanying the wife of an American colleague who really sings very well. Old Italian lieder, Rossini, Mozart, Debussy. Also a few violin sonatas were played. But all the pianos here are bad—probably due to the hot, humid climate. Music here is only half as much fun. On these uneven pianos, I am playing even more inexactly than at home.— . . .

Monday noon [July 10]. . . .

Especially now that I am not quite feeling well, I have a great longing for news from all of you.

I am reading in the papers that, at least for the next weeks, there is no danger of war. That is a great relief to me because of my travel home. It is now pretty much half time since my departure from Leipzig. So one can almost count the days already. Just take good care of yourself and the little ones. Greetings to them all, especially our youngest, whom I don't quite know how to picture now. Every good wish!

Yours, Werner.

Elisabeth to Werner

Saturday evening [July 8]

My dear, good love!

Yesterday I missed a ship for the first time. I am very sad about it. . . . I am having great trouble finding any willing and able help. Unlike the first one, I do not like any of them without reservations this time. But I must probably shift gears and take a simpler person with no other ties to our family. She has a fabulous reference, spent five years in her first position, and had to look after two children there from birth onward; she is perfect at cooking, ironing, and serving meals. The advantage is that we will be undisturbed, without always having a stranger around, while the disadvantage is that I will have almost no conversational outlet when you are away. . . .

Be well, you dear, good love! Yours, Li.

. . . Love, I have now taken the one I wrote to you about, after another one presented herself here today who would have very much liked to come. But she made too much of her aristocratic relatives, and basically thought she was too fancy for everything.—Well, I hope you are satisfied with my choice. I will have to make quite an adjustment, because having two domestic workers is very different from before. But I have considered everything in detail and think it should go quite well. . . .

Tuesday morning [July 11]

. . . Today I have a huge program for the day. I have to buy dishes for the helpers and all kinds of household things, so that everything is in place for when the new girl comes. If the two of them are to eat and spend time in the kitchen, it should be nice. The whole organization is getting changed upside down—I am very curious to see how it will all turn out. . . . The letter has to get out this morning. So I will close! With all my love and best wishes from your Li.

Werner to Elisabeth

[Lafayette], Tuesday, July 11
Dear Li!

. . . My lectures are going along quite nicely and people are paying very close attention. I am enjoying lecturing here. In Leipzig one would meet in the same class only a tenth of people who really understand the material.

Wednesday evening [July 12]

Gradually here, too, the number of obligations is increasing to a level where I have too little time, just like in Leipzig. In addition, I am now progressing from the material in my lectures that I have already given in Leipzig to the one I still have to work out. I need more time for this than people here are allowing me. . . .

I am once again consoling myself, as I often do, with the Walchensee. Sometimes I worry a little that in the beginning it will have to be terribly uncomfortable because, of course, everything has to be done over. But it might be also quite nice to work as a gardener and handyman for a change. What is the state of affairs now with the house, how far has the work on the terrace progressed? I would love to once or twice be able to check on things from here, but now I have to leave everything to you. By the way, one can do the math: today half of the separation time is over, isn't that nice? . . .

Thursday afternoon [July 13]

. . . This morning I again had a long talk with the head of the department, who would like to invite me here more often. Also, I have been asked by others a few times under what conditions I would permanently come here. The two aspects, light and shadow, are so immensely clear.

I am treated fabulously in every way. I would have ten times as many bright students as where we are. It would probably also affect the results in my work positively. But we just are not at home here. The children would speak English and grow up in an atmosphere that is foreign to us. That would not be nice at all, and so we are just staying put.—

We finished with the music now, all Italian, French, modern Dutch music, that is fully unknown to me. The French lieder are incredibly affecting, intriguing in their harmonics, but also "slightly suspect." (Mean people might say: champagne with whipped cream.)

In my thoughts I am so much with you all. Take care! Yours, Werner.

Elisabeth to Werner

July 11
My dear, dear Werner!
Today was a good day. Above all, the letter you wrote on my birthday came. How lovely, that you have such a nice time! How I would have liked to have been with you in those woods. Now you have another memory all to yourself. Do you suppose that one day we will experience together something that strikes that chord, or is that not possible? Tell me about it sometime at the Walchensee, right?

Everything is in order there, Bodmer [an area contractor] was there. The terrace is almost finished; the work inside will begin on July 17. . . .

We are packing boxes and crates for the Walchensee. It is an efficient operation. . . .

With Mutti it works out so perfectly. It is simply great to have her here. Good night for today! Yours, Li.

Elisabeth to Werner

Thursday, July 13
The "treasure" arrived today. Her name is Elfriede and she makes a pretty good impression. I have furnished the small chamber for her, and she was very happy about the nice room. She appears to be calm, clear, and reliable. Her hands are expressive and nice, which inspires my trust in her. The children have accepted her already within these few hours. I believe this was a good choice. And my mother is telling me just now that the way she is dealing with the children shows her great experience and confidence; and yet she also appears quite unassuming by nature. Tomorrow my mother will be leaving.—

And when you receive this letter, you will already be in New York. And in four weeks you are almost back here again! That is good. Just enjoy the rest of your time there, my love. . . .

All my love and best wishes to you! Yours, Li.

Werner to Elisabeth

[Lafayette], Friday, July 14
My dear, little Li!

It is almost midnight, and I am calculating that the sun is already up where you are, that little Jochen is maybe hungry already and disrupting your sleep. It is in some sense strange that day and night are different here from where you are. In a poem from the youth movement booklet, which you know, there is the verse: "The luster of the day that gave us joy moves around the world silently and brightly."

How true that is! I hope everything is well with you all. We are having some wonderful weather here today after, just the day before yesterday, the thermometer climbed to 37 Celsius in the shade. The air is cool today, and outside there is now this genuine, fresh summer night. We have played music for a long time with acquaintances, this time some really good music, and then we listened to records of Mozart and Beethoven. The violin concerto by Beethoven has made me come alive again, just incredible music. In the winter, we must listen to a lot of music and play it too. . . .

Sunday night [July 16]
Today I slowed my pace in the most agreeable fashion: slept in, read the paper, wrote letters in the morning. At noon I was invited by the Nordheimers [U.S. colleagues]; afterward we drove around the area a little. Then we listened to the *Magic Flute* on records; in the evening the whole institute was invited by the head of the machine shop. He owns a charming house, has an excellent library, piano, and record player, and considers himself an equal of the professors, which he actually is with all that. The evening went splendidly: people played table tennis, made music (violin and piano), listened to gramophone records (Handel, Mozart, Liszt). The fact that such a thing is

possible makes for America's real strength. Class distinctions, at least in this place, do not exist. And whoever is proud of his work is not going to be tempted to envy others. . . .

Now have a very good time during those three weeks, you all! The letter must go out today to make the airmail. Many, many greetings! Yours, Werner.

Elisabeth to Werner

Friday, July 14
Love—

I now often have a terrible yearning, counting the days and the hours. God willing, you will be back here soon. . . . The children are in marvelous shape. Jochen is becoming more delightful with every day. He has big, dark, thoughtful eyes. And you can already detect tiny traces of his soul and his mind in them. And it seems to be a friendly, fortunate little soul. At least, whenever I take him out of his little basket—whether he had been awake or was fast asleep—he starts, in his love of life, to kick his feet and to laugh. . . .

Elisabeth to Werner

Sunday, July 16, early morning
 . . . Here in the house, everything is working out quite wonderfully with the new girl. I feel as though I am in paradise, am finally getting around to organizing my own things too, and no longer feel that the work I have not yet done is looming over me like an impossibly high mountain. It is just that I am very much alone right now and have too much time. I get caught up pondering the dark picture everybody is painting. How fortunate that the children do not know anything about all this and are so unencumbered and jolly, so enterprising and full of life. . . .

Hopefully, you will find more joy in playing music at the Walchensee than right now. The piano is not so wonderful either, but it is better than none at all. Good night for now! Yours, Li.

Werner to Elisabeth

Lafayette, July 18

My dear Li!

Sometimes the mail is incredibly fast: today I got your letter from last Tuesday; it took less than a week. Many thanks for everything you are telling me about! I had the feeling that you are a little overworked and that the whole job with the children is making you too tired, after all. I hope you have good help now; that is, I hope the new helpful soul you hired is coming through for you. I am so curious about everything new when I return.— . . .

By the way, I think I have not yet told you about our musical evening on Monday: the "boss" had found a cellist, so that we could play quartet with him and a violinist he knew. We went over the Beethoven and the two Mozarts; that was such a great delight. In spite of the bad piano (on some keys the ivory was missing, in the higher ranges the tone was reminiscent of a stone axe), I believe I played quite decently. It definitely was fun, in the absence of a Jacobi, to properly direct such a quartet myself. Probably we will play again today or tomorrow; since the cellist is unavailable, trios will be tried, where the viola substitutes the cello. We have found out the other day that, with Schubert, that works out quite decently.

When you get this letter, you will be most likely full force into preparations for the trip to the Walchensee. . . . It is amazing how competently you are accomplishing the whole organization of the trip, in addition to the work with the children. . . .

Now the letter must go out to reach the airmail. Greetings to the little ones, especially the youngest, even if he does not always want to cooperate. All the best to you from your Werner.

Elisabeth to Werner

July 24

My love!—

To my greatest surprise, I received another letter from you today, namely, the one you wrote and sent before the one I received yesterday. It is impossible to know what happened to it. Anyway, I was very, very happy about this letter, and do thank you very much. This letter here has to go out before evening; and it is already late, because we were again very busy today. We were canning a lot, to make use of all the beautiful fruit. The berries this year are unusually abundant. I also gave Mrs. Jacobi some, and still the bushes are so fully loaded that I hardly know how I am going to fit them all in.

Today I became very frightened about myself and about the great, great challenge of bringing up children. We had the twins together in the bathtub and washed their hair. In order to rinse out the soap, I turned the shower on and, from behind, sprayed the boy's head. The poor little thing was so terribly shocked that at first he did not react at all but was then perturbed all evening. . . . I still have so much to learn—also about how infinitely tender a child's soul is; one has to think of this at every moment. I need a vacation because at the moment I do not have the calm and the flexibility the children need.

For me too the Walchensee is like a little treasure chest that contains the fulfillment of every wish. Love—fear not that it might be too unfinished. We can leave ourselves as much time for the work there as we want. We can definitely turn the work into pleasure. But just imagine us having breakfast in the morning out on the terrace, the children playing there, and no other person to disturb us, while everything around us belongs to us, even the beauty of nature in that place.— . . . —All my love. Yours, Li.

Werner to Elisabeth

[New York], Monday, July 24
My dear Li!
This time you get a somewhat shorter letter than usual; in the days before my departure to here, I had no time to write at all. On Friday the day went by with packing, then my lecture, and saying my good-byes at a gathering with friends that lasted until almost 1 o'clock. On Saturday I lectured again from 10 to 11 and then quickly got in the car; we drove the four hundred kilometers to Ann Arbor straight through, almost without a break. There we arrived at 7 o'clock. We were passing through a hilly, partially wooded terrain with many fields of grain; in between there was a

region with many lakes, similar to Mecklenburg. In Ann Arbor I met up with the Fermis right away at a party, and they told me much about their experiences during the recent months. I also met their children; they already spoke English rather well. To see a few old acquaintances again gave me great joy. Much has changed there, but the friendly calm of this town, with gardens everywhere, has remained the same. I did not pass by my old apartment from way back, regrettably. Until Sunday night I stayed there, spending the afternoon with the entire Italian colony: Fermi, Amaldi, Fano, and others. Last night then I got in the sleeping compartment and woke up early to a cloudless sky, just as we were traveling along the Hudson.

During the night we had also crossed a very wide river, but I have not yet found out where that was. Probably it was the Niagara, but in the dark I could not see the falls. Here the first enjoyable event was finding your letter; many thanks for that! How nice that you are all doing so well. I am also happy that you are pleased with the helper; let's hope it stays that way.

Tuesday afternoon [July 25]

In an hour I will give my lecture, and then I have to hurry to catch the train to Larchmont. So I must finish this letter quickly. A week from today I will already board the ship. . . . Till then I will have a very nice time here at Uncle Karl's, for sure. I will be living there in the country, from every window one looks out at high trees, and in the morning one is awakened by singing birds. Also, the resemblance of Uncle Karl to my father, though slight, makes me feel right at home.—

So give the little ones my love, and when you get this letter, it will only be about ten days till I am back. Take care. Yours, Werner.

Werner to Elisabeth

New York, Sunday evening, July 30
My dear Li!

Once again I have received a long letter from you and you won't be able to write me again before I leave, but perhaps I'll get news again in Cherbourg. I am so happy that everything is going so well with you all, that little

Jochen is thriving, and that you are looking forward to my return. I am now more excited day by day about seeing you all, it is now only a few days until then, and when you get this letter, I am probably just a thousand kilometers off the British coast. The ship I am going home on is already in the harbor, tomorrow morning I will pack my suitcase, the day after I am off to go aboard. . . .

Tuesday morning [August 8]

In the meantime, I have strolled in the city once more all by myself, and looked at the sights I still wanted to see: after I took care of all my papers at the customs office, I went up to the highest building (four hundred meters) and looked at everything from above in clear weather. Then I ate lunch up on the eighty-sixth floor—it is considerably breezier there than on the Europahaus— and when I stepped out onto the open-air terrace, my briefcase almost was ripped from my hands by the wind. I like these high towers more than everything else. They stand in the city like giant rocks. Compared to them, all our high buildings are just toys. If you want to get an approximate impression of the buildings here, you should think of the rocks in the Dolomite Mountains— the little Zinne or the Brenta. And by night they all are unbelievable fairy-tale castles with a thousand lights. So—tonight I am saying good-bye to this world of man-made rocks to return to the friendlier mountains, formed by nature. But one thing I still have to tell you, so that you can get a better impression and can understand why I am referring to "rocks": yesterday I was walking through the streets and looked up at one of these buildings. There was—like so often in the mountains—a cloud clinging to the top portion of such a tower that obscured the summit totally for some time, and only when the wind picked up did the top portion reappear, glittering in the sunlight from the moisture. From up above, I have also spotted the ship in the harbor that brings me to Germany. Tonight I go on board and after midnight we will depart. I am looking forward to the sea voyage, and of course so much more to seeing you all again.—Uncle Karl and Aunt Helen also are sending their best to you all. So, in one week I will be with you again. To a happy reunion, Li! Yours, Werner.

WERNER RETURNS TO GERMANY *at the beginning of August and moves to the new house on the Walchensee with his family. Four weeks later he returns—together* with his mother—to Leipzig. *The war has started, and in the general uncertainty about what will happen, it makes sense to leave the family in Urfeld.*

In mid-September a new nanny, Edeltrud Olvig, joins the household, providing Elisabeth with company and domestic assistance. Thus she no longer needs to depend solely on the unsatisfactory Marie, who was on her one year of compulsory community service and had come at the recommendation of the innkeeper in Urfeld, Mrs. Brackenhofer, but was often more trouble than help.

When it turns out that Werner will be commissioned to the uranium project in Berlin, not drafted into military service, the couple decides the family should return to Leipzig. The two consult on these matters by letter and, occasionally, by telephone. Werner returns to Urfeld for one brief weekend, but then the house is shut down for the winter. The Leipzig house undergoes a makeover for wartime, and after the end of October, the family is reunited in the city.

Werner to Elisabeth

Leipzig, Monday evening [September 11?]
Dear Li!

We have labored terribly hard since yesterday, and now the most important things are halfway in order. The journey here was very nice: a wonderfully clear day, the fields everywhere completely peaceful. Not much talk about the war. And yet it reminds me in some way of the time twenty-five years ago, which still is in my memory as distinct as if it had been yesterday. On the journey I sometimes had a similar feeling to the one you have when you return to a house you have not visited for a long time and suddenly you notice the old smell again. In Munich, I visited Sommerfeld. The walk through the completely dark Schwabing under a cloudless and clear starry sky was splendid—Ernst Sommerfeld, who visited us recently, is at the front, probably in Poland. . . .

Here in the house, things are not quite right when you are not here. I am always missing something; I do not hear your voice, the children are not squawking, and it is far too quiet to be a home.

If I have to, or am allowed to, stay here all winter, I think I will be far too lonely and I would really like to bring you all here again. Perhaps I will be able to find out something about my future in the next few days. At any rate, I want to come to Urfeld again in three weeks. We can then discuss everything, and you should remain out in the countryside for some time anyway.—If there is anything urgent to discuss, call me, because the mail takes a very long time. And tell me how things are going out there.

A thousand good wishes! Yours, Werner.

Elisabeth to Werner

Thursday evening [September 14?]
My love!

Now I have not written a single word to you for an entire day. But you have no idea how I have slaved away. I think I have never worked so hard in all my life. From 6:30 in the morning until 11:30 at night, almost without a break. Today was a bit better, as the weather cleared up and the children played outdoors by themselves for a while. I used the time to set up Miss Olvig's room. She arrives tomorrow morning. I am enclosing her letter— just so you get an impression of her . . . !

Suddenly in the middle of work, I am often gripped by a terrible fright—everybody, everybody who has visited us here has left. And who will return? I can only, very gradually, comprehend what war means, actually, only since you have been away, and maybe just since Miss Olvig's letter. And now I also understand Wiechert's book much better.

There is no end to the things I could tell you about these two days. One thing I have learned: namely, the risk involved with raising children is infinitely higher when you cannot afford help. Several things have happened where the children were endangered. The worst one happened recently, when I was talking with the painter for a moment. Wolfgang had run off, quickly, to the water, wanting to throw big rocks in—you know, near the private house, where it gets very deep immediately. Since then I have had the children on a tether. And today, I had sent them with Marie to hang up laundry. Marie came back by herself. When I asked her where the children were, she said, "I

The Urfeld house

don't know!" We searched frantically, then found them sitting quietly by the garden gate. . . .

By the way, I think that he [Wolfgang] is really musical, because he listens so very intensely when I sing. There's no knowing with Maria. She doesn't ever reveal what is going on in her heart and mind. But she too is a sweet little person, and the two of them now will often horse around together, so that their laughter rings throughout the house.

By the way, I would like to ask you to get a children's picture book for us. You have no idea how much the children like the pictures above their beds. Every evening they stand chattering in front of them and point with their fingers, as though it all meant something. . . .

Thank you for your long letter. . . . I sometimes think—although it is so awful: you in Leipzig and I here—that it really is the right thing. It seems awfully difficult all around in Leipzig. I am sending margarine, right away, with this. It is a precious commodity here too, but I can get enough fat. I can get boots for children under three without a coupon. I will have to see whether I can get some in Kochel in the next few days. . . .

Good night, love of my heart! Yours, Li.

Werner to Elisabeth

Leipzig, midday Friday [September 15]
My dear Li!

Thank you for your letter. How much work you must have now! Hopefully, in the meantime, the help from Nordhausen has arrived. I find it troubling that I have heard from you only so late. Now and then you should perhaps give me a call at night. . . .

It is so good that you in Urfeld are far from the war. If you had to look after the three little ones here in Leipzig as well as stand in line for food, I do not know how you could manage it. Mama has an awful lot of work here. One runs to the shops every day, and then only gets referred to try again the next day. But of course, these things are minor compared with the actual burdens of the war.

I had very sad news yesterday: the brother of Karl-Friedrich von Weizsäcker was killed in action in the night of September 2–3. His parents sent me the notice. Heinrich v. W. was a very nice man, chivalrous and upstanding, certainly one of the best officers you can imagine. I have often played music with him; he was a very good cellist. The news made me think of Wiechert's book; of the place where he writes about the old Prussian clans, who always sacrificed their best blood in the battlefields. This will also be very difficult for Adelheid, who was particularly attached to this brother.—I have written to the parents and also to C.F.

Bonhoeffer was in Berlin yesterday. He said that he had heard through Debye that in the next few days I would be commissioned to Berlin to some military armament agency or something similar. Tomorrow in Berlin I will hear more. If that is right, I would perhaps be based in Berlin for a longer period. I am not entirely comfortable with this thought. You do not have a very good conscience when you live a comfortable life during this period. But perhaps the war should be left to younger people. By the way, I heard that voluntary sign-ups were happening nowhere, and that people are subject to decisions from up high. One can perhaps draw some comfort from this.—You may well wonder how illogical all this writing is. But in these times, one will discover how terribly difficult it is to reconcile feeling and thought. And even one's feelings are riddled with contradictions.

Yesterday evening, the Watanabes said good-bye to me. He told me that he had to go back to Japan now; however, he had no more money, also the route via Siberia was blocked. He wanted to try to get to Norway and from there to America by ship. Of course, this is also dangerous because of the war at sea. On this long journey, he will take his four-week-old baby with him, of whom he showed me some lovely photos. All this he told me with a smile, a true Japanese, as though he were talking about a Sunday outing. He also brought along some wonderful presents for you and me: for you a big red kimono of Japanese silk, for me a very handsome cigarette case. You will find both here, when next you come here again. . . .

I am in Berlin until Sunday evening. If you do not have time to write, please call me sometime, so that I can hear how you all are. I hope very well! My best! Yours, Werner.

Elisabeth to Werner

Friday [September 15?]
My Love!
So: she is here! And her fiancé was not killed in action at all, but just left her—the mother-in-law got in between them; just now she told me every-thing. She looks very lovely. In the beginning, I was very enthusiastic, and still am, just that there still are certain difficulties—you will see once you come here again. Her family background is strong, her father is in the [Nazi] Party, semiofficially, her brother, whom she adores, is full-time. She is very upbeat and optimistic. She is a straight, honest person, a great idealist, who needs this idealism to live and incorporates it actively in her work.

It is good not to be alone any more. One almost has disappeared in the horror. The only distractions were Marie's awful stories from the lunatic asylum where she worked for a long time. The rain is streaming down—soon it is winter.—I am coming to you. In my heart I am singing, "If I Were a Little Bird" all day long. Do you know all the verses? "No hour of the night goes by . . ."

My dear heart! Yours, Li.

Elisabeth to Werner

Monday, September 18
My Love!—

Yes, it was after midnight again yesterday. It is not good at all that it is always getting to be so late. But overall, I am now in decent shape. The children are well. Edeltrud, however, is a little despairing about how difficult it is with them now. They open every door, get into anything and every-thing, and you cannot really ever leave them alone in the room. And since the weather is nasty and rainy, they have to be in the room all the time. She finds Maria in particular definitely difficult to train. It is difficult on account of Maria's clingy behavior with me. When I am not there, she runs around the house calling: Mama. And when I am feeding Jochen, she will find a way to escape and also come into our bedroom. And I am the only one who is allowed to touch her, wash her, and feed her. And then Wolfgang gets jealous and starts to complain.—

Thank you for all the things you sent. . . . I am very busy getting warm clothes for the children. But it is a lot of work when you do it yourself. I could no longer get any boots in Kochel. I will write to my mother, immediately, whether she can find me some in Berlin. In Kochel, I sense that the attitude is no longer so rosy. People are starting to believe the war will be long and they are afraid of it. How can it be that the British have not yet done something of consequence? . . . All my love. Yours, Li.

Werner to Elisabeth

Leipzig, September 19
My dear Li!

In the interim, your margarine package has arrived together with the letter from Saturday. . . . How nice that the little ones are cheerful. I hope no real problems arise with Miss Olvig, but she seems very nice, according to your letter.—It was very comfortable in Berlin, but the political conversa-tions, which were unavoidable, gave me much to think about. Your mother revealed a very deep-seated hatred of England, beyond all rational thinking,

Elisabeth with Jochen, born in May 1939

which probably stems from the time of the Great War and has since been barely forgotten. But all other people also appear suddenly different, when it is becoming serious. It may well be one good side of the war, that everywhere the original and the roots become visible more distinctly.

Nothing certain is known yet about my use in the war. Two departments want to have me, but none have definitively claimed me. Meanwhile I am still teaching here. Tomorrow the lectures are scheduled to begin. I am very curious which students are present. Of those from Leipzig, only Hogrebe has been drafted. He is in the antiaircraft unit in Bitterfeld which, although not dangerous, is not very enviable, I imagine. Volz is in the Black Forest and so, for now, is not involved in any campaigns. Krekel is in Poland. Of the

Weizsäckers, the youngest is in the same regiment as the one who died on the front. The same for Adelheid's husband. Only Carl Friedr. is still in training in Küstrin. Heinrich v. W. was buried in Stuttgart on Saturday.—

Here in Leipzig it is monotonous, the weather is gray on gray, and I find the house terribly bare without you and the children. In ten days we will have to determine in detail what to do. One may well have to count on several years of war.— . . . By the way, from September 20 on, we are no longer allowed to use our car (however, it may be that I will be allowed to take the car to Berlin, if I will be there with the army).—In case of urgency with the children, however, you could probably summon the doctor in Kochel by telephone. All of you stay healthy and cheerful! Yours, Werner.

Elisabeth to Werner

Wednesday evening [September 20]
My love—

A good night greeting! Little Jochen is lying in his crib next to me and looking on with big eyes. He is an enchanting little fellow, always friendly and patient; and his eyes show such an infinite trust that everything inside me tightens when I think of the insanity in which the adult world is now ensnared.—Maria was actually much more compliant today, and Miss Olvig was also cheerier, must have adjusted her expectations now. Maria was even extra special all day, so peaceful, compliant, and affectionate. She really can be delightful. You know, the ever-new stream of people she has always had to obey has really derailed her a little. . . .

Werner to Elisabeth

Leipzig, evening, September 21
Dear good Li!

Today everything is gray on gray for me, and perhaps I should not write to you at all in this mood. But it is a consolation to tell you things even when you are not here with me. I am finding the uncertainty about the near future so tiring. Whether I shall be working in Berlin in the coming weeks or lecturing here is completely undetermined. The summons yesterday was, as it were, only about "readiness" and did not come from the place I had expected but from the scientific office. They then sent me back here for the time being. But it may well be that the other office will want to have me yet. Most likely now, however, is that I should simply remain in Leipzig and only go to Berlin occasionally.

I should know at the beginning of next week. If this happens, I would very much like you to come back here around the end of October. I would then come to Urfeld next week, as planned. But is it good for you to come here? It is better for the children to grow up normally in the family; but they would get less to eat here.

It is also quite likely that the air war will become worse. The Führer's speech points toward that. Then it might actually be irresponsible to bring the family here. Therefore, uncertainties in every direction. Let us wait until next week. I hope you are all well in Urfeld, that is the most important thing. . . .

So stay cheerful, and write to me often; to here, for now.

From my heart. Yours, Werner.

Elisabeth to Werner

Kochel, [September 23]
My dear, dear heart!
Just as I was going to Kochel, I received your lovely, lovely letter. And since I have another three quarters of an hour before the post bus comes again, I bought some stationery to write to you quickly, just a little.

You know, love, I am also in a terrible state, am quite out of sorts, because you are not here, but am, hour by hour, more excited about your arrival. If only it will not be changed again and you must suddenly go to Berlin after all and stay put there. Just now I have picked up the food coupons. That is a whole library. Takes a while to get your bearings. Aside from that, I have picked up two harmonicas. Wolfgang came across the harmonica of Miss Olvig, sat all afternoon in one spot, and played it. And he was completely immersed in trying it out, was beaming and joyfully shouting. . . .

Only one thing concerns me with little Wolfgang. He will cry during the night two or three times. I do not quite know why. I almost assume it is fear. He also does not want to go to bed at night, and it gets so bad during the night that I often will bring him over to let him sleep in your bed. Then he is all peaceful. I am thinking he might be dreaming. For last night, when he lay next to me, he suddenly also started crying, and when I then spoke to him and stroked his hair, he calmed down at once and fell asleep again. Being stern may not be the right approach there. But my own sleep does not exactly benefit from it. It may well be the reason why I so often do not know anymore what is going on within me. You know, if you are going to stay in Leipzig, I also think we all should come to you, at least for November, December, January, February. Then one could perhaps move up here again. . . . With love. Yours, Li.

Saturday night

In the meantime I have written you from Kochel at noon. At least you have heard from me a little.—Here it really has become fall; Kochel was under cloud cover, foggy, and windy. In Urfeld the sun was shining, the lake glistened in its deepest green, the mountains barely visible in the light haze of clouds; everything in the distance was a deep blue. I had never seen it this way.

. . . In the afternoon I sent Miss Olvig to Kochel again to find some more crisp bread. But almost all was gone. Everybody is stockpiling, I do too. My little provisions cabinet is nicely filled already. Twenty pounds of flour, twenty pounds of sugar, eight small crisp breads, ersatz coffee, malt coffee, noodles, and all sorts of other things. . . .

In the evening we both knitted stockings. At the same time I read aloud to her, so that one is not only chatting. I read *The Simple Life* to her. It is the only book here that is appropriate for her. I hope it will be different in Leipzig. Here—and this is only natural—I spend every free minute together with her. Thus, to my sorrow, I do not even manage to get to any letters.

. . . With love. Yours, Li.

Werner to Elisabeth

Leipzig, September 23, evening
Dear Li!

My telephone conversation with you brought me some consolation. I know at least that everything is alright with you all, and besides, I do believe that I can travel to Urfeld next week. If I am unlucky, there might be a meeting in Berlin interfering, but then I could travel the following week. A permanent engagement in Berlin is not very likely, I believe; but there may be surprises. Today I had a brief telephone conversation with Miss Oertel. She had been, if I understood correctly, in Munich, and also made the point that shortages of foodstuffs are so much worse here than in Bavaria. For example, there are no eggs here (with or without coupons), milk is only available for children. I have not been able to get Granovita flakes anymore. There also seems to be a great shortage of coal. . . . Yesterday I harvested the second apple tree, it bore huge beautiful apples, about a whole *zentner's* [one zentner = 110 U.S. pounds] worth, I would guess. . . . However, nobody here believes in a brief war anymore, especially after the shortened rations of the latest food coupons. The recent speech of the Führer also did not indicate this anymore. An article in the *Black Corps* deals with this topic as well.—All my best to the four of you! Yours, Werner.

Elisabeth to Werner

[Urfeld, September 24]
My love!

The letter that Edeltrud was meant to take with her today was left behind, unfortunately. So you will have waited a long time for news. I am sorry! But it was not my fault. My sympathies for Edeltrud have been dealt a blow today. I do still value her as before, but you are right: she sort of has small cracks. She wants to be a martyr. And since today I would not allow her to continue to work on what should have been her full afternoon off, she put on a great performance for me with many tears and tragic-looking facial expressions and deep silences. Now everything is straightened out.

Fortunately, these moods apparently vanish quickly. And outwardly everything is as it was. But inwardly I have dissociated myself from her quite a lot.

. . . I will go to sleep now; more tomorrow! I love you so much!

Yours, Li.

Elisabeth to Werner

Monday, September 25

My love!

Oh, I had such trouble! I am now really getting to know the problems with maids. Marie is so sloppy, one cannot imagine it any worse. She no longer is doing any work at all. . . . If I didn't know that Edeltrud is getting sick, I would not really care; but now—She says that if her hip problem comes back, she will be done. And I do believe her. She has gone through such terrible difficulties and is basically completely despairing and has neither courage nor strength. She has nothing to lose. Also, her youngest brother took his own life. It is her mother's fault. I cannot tell you how much horror she has endured from her.—

Forgive me, love, for telling you these kinds of terrible stories. But ultimately, these things are in my immediate environment and do take up a lot of my mental energy. . . .

Fortunately, the children are here. How delightful Wolfgang is now! He has actually discovered music and is playing it properly on his harmonica. Up and down and always just one tone, not the full chord, very carefully and listening in complete abandon. And he likes playing on Edeltrud's harmonica much better, because it sounds much nicer; and he will run out of the room when Maria produces her loud and monotonous noise on her harmonica. Miss Olvig says she had never seen such a young child use this instrument so appropriately and really beautifully; if three- to four-year-old children were playing this way, it would already be something special. One really enjoys listening to him. And at the same time, he is also such a rascal and a true boy, which gives you genuine pleasure. Maria is difficult. If you are stern, she builds a wall around her. If you are very, very loving toward her, she opens up, but easily goes too far then. Bringing her up is a true art.

What about us, my love? Must I really stay here all winter long? . . .
Enough now, for today! With love. Yours, Li.

Werner to Elisabeth

Leipzig, Tuesday evening [October 3?]
Dear Li!
The days at the Walchensee were so nice that the return to Leipzig is
particularly dreary. Added to it are several contributing factors—a terrible
cold, bad weather, etc.—so that I am in a true hangover state. Tonight we
are also expected at the Jacobis'; so this letter will be brief. I must not forget
an important question: where is our flag kept? I have desperately been
searching, because we ought to hang it, but could not find it. Please write me
immediately where it is. I have searched all the upstairs rooms, asked
Mrs. Frels also, to no avail.— . . .

Mama returned from Dresden, quite cheerful, all seems to be going well
there. Erwin, at any rate, has not been drafted. Nobody knows how this war
will continue; most people believe there will be more intense fighting from
the air against the western powers. Thus it is good that you are there so far
out of range. Today I have inspected the air-raid basement with Mrs. Wie-
gand [probably the housekeeper] and discussed improvements with her.
Mama has to sew some sandbags.

Otherwise nothing new here, and I can barely think straight. Please
write regarding the flag and photo equipment! Many greetings to you all!
Yours, Werner.

Elisabeth to Werner

[October 4]
My love!
Today your rather plaintive letter arrived. I hope that it was at least nice
at the Jacobis', so that you became somewhat more cheerful. For me too it
was difficult to get back to my lonesome muddling along; on top of that,
there was the disappointment with Edeltrud, so that I felt even lonelier. . . .

The children are asleep now and Edeltrud is at the Brackenhofers' listening to Hitler's speech. I am sitting here with an unquiet heart waiting for her. Will it be war or peace? And you write: it is good that we are a long way away? Should I not come, then? I am becoming quite sad here over time. . . .

Edeltrud has just come back. Things will come to a head now. What will the British do? Can we hope for peace? The alternative is unthinkable. Is England feeling weak? But no one actually knows. In any case, it has turned out like you said. What else do you say now? If there is a war, it will certainly be much more terrible than before. Oh, my dear, dear heart! If only one could talk with you.—

Edeltrud returned very joyful and reassured. She reported that Hitler said we would definitely not lose this war. She had been somewhat concerned about it, but is now fully confident again. . . .

All my love to you! Yours, Li.

Werner to Elisabeth

Leipzig, Tuesday evening [October 5?]
Dear Li!
Your letter today sounded as gloomy as my last one—hopefully things have gotten better again since then. The children probably have the same cold that I have. Hopefully they will get over it quickly.—In the meantime, I was busy and active on behalf of the household: the beds are coming tomorrow; I have ordered the bed linens and the pillow from Friedr. u. Lincke [a store in Leipzig]. The search for canned food was totally in vain, the sale of canned food is forbidden. Flakes of every kind (including Granovita) are only available on coupons. The only thing I could get without coupons were 20 pounds of potatoes. Tomorrow, weather permitting, I will pick some more apples.—On Monday and Tuesday I have to be in Berlin again, so will be staying with your parents probably.—I had a letter from Wolfgang Rüdel with questions about Jochen's baptism. What do you think about it? We have not really discussed this enough. Possibly one could have the baptism on Friday, October 20, in Urfeld. We aren't leaving there until the 22nd. But

maybe the baptism so shortly before the departure is too impractical. So please write me about it sometime. My best! Yours, Werner.

Elisabeth to Werner

Saturday, October 7
My dear, dear husband!

It is already long past midnight, but I must still talk to you, because since I was married, I have not been as desperate as I was today. To start with the end: Edeltrud is dead unhappy here with me, and it can only be a matter of very little time before she goes, unless there is a complete change, which I do not believe.

I spent the whole evening up to now talking with her, because her mood became intolerable for me, and her answer to my every question was "I don't know." She was becoming more listless and overly work focused by the hour before I confronted her.

Basically, there are three reasons. The first is our sweet little Maria. You know, the child is so extremely attached to me. She simply does not let Edeltrud come close. And it reaches the point where Edeltrud deep down just hates her. The poor eating behavior is simply seen as her terrible naughtiness, whereas I can see so much else going on and can therefore excuse it much more. . . . The second point is me: she is afraid of me, and does not feel understood, and is entirely opposed to my pedagogy. . . . Well, yes, I did say to Maria once, when she was very sweet: "Right, you are not really as difficult to deal with as E. thinks?!" and I have also rejected some of her suggestions. I also said once, when I was telling her about Miss Oertel, that ultimately I wanted the education to be my own business. All this has discouraged her and made her shy away from me. And then, I also am inclined to think that she simply does not like me, although I have taken pains to make everything nice for her and create a real home for her.

And the third reason is she herself. She says of herself that her sister once told her that she could not go and work in a family; there she would fail. And on day 3 she already knew that she would fail here. Because she could only either be in charge or just submit. Anything in between would not be possible for her. And the "just submit" was not making her happy. . . .

Oh, I am so desperate. . . . And I am sitting here, completely helpless. To get anybody is practically impossible, since all girls age thirteen and up have to make themselves available to the Labor Service after October 15. Good night! Love of my heart! Yours, Li.

Elisabeth to Werner

Sunday, October 8
My love!

I have now been rethinking all this during the night, back and forth. And I was very astonished what a sensitive little soul our Maria is. When I came in the room, her little bed was all crumpled up and she lay there wide awake, and later on she cried off and on, something she had never done before; she only calmed down when I put her next to me in your bed. There she slept soundly till this morning. I am firmly convinced that this restlessness only stemmed from my thinking so seriously about this child. Actually, I did battle intensely within myself over her because, when you are told that Maria is so difficult, unlike any child she [Edeltrud] has known, one has to do quite a bit of soul searching. . . .

For one—can I not come home at the end of this week already? . . . The baptism here is out of the question. How are we supposed to get to Kochel? As for doing it at home, the weather is too poor, and Marie too unabashedly sloppy. You cannot imagine how she is running around, in completely tattered, dirty clothes, all day in her slippers. It is crazy with this unbelievable sort of woman. . . .

And also—there will likely be a definitive decision made this week about war and peace. In this one point I am filled with hope. I cannot and will not believe that the British will wage such an insane war. And aren't the offers acceptable? . . .

Thirdly, I have pondered myself, and am posing this question to you, whether it might not be good for Maria to go to Berlin for a time, so that she can forget about me a little more. She lays claim to me, totally, and I just cannot be there for her totally, I have to be there as well for Wolfgang and then too for Jochen. It is torturing her. To boot, if yet another stranger will again come up to her in my presence, my child will get completely confounded.

I am sending this letter to Berlin by express mail. . . . Your little Li.

Werner to Elisabeth

Leipzig, Tuesday evening [October 10?]
My dear Li!

After your desperate letter from Saturday, I must quickly reach out to comfort you.—I can easily imagine that Edeltrud does not want to stay with us for any length of time; I have the following impression of her: she is a very nice, somewhat difficult person who has, however, already had quite a lot of misfortune. She feels mistreated by fate, and has settled in being content only when she can have the feeling of sacrificing and being used. The idea that she is worse off than others and is sacrificing more is a central part of her life. So you most likely affronted her when you wanted to force her not to work on her afternoon off. If you, so to speak, want to force such a complicated person to be happy, you will rob her of her firm ground of safety. She still might settle down–only for a brief time. But in the long run, she will not easily enter into a relaxed relationship with us; for we want to be just simple, joyful people, for her to join in—but that just is not working. For people such as Miss Olvig, life can only become whole through a strong conviction—as for so many other people. Since we do not share her conviction, even though we respect it—she will always be different from us. This has nothing to do with little Maria; little Maria, however, has an injury from this summer: because of Jochen, you suddenly became somewhat removed from her; then Miss Oertel was taken from her. Now she is simply scared you too might leave, and she feels you are the only person who really loves her—I myself am, unfortunately, not around the children enough. I believe these difficulties will lessen quite a lot when I can be another caretaker.

Tomorrow you will probably be calling me. I have talked with Mrs. Frels in the meantime—I can tell you more about that then. In Berlin it was nice;

I have enjoyed being together with your parents and Ernst.—After the newspaper reports and Hitler's speech, I do not, unfortunately, consider peace likely in the near future. We will have no choice but to pass through this purgatory.—So, till tomorrow's call—eventually, everything will be fine. Just keep up your chin, especially in wartime one must learn to become secure and calm. All my best, yours, Werner.

Elisabeth to Werner

[Urfeld, October 11/12]
Love!

Today we were in for real luck! I want to tell you more in some detail, because on the telephone you could not hear me so well. Didn't you perhaps see those twins here, two identical boys, nice blond eight-year-olds? Their mother—she lives in the house at the Kesselberg road—came to me today and said she had heard I was looking for a girl. Her daughter, who had apprenticed at the Brackenhofers' as a baker for two years, was looking for a job, since there was not enough work there anymore. Although she could go to Mannheim for the third year to get her diploma, she, the mother, did not want to let her go now during wartime. And her Fanny would be overjoyed at the thought of getting to go to Leipzig. So I asked for Fanny to come over to meet me. She is terrific: tall, beautiful, joyful, and friendly, and she appears very intelligent. I told her about all the drawbacks of Leipzig, but she thought she would be with us then and would be quite content. Of course, she is still a child who has never left home and perhaps gets homesick; but we will soon be back down here, anyway. . . . —You know, we have really been lucky. And it is important that she should feel good about staying with us. We would not have found someone like her in Leipzig, probably. . . .

My love, today in one week you will already be on your way to me. That is wonderful. . . . All my love, yours, Li.

1939

Werner to Elisabeth

Leipzig, Saturday evening [October 14?]
Dear sweet Li!

Your cheerful letter today was a great relief. . . . I am very much looking forward to a regular family life now. Ever since I have been living alone here, I can get a better understanding that for you it was much more difficult, while I was in America, than for me. The one who stays back senses much more that something is missing, and the monotony of the city is weighing on him more than it does otherwise.—

Your packages have arrived; the contents are fabulous; I have temporarily put them into the kitchen cabinet, only unpacked the items that needed to be. That you are so happy about the new girl is wonderful. Of course, later on there will arise bigger or smaller difficulties—nothing is without those—but that will not matter.

Today I have picked the last fruit trees bare. The whole cellar is full of apples, also one crate of pears, filled to the rim. I passed some of the apples along to Mrs. Busch [a neighbor] again, but still we are left with riches that are almost overwhelming. Now, in war-time, such a yard with fruit trees is indispensable, particularly with the children.— . . . Tomorrow, Sunday, I want to take Mama out to dinner, in the afternoon we go to have tea at the Frelses', and at night, after 8, we go to the Jacobis' to play music. Aside from that, I have to work on my Coronella talk for the night after tomorrow. This talk is interesting to me the more I think about the topic and study it. Unfortunately, the time is too short to penetrate into the particular questions. The main topic is the relationship between living and dead matter—the wisdom of Bohr. I am quite interested in the reaction of the biologist (Buchner) and of the medical doctor (Catel). Otherwise, there is nothing else to report. So, say hello to the children, I will see you again soon! Yours, Werner.

Elisabeth to Werner

October 14

My dear heart!

Just now I have played music for a long time, dug up my beloved Schubert sonata and practiced portions of it. If only I were better able! I would love to take lessons again, but from whom?—

I needed the music badly, to calm my fury, because I was once again so very infuriated over E. Every time it is not going all smoothly with the children, when they wet themselves more often and become whiny, she puts on an indignant air and laments how terrible this work is that her desire for children has completely gone during her stay with me, and more along these lines. And all this, after it had been such a beautiful day, and the children had been playing together so nicely outside. I told her today that if the work were so terrible for her, she would have to find more suitable duties elsewhere, because her attitude was just not good enough for my children. She did not make a reply. If necessary, we will take the compulsory service girl. Now, with Fanny, I am no longer worried. She is straight and vigorous and on board with my ways, I am certain of it. And she will work very hard too.—

I walked up to the Parapluis today because the weather was so beautiful. I spent a long time looking down on the glowing and colorful plain; the sound of bells reached up to me, carried by a slight wind, and I felt comforted that the world remains so wonderful, in spite of the hatred and insanity of mankind. . . . Much, much love! Yours, Li.

Werner to Elisabeth

[Leipzig], Tuesday evening [October 17?]

Dear Li!

Now our family's return trip seems assured, as long as our car will still run; thank you for your letter. If you have the time, could you drive to Tölz for the permit and, at the same time, have the air, battery water, and possibly the oil refilled. If you do not have time, I can, of course, do it myself on Saturday, but we will have many other things going on then.

Thinking about our trip home, I had some slight doubts whether we can complete the trip in one day: the driving time by itself is . . . at least nine hours. (No more than eighty kilometers per hour is allowed.) It will be daylight eleven hours only . . . , so that we would only have two hours, for all the breaks combined. That could only work if one keeps rigorously to the schedule, without consideration for sleeping children, etc. In principle it will work, but it will come with much unpleasantness and crying children. Another possibility would be to leave Saturday afternoon, . . . stay overnight in Nuremberg . . . , and on Sunday drive comfortably to Leipzig. A last resort might be to lower the light beam and risk a trip into the dark. I would find it very unpleasant, given the current state of street lighting. I myself am dead tired, it got late last night; also the institute presented me with some human problems to resolve, which is always exhausting. I am looking forward very much to all of you arriving, and before then to a few I hope nice days in Urfeld. I am dreading the car trip a little still. So, if I do not write you anything else, good-bye till Friday morning! Good wishes! Yours, Werner.

1940

TIMES ARE GETTING TOUGHER. *The war—although its progress is constantly couched in terms of victory—is demanding concessions. Official decrees and regulations are on the increase: dwellings have to be modified for air-raid protection; cars may be used only with special permits; coal, groceries, and many other necessities of daily life are no longer available without eligibility coupons. Thus life now includes the tending of a new vegetable garden, holding in reserve whatever will keep, exchange-of-goods excursions, and numerous appointments with bureaucrats. No wonder that the letters of the couple are replete with such daily concerns.*

Elisabeth is also burdened with the care of two households, in Leipzig and in Urfeld. Although she often has help from a nanny and a housekeeper, these bring their own problems: it is difficult to train inexperienced girls doing their obligatory one-year duty, and turnover is high.

Werner's professional situation has fallen into a routine: he is in Berlin for the first part of the week and in Leipzig over the weekend. The commuting and the increasing air raids weary him; management of the household is left to Elisabeth for the most part.

The plan to spend summers in Urfeld continues as envisioned. Since Elisabeth is expecting her fourth child, only the active support of Mother Heisenberg and the Schumacher parents make this feasible. In June, Elisabeth, Jochen, and the trainee girl Gerburg travel to Urfeld to prepare the house for the summer stay, while in Leipzig Mother Heisenberg, aided by Lisa, the household help, is looking after the twins.

Elisabeth to Werner

[Urfeld, June 9]
My love!

We already are calling it a day! It is ten minutes past 1 o'clock!! That means we have made quite a bit of progress with the moving in and are waiting till Mr. Jochen deems it appropriate to wake up. I think we may have to wait a while; the poor little guy was so terribly tired. He has a hard time with the change, looks unwell, is pale and weepy, and cannot get to sleep at night, . . . so that I took him into my room, which calmed him noticeably. . . . It will improve over the next few days. Also Gerburg, the child, is quite *"down."* In her state of homesickness, she is doing the worst things. She is not really a big help to me yet—although she is touchingly ready and willing to be helpful—yesterday we watered the vegetable garden till 10 o'clock.

I am still very much fighting the difficulties of daily life. But I am managing, and am proud like a peacock about every success. For instance, I had no idea at all where I would get the water for watering. So, after several unsuccessful attempts, I climbed along the whole pipe till I found out. This kind of thing happens with a lot of other matters. At home—how quickly I always would call for your help! But now I have to cope by myself. I think that will be very good for me. I will also pay attention, not letting all the people around me have the power to intimidate me so much anymore. That friendliness is available only in exchange for money has become clearer to me once more. . . .

Tomorrow I go to see Weitzmann [a building contractor] for a talk. I will ask him everything I want to know, and my damn worry, that I, in my North German manner, will step on the toes of the Bavarians here, will simply be laid to rest; it makes me all insecure and dumb, and the sly guys are clearly aware of it.

I want to start tomorrow, or the day after, with painting. First the flower boxes, into which they have planted not cress but petunias—regrettable! Probably to get more money! It is a really wretched and shrewd gang. They claim (Schlosser, the gardener) that they did not know of cress here! Such a racket!

Today I have changed quite a few things in the house to my tastes. I threw out quite a lot, closed my eyes throughout, because I could see your appalled face about my unscrupulous, destructive drive. But if one stops to think about the possible, yet very dubious, value of all these things, one will never get rid of the Corinths' leftover stuff. With each piece, I breathed a little easier. I also removed all the plates above the windows—not smashed them, but stacked them in the leftovers shelf of the cabinet for you to take a look. I think it looks much better now, much more fitting for us! And I am certain you would think so too.

A last, the Jockerle has woken up. I am afraid we will no longer get a meal at the Brackenhofers', it is so late now. Till tomorrow, my love! Give the twins my love. I am almost forgetting the war altogether. It is nice here. It was great that you called yesterday, you my beloved love! Yours, Li.

Werner to Elisabeth

Leipzig, June 11
Dear capable Li!
You seem to be in complete command in Urfeld, to get house and garden up to speed—if it is not too much for you, I will only be too happy about it. Do not get too mad about the greed of the Bavarians but stand your ground calmly and emphatically. . . . Jochen has probably begun to settle in; I cannot imagine him tired and unhappy. The twins are in excellent shape; they were outside all day long in the garden, naked and with a dark tan already; aside from that, by nighttime they were covered from head to toe with clay and soil and thought it was terrific. Mama has bought them a—fortunately little—pump fountain for water play, which is currently the main attraction. Gymnastics, with Maria's participation, is already going much better and is viewed by them both as entertainment in front of people, and also as a good opportunity to storm my room. Gymnastics in the children's room "does not count."

—Lisa manages the household fabulously and smoothly. Tomorrow morning the cherries will be picked; to this end I have borrowed, with much trouble, a ladder from Wild. . . .

—Tomorrow at noon, I will probably have dinner with Bothe in the Ipa restaurant; at night I am at the Gadamers'. Thursday I may have to go to Berlin, and possibly, but it is not yet certain, afterward to Copenhagen. So possibly I can write my next letter only in a few days.

—Today I spent almost all day at the institute. In the morning I discussed the measurements with Döpel; all week long a mistake had made all measurements useless. In the afternoon there was a seminar, afterward I spoke with an inventor of perpetual motion, eventually I returned to Döpel at 7 o'clock; now everything is running impeccably, I was very proud.

Now it is almost midnight, and I am very tired, mostly on account of the hay fever. But you, you must rest as much as you can. With many good wishes, yours, Werner.

Elisabeth to Werner

[Urfeld, ca. June 11]
My love!

Today was a strenuous day; it already started miserably, as Gebe [Gerburg] made one foolish mistake after another. No, today I was really despairing about her. Such slowness is unbelievable. But the beauty and tranquility of the evening has softened my emotions completely, and, in addition, Jockerle makes sure that I will not be down in the dumps for long. You know, Jockerle has made me much more secure and calmer; somehow, I owe to him a strength and confidence that I did not previously know. I am also infinitely happier here than I was last year, and being alone does not open up such an aching deep hole. The weather now is really perfect—not very difficult to love it here! Lilac and golden chain are in bloom, although skimpy, but all the more impressive in this rough native environment. The slope toward the vegetable garden is covered with splendid columbines. I have never seen them growing wild. There are so many that I could not count them, and new ones keep coming up all the time. And the vegetable garden is itself a source of joy for me; probably it is also the reason that I am feeling so much more at home. A piece of land to take care of and cultivate is remarkably enchanting. I look forward all day long to watering it in the evening. . . . The story about the cress also resolved itself. They are not really such scoundrels. Schlosser was here yesterday for about an hour, and we talked. He thought we were talking about garden cress, since the flower would be called Capuchin cress. And he confessed to being surprised about our idea to sow vegetables in the window boxes, and he preferred to plant petunias. . . .

I am busily painting: four tables in dire need, the bathroom door, and I began with white on the flower boxes. I hope you agree. . . . I will have to buy more of the white, though. I did not have enough. The boxes soak up a lot. I got it at Blessing's, where I had a very sad impression. The woman has, now that her husband is gone, totally gone downhill. She drinks and is always drunk, can barely conceal her slurred speech. Her face is puffy; the eyes dull, a terrible impression. She also did not recognize me again. The only one in all of Kochel. . . .

The radio and the money have arrived today. I have not unpacked it. My desire for it is not great. But it is good to have it, anyhow, as long as you only turn it on in the most urgent of circumstances.

Good night, love! Greetings to Mama and especially to the children. Yours, Li.

Werner to Elisabeth

[Leipzig], June 12
Your letter today sounds, actually, very cheery, I am so very glad about it.—Only what you wrote about Mrs. Blessing made me really feel sorry. To see in individual cases all that the war is destroying!—

We here had a hectic day. Horn had not come, contrary to our agreement, so Lisa tried, in addition to all her other work, to also pick the cherries. . . . I myself had to leave presently to my lecture, after which I had a visit from Bothe and Gentner from Heidelberg. At noon I ate with them in the Ipa restaurant—I could not possibly impose more work on Lisa—and when I returned at 3:30, I had been in the open air way too long and had terrible hay fever. There was now great chaos. Lisa was alternating between picking cherries and removing the pits with Mama, and she really did not know anymore where her head was. That is when I got into the tree, was constantly in danger of falling off the ladder with all the sneezing, and picked cherries for almost two hours. Altogether, we have more than twenty pounds now. In order to protect my suit and considering the heat, I did it, by the way, in my bathing suit, following the neighbor's example.

Afterward, I climbed in the bathtub with completely inflamed eyes and constantly sneezing, took much Ephetonin, so that now it is again sort of fine.—I may not yet have to go to Berlin tomorrow morning; I am so glad not to have to travel again right away. Also, the matter of Copenhagen seems to be drawing out. . . .

Tonight I must still go to the Gadamers', I am a little too tired for it. But you should rest a lot up there! Be well! Yours, Werner.

Elisabeth to Werner

[Urfeld, June 14]
My love!

Today I am really proud of my achievement. The room for the two little ones, for Jochen and the baby, is finished and it has turned out so appealing and pretty that it is truly a joy. Nothing is left in them reminiscent of the Corinth taste. And it is all practical and bright, so that I think last year's appalling Bohemian lifestyle will not repeat itself. I cannot understand myself at all how I could have been so remiss last year. A few little things are enough to correct the severe deficiencies of last year! A bit of color, a few new purchases (soap dishes, buckets, etc.), and the courage to throw out certain items! Today I also took some pieces of furniture into the shed. You will not miss them! I was particularly proud about my efforts with moving some furniture. How I managed to slide the heavy cabinets across thresholds so easily on planks should serve as an example to any moving crews. A little careless it was, admittedly, to do it by myself; but your wife is endowed with an indestructible health! I compensated by going to bed very early. . . .

I am also making some connections to Walchensee. In a certain sense, one can get more there than in Kochel. Slowly one is feeling more native here. Everything is already going much more easily and enjoyably than last year. . . .

To you and the children much love, and many greetings to Mama and the capable Lisa.

Yours, Li.

On Friday

Just now we hear the news that we are marching into Paris; accompanied by unbelievably insipid music. How much I would like to talk with you! Y., Li.

Werner to Elisabeth

Leipzig, June 14
My dear Li!

The mail from Urfeld goes amazingly fast—today I got your letter from yesterday, but the reverse does not seem so fast. . . . —Jochen appears to have gradually accepted the new environment—I believe it will work out well for him, overall, to begin walking up there. I am curious what you will think of the twins, who are simply outside all day long in their shorts. Their bodies are already completely tanned and they look fabulously healthy; they are happy through and through in the fresh air and sun. Since you left, by the way, there was not a day of rain here, almost always a cloudless sky! Hopefully, it is the same where you are too. . . . —This afternoon sixty zentner coal was delivered, which is at least a start. The children found the performance of the coal-carrying men so interesting that they both sat down on the lawn near the roses and observed each basket intensely. In the end, the coal carriers started a conversation with them, which they then talked about for a long time afterward. The roses are in full bloom, it is time that you come back again. . . . —My Berlin and Copenhagen trips seem to be postponed further, I do not know yet for how long.—Say hello to Jockerle and get a good rest. Yours, Werner.

Elisabeth to Werner

[Urfeld, ca. June 15]
My love!

Today I had intended to go to sleep very early on, but it did not work out that way, due to a very annoying occurrence. The ants have invaded the basement; and they crawl through the openings in the screened cabinet; just now I must have taken out one hundred drowned ants from Jochen's milk, and now the poor child must drink thin oatmeal for breakfast. . . .

Today we went to the Brackenhofers' for midday dinner. Just think, they served me a much more expensive and better meal than I had ordered, and I did not have to pay. I was truly astonished. I believe it is the Jockerle. He laughs himself into everybody's heart. And he gets admired in the whole village. Ever since our Jockerle has gone out into the world at large, he is as if changed; he swims in it like a fish in water, is completely unfazed by large numbers of people, and loves to get close to beautiful women. We do have a daring fellow there! He now has a habit of really hitting me hard. When I then give him a little slap or make an angry face and chide him, he starts to sidle up really affectionately, so that I cannot help but laugh, after which he considers the whole thing done with.

Now good night for today. More tomorrow. . . .

In a hurry, yours, Li.

Werner to Elisabeth

Leipzig, June 17
My dear Li!

. . . Tonight your mother will come to take the children to Urfeld. I am having a really difficult time with giving up the two of them; they are making the house come so alive, are almost always cheerful, and enjoy life in a way that we adults probably no longer are capable of. The good thing is that you yourself will return soon too. My trip to Copenhagen is getting postponed all the time; perhaps peace will come before it takes place at all. France did capitulate today; I am curious what England will do. . . .

Rest up in Urfeld, but also come back here soon! Yours, Werner.

Elisabeth to Werner

[Urfeld, ca. June 19]
My love!
This will be the last but one letter. Then only a note which train I will arrive on and how the twins have arrived here. If only the weather would improve by then! All morning long it has poured as only here it will. . . . Oh, you in Bavaria do have crazy weather!

Yesterday I was in Kochel and heard the special report at Bergdorfer's. Now France has stopped fighting! The whole of the Maginot Line is broken and Verdun was taken—all of it completely incomprehensible. One is torn between joy and concern. Love, I am so glad to be with you again soon. Here I have accomplished pretty much what I wanted. It really was a mountain of work. . . .

Evening
In the interim I was in the strange village of Walchensee, which is a conglomerate of professorial families. In the stores lots of the old wives of professors. They all look so terribly distinguished and fancy. I had much rather be here in our solitude afterward. In the evening it began to clear up marvelously. The sun was gilding everything; the mountains were gloriously high and mysterious. It really is particularly beautiful here! I am also pleased with my work, finished painting the last bit—until 10 o'clock at night! The little house is very much changed, so pretty and neat and clean, quite statcly. Not much more is needed to make it *our* little house. . . .

ELISABETH IS NOW *anticipating the arrival of her mother with the twins in Urfeld before she herself returns to Leipzig, taking Jochen with her. Four weeks later, she moves in with Werner's mother in Munich to await the birth of her fourth child. It is delayed until early August, much to her dismay. Since Werner has his vacation in August, he can be in Munich during these days, but then he immediately leaves for*

View from the Urfeld terrace

Urfeld to be with the rest of the family. There the Schumacher parents have been taking care of the three older children, assisted by Lisa and Gerburg. Elisabeth's sister, Edith, whose husband, Erich Kuby, is serving in France, also comes to help out for a time when the family is struck by an influenza outbreak. So the house is filled with people that summer, which allows Werner to take off to the mountains for several days, where he is joined by Elisabeth's brother Ernst.

Werner to Elisabeth

Berlin, Friday noon [ca. July 12]
Dear Li!

Since last night I have been trying nonstop to reach you. At first they said the lines were too busy, and then I heard the connection was disrupted, with no way of knowing as to when talking could resume. So that you should not wonder why I am not calling, I have now sent a telegram—maybe that will get through. It is easy in wartime to find different explanations why a telephone line is not working. Hopefully everything in Munich is fine. . . . How much I would like to know how you fared on your trip. Now I will probably have to wait until the day after tomorrow to find out. I intend to travel to Hamburg tomorrow and return Sunday night to Leipzig. . . .

I find the work in Berlin so far not very enjoyable. Too much talking and little actual work. But maybe I can change something about this situation. The Dahlem people seem to me to be living off of university politics and chatter.——By the way, I am staying there in the Harnack House, in a nice mansard room with a view of Grunewald, air force barracks, and subway. The gardens are full of many lovely flowers; a friendly housekeeper has placed a big bouquet of snapdragons in my room. I have also tried calling your house, but so far no luck.——Warm greetings to Mama, have a good time together in peace, and take good, good care of yourself! Yours, Werner.

P.S. Please write how little Maria is doing. As soon as I can, I will call Munich again.

Elisabeth to Werner

Munich, July 12
My love!

It is quite disheartening that your call cannot be connected. I had been looking forward to it so much. And you have been without news for so long! So, everything was fine. It is true that it was quite strenuous, but not as bad as the trip from Urfeld to Leipzig had been. We arrived in Munich twenty minutes early, just think! We also got a car right away and were comfortably getting home, where at first, of course, my head was throbbing some. Today I called the clinic. Dr. Albrecht will leave for vacation on the 20th. After that only the assistant doctor is there. So before then Baby should have made an appearance! . . .

Today—just now, my father called from Urfeld. The children are better, Maria too. She was up already today. Only Mama is still having a bad case of it. But Edith is now there and is taking care of everybody. A big nuisance that I am so laid up. It must have been a terribly infectious thing, but the doctor says if it were dysentery, he would have been notified at once.——

Here it is gray and cold. Your Bavaria is a pitiful state with its constant rains! But in other respects—here one actually lives as if in paradise. The strawberries, fist sized and shiny, are in front of the stores in their baskets. Blueberries, gooseberries, all the nicest vegetables, mayonnaise, nuts, vermouth, juices—all this I could spy with my Argus eyes today, and I acknowledged it with a heart full of envy. On top of it, cookies in every store, and tortes to make your eyes bulge. The Munich folk are quite a spoiled people if they are complaining in the face of so many wonderful offerings!

Otherwise—I have folded myself all up into myself and am, as much as I am able, the compliant and well-mannered daughter—in-law. Although: the fact that I am still reading Stendhal—the life of an eccentric, an autobiography—has made Mama a bit indignant. It was she herself, however, who brought it up right away. . . . And now, a thousand greetings to you! Lisa will come on Saturday. She stayed that extra day due to Mutti's illness.

Oh, you, my love! Be well! Yours, Li.

Werner to Elisabeth

Leipzig, July 15
My dear Li!
Yesterday at midnight I came back here; I was so glad to find good news from you. At the same time postcards from your parents were here also, saying the children were very well again, and Lisa told me in detail about this illness of the entire family. How good that now everything seems to be getting back to normal. Now you must see to it that you have the baby without any problems and then rest well. I can get vacation time in August, but must probably be back in Berlin in September.—

The trip from Berlin via Hamburg to here was actually quite a strain; at least I do not know if I can keep up, long term, the disruptions of traveling back and forth, because nothing much can become of my real work. But during wartime, one may have to take that in stride. In Hamburg I got in on Saturday afternoon; until 8 o'clock we had a conference, then I was invited together with many others to a truly Lucullus-like dinner at a colleague's house. There actually do still exist some people who have reserves—all the more admirable that they invite others to share. Only at 12:30 at night one dispersed. When I then wanted to go to bed at the hotel, there was alarm and sleeping had to be postponed again. Since the attack did not seem to spread into our vicinity, I could not but watch the happenings from the window.

The shooting of antiaircraft weapons reflected in the clouds like a nighttime thunderstorm, just the noise is briefer and more mechanical. The attack appeared to be quickly over, so I lay down to sleep and was awakened again at about 3 o'clock by more sirens, this time just to signal that one was allowed back into one's home. The Hamburg people told us the next day that it is usually much worse. Also that the British had the practice of dropping bombs with delayed explosives, which lie about somewhere for half a day and finally burst. Near the railroad station, one was still on the ground, packed up carefully in sandbags and peat moss. About the successes of the antiair-craft weapons, the people of Hamburg could not tell us anything glorious. At an attack from twelve airplanes a few days ago, the British supposedly turned on their lights in the end to demonstrate where they had been. But maybe this is only already fabrication, a kind of "seaman's yarn."

. . . So, now you keep up your chin, and look that you and the baby can come to the little Ötz castle; and greetings to Mama! Yours, Werner.

Elisabeth to Werner

Munich, [ca. July 16]
My love!
Today's conversation with you was like a sip of cold, fresh water, really! How good that such an institution exists!

Tell me, what kind of a person am I that I find it so hard to keep my equanimity in the face of Mama's kindness and love? I can barely compre-hend it myself; am full of explosive energy and constantly have to contain myself.—But I am terribly excited to get your next letter. You bad, bad man that you would not go to the basement during the air raid! But powerfully captivating it surely was!

Today with Dr. Albrecht it was interesting, in that he is in every respect the opposite of Hirschberg. H. is short and not handsome; A. is tall and gorgeous (almost all gynecologists are gorgeous, a strange phenomenon). With H. everything is factual, brief, and modern, very energetic and robust. A. lives in an old Biedermeier-style house. The rooms are at ground level and have the pretty, poetic proportions of the Biedermeier times. They are furnished entirely in the old style, very tastefully. Antique, beautiful pieces hang on the walls, which are clad with beautiful fabric. He himself sits at an old desk made of precious wood, a bouquet of bright red roses next to him under the lit lamp. One gets the impression that he is completely nonfactual. Chats, gives compliments, touches your hand in a fatherly, benign gesture, yes, even puts his arm around you to demonstrate his fatherly concern. That is Dr. Albrecht. Is there any greater contrast than between these two doctors? However, I prefer Hirschberg, although one really should not compare, but let each in his unique way live and let live.—

So much for tonight. I will read a little more in the *Life of an Eccentric*. A very strange book. There is a broad stream of life pulsing through it, and yet it still feels very foreign to me. All my love, you most beloved! Yours, Li.

Werner to Elisabeth

Leipzig, July 17
My dear Li!

While you probably consider the waiting time in Munich monotonous, I am here in a constant, terrible hurry—I have to go to the institute later on, from there to the train station and back to Berlin. This life of an industrial tycoon is no fun for me at all; I need tranquility of the soul to be reasonably productive. In addition, it is now way too lonely for me here, I long for you and the children. I do not like dealing all day long only with things instead of people. The other day in Hamburg, before the meeting, I went to a flower show for half an hour; glorious roses and colorful beds thick with shrubs, all the while fantasizing about our future house and garden. It would be nice to one day have a spacious house with a really big and well-cared-for garden. Of course, the children must be allowed to play in it; but one half would be full of the loveliest flowers; particularly many roses. . . .

Just now your letter from Monday night arrived. . . . Your description of the doctor was amusing; I imagine that the most factual doctor is always also the most suitable one. Give Mama my greetings, and tell her not to think of the war too much—in any event, she will have the baby to look forward to now. . . . All my best! Yours, Werner.

Elisabeth to Werner

Munich, July 17
My love!

Now I have been here for almost eight days already. How the time passes even in idleness—it is wild! Will it keep on going like this much longer? Thank you for your thick letter. . . .

I had a really very nice letter from Gerburg about the children, the garden, and the housekeeping. It seems that everything is going along splendidly. . . . However, Edith writes about Jochen that he is not quite happy, that he still must miss me a little. The dear little guy! If only I could be with him instead of sitting here with nothing to do. And when I finally come back, can I be for him what he needs? If only this delightful, intense cheerfulness does not get lost! . . .

Good night, my dear heart! Yours, Li.

Werner to Elisabeth

Berlin, Thursday night [July 18?]
My dear Li!

Here in Berlin I am even further away from you, not merely in terms of space, because at home you are still very much present in the house, but here in Berlin I am simply foreign. Also, every few hours I have to deal with all new people, which makes it somewhat tiring. . . .

This afternoon a few regiments from France marched in, which are getting back to their garrisons. The city flags were flying; all party formations had to stand at attention along the way. But there was no actual excitement noticeable in the people, it seemed to me; whoever is glad about the return of a relative does it quietly by himself and tells nobody about it.

—Although the Berliners usually claim to know the politics of the next weeks so precisely, I have not heard anybody tell me something about the future course of the war. Also, the next general assembly of the Reichstag is no longer a topic.

How might our children be doing? You must have a connection to Urfeld, or can at least easily always make one. I miss you all a lot right now, and am counting the days till my departure to Bavaria. Say a warm hello to Mama!

To you all my best, from your Werner.

Elisabeth to Werner

[Munich], July 19
My love!

Regrettably, I still cannot report anything real. Will Baby let me wait till August? It would be not nice of him. Today was a beautiful summer day—outside; it does not reach into these dark city apartments. What a barbaric establishment such a city is. Outside there is nature, pouring out all its blessings, and here, between these high houses, one can barely have any inclination of it. You know, people here are so very alienated from nature that it must be quite impossible to make a well-rounded human of yourself. . . . The change of the seasons, the blooming and drying up of flowers, the ripening of fruit—it is good to be surrounded by it all the time; one is reminded so much more of the laws of nature and does not cling to human laws. Love, isn't that right?

You know, in the Ötz castle I would like to read *David Copperfield*. . . . Now I am still reading Stendhal. And he gives me comfort. Goethe says of him: "He attracts, repels, interests and annoys, and so one cannot get rid of him." That is a really brilliant assessment. Exactly what I am feeling too—could not express it the same, of course! But the wide stream of life that courses through these people imparts itself beneficially to you.

Much love to you! When are you coming? It cannot be much longer now! Warm greetings from your Li. . . .

Elisabeth to Werner

[Munich, ca. July 20]
My love!

Thank you very much for your call. In eight days you will come; how happy I am.—We have talked completely openly today, Mama and I. Since then the air is cleared, and everything is going smoothly without effort. I believe Mama is happier as well. We walked in the beautiful and hot summer weather in the English Garden, which was actually quite nice.—I am beginning to have a terrible longing for my children. Until now, I had none. But now it itches and prods me everywhere. How much longer will it take! Oh, I am afraid I will have to wait much longer still. Also, today Dr. Albrecht is leaving. Then there will only be a very young assistant doctor. That is not a very reassuring thought either!

Now I will say good night to you. Keep on loving me! Yours, Li.

Werner to Elisabeth

Leipzig, July 22
My dear Li!

Today I clarified my vacation schedule and told the Armament Division that I will be going on vacation from July 30 to August 31. A longer time is difficult to justify, but maybe I can come to Urfeld once more for eight days at the end of September. A brief time like that might just somehow get added on. I myself find four weeks abominably short, especially since you will not be in Urfeld for part of the time; but others have even shorter vacations.— Unfortunately, at the moment our work here in Leipzig is going rather poorly, it is taking much longer than we anticipated, and I do not know if we will be able to finish by Sunday. This week I want to go to Berlin only from tomorrow evening till Thursday in order to get the work here up to speed. So overall I am really busy, have stood this morning in the laboratory in a white coat and learned from Mrs. Döpel how to make metal tubes airtight. In an hour I will go back to check if the tubes are working out. I enjoy the opportunity to learn the basics in experimental physics.— . . .

When I get back from Berlin, I will call again. Many good wishes! Yours, Werner.

1940

Elisabeth to Werner

[Munich, end of July]
My love!

How good that you will come soon. Thank you for your call! . . . Did Mama write to you so full of woe? Yesterday I had a nice long talk with her about aging and the position of young people vis-à-vis old age. I do think it pleased her a little; but I am not suitable to really be of help, of course. I am just so terribly sorry that she considers old age a shameful blemish, as she put it herself. Yet it is anything but! And I am inclined to think, Werner, that young people would have so much more respect for the aged if they could age and stay accepting and harmonious. Can you not help Mama a bit in this respect? She loves you so much and keeps every one of your words in her heart. I want to believe that you might help her if you were to talk with her about it from time to time. She no longer has a husband who helps her; you have to stand in for your father.

And I myself—well, you will not find your real wife. Not the one I should be and maybe sometimes also am. The time here has not been good for me; I am like a plant whose leaves are drooping.

And you too will most likely not be at your best either. So we will just have to recuperate together, one for the other; it will work out! In the English Garden; and at night we will walk through the quiet streets of the sleeping city—I love that!

Much, much love to you! Be well! On Sunday—how nice it would be if you were here by then. Yours, Li.

ON AUGUST 7—*later than expected—Martin is finally born. The advantage of this late date is that Elisabeth has her husband nearby and the two can share the joy of having their little son before he travels to Urfeld. About ten days later, Werner takes his wife and the newborn to the Ötzschlössl, a little guesthouse in Pessenbach run by a Miss Penzberger, where mother and child will have some time to recover and bond. There Elisabeth encounters two women from Werner's circle of acquaintances, referred to only as the "Evers ladies." Pessenbach is not far from Urfeld, so Werner can often visit his wife there. Letters become necessary once more only when*

Werner has to return to Leipzig and Berlin at the end of the month. Elisabeth stays at her retreat until mid-September, after which she returns to Urfeld to resume the household responsibilities. On September 15 Annalene, a new nanny, starts in her position, allowing the Schumacher parents to depart. Now the children as well as Lisa, the household help, have to get used to yet another new person in the house. At the end of the month, Werner comes to visit once more for a few days. But in mid-October, the house is closed down, and the whole family moves back into the Leipzig home.

Werner to Elisabeth

[Urfeld], Sunday night [ca. August 11]
My dear Li!

Today we were quite busy: in the morning we mounted a little gate in the passage behind the shed to close off the area to Jochen. . . . Around 11 o'clock I took the twins with me down to the lake, where I met your father and Ernst; the children then played at the sandy shore across the lake. They threw rocks in the water, set out little boats to swim, and on the slope above the road they watched some cows. . . .

Jochen was really cheerful throughout the day. . . . He always wants so much to play alongside the twins but is often treated poorly by them. In the afternoon the two of them played "hair washing": Maria had found an old brass faucet in the shed. Woi [Wolfgang] had to lie down on the old rug in front of the house; that was the bathtub; Maria held the faucet from above and turned it on and off. Jochen always wanted to lie next to Wolfgang; a battle ensued until all three were rolling around, entangled, and crying.—By the way, it was overcast and misty today, but we were outside almost all day, regardless.

How might you be getting on? . . . If nothing is planned differently, I will pick you up in Munich on Saturday. I hope both of you are really well! Good-bye! Yours, Werner.

Elisabeth to Werner

[Munich, in the clinic], August 13
My love!

Thank you for your letters! Now you are high up in the mountains somewhere—I cannot quite imagine it from here in my bed. But next year I too will come along! . . . Martin and I are well. Of course it still varies a little; particularly the cuts are painful sometimes, enough so that I cannot sleep even with a sleeping pill. But all that is not a real problem, except that then the milk immediately is reduced, which is very regrettable for Martin's "imbibing soul." . . .

Yesterday Mama was here, and today Edith, for the whole day. I am again in awe of so much beauty. How one wishes that she could transfer this kind of beauty also to a more fulfilled life. . . . I am very happy and have even come through those critical days without tears. Only today a touch; but when I wanted to enjoy wallowing in them properly, they dried up immediately, and I had to start laughing out loud. I really feel as if I had climbed a very, very high mountain. You only have to love me a lot; then all will be fine. Yours, Li.

Elisabeth to Werner

[Pessenbach, August 31]
My love!

Now you are in Berlin! I hope you do not have to suffer too much on account of the air raids! One hears constantly these days of attacks on Berlin.—The two days alone here have passed quickly. Martin is taking up so much of my time that there is not much left to feel lonely. Only on my walks I notice it. Yesterday, in the woods, I was singing a little bit to chase away any loneliness. Unfortunately, the two Evers ladies heard it, causing me to be the recipient of some general playful teasing at dinner. But it was a nice evening, and we sat together for a long time. Today we had a cool, wonderfully bright fall day. I was thinking of you, how you must have driven with a heavy heart through the sunny landscape before you arrived in the dark and troubled city. . . .

My little boy is good and splendidly well. I have a fair amount of milk for him so that he can really get enough. And when he is so completely full, he will often be awake for hours and look about with wide-open eyes. He will often actually be looking; one can tell quite distinctly.—Every bit of my hard-fought security has vanished during the past few months. Now I have four children and feel often more underage than ever. When I am back on my feet, I may regain a little more courage and ease. I am very curious how everything will work out when I get to Urfeld. Many, many greetings from your little Li.

Werner to Elisabeth

Berlin, Tuesday noon [September 3]
My dear Li!

For the first time since my arrival, I have half an hour to write to you. That is, had I been smart, I would have used the one night in the air-raid bunker to do it, but there I was too tired and hungover. All other times I was incessantly under pressure, so many people to talk to, talks to listen to, institutes to visit. Perhaps it is good that there is so much work, otherwise the end of the vacations with you all would have been even more difficult for me. On the train I was, despite the nasty overcrowding, in a strange emotional state, as it always will happen after any great external alterations. Eventually, it was recalibrated and balanced by way of a very jolly group of people—during eleven hours one practically has become a group—, in particular two extremely vivacious young female students who took care of the sunnier side of life. At my arrival, though, I was so beat and tired that I went to bed shortly after 9 o'clock. Around midnight then, there was a pretty intense air strike, from the basement one could distinctly make out bomb explosions in addition to the multitude of air defense weaponry. By the way, the strikes were aimed on the north side, Siemens town, etc. Talk the next morning was that a lot had been hit, but I myself have not yet seen any traces of the raid. From 2 to 7 o'clock I could go back to sleep, then I had to get up for the meetings at 9 o'clock. I talked to innumerable physicists, sat together with the Kienles at night, and came home only at midnight. After 12:30

alarms started up again; I got dressed and lay down again to wait until the shooting would begin. I must have fallen asleep; at any rate I awoke from the all-clear sirens and quickly got undressed once more.

Yesterday afternoon and evening I was at the biology department in Buch and met a very interesting Russian. The Russians have something innately free and carefree about them; they can make jokes and sarcastic remarks while being quite serious. They are very different, but it is nice to listen to them.— . . .

Greetings to little Martin, and get well soon! Yours, Werner.

Elisabeth to Werner

[Pessenbach, ca. September 3]
My love!

I did not write to you yesterday. It is despicable of me, since you surely will be very eager to hear from me—in all your loneliness! I am concerned that, in addition to all the unrest of traveling back and forth, you now have these nightly alarms. The strikes on Berlin are reported daily. Last night there also was one on Munich; one could hear the roar of the ordnance all the way here, some claim also to have seen the fire reflection. Here everything is wonderfully peaceful and we had lovely sunny days. It is cloudy today, but nice enough so that one can sit outside; and Martin too is outside all the time. . . .

Often in the evenings or at mealtimes we talk about the war. The opinion of this elder Mrs. E. is incomprehensible to me, and so counter to everything I believe, that I cannot grasp how a woman can even think this way. If it were a man, an officer—by all means. . . . Such is my life here, and I have enough to see and to think and to experience.

I am soon finished with *David Copperfield*. It is a little too simplistic in the end. The good are rewarded and the evil punished and there is nothing left over in that world order. If it were like that, we would have much less suffering. But fate is not quite such a simple example in arithmetic. This is like Reuter writes too: all is so wonderfully balanced out. Every pot finds its lid, all virtue is rewarded, the evil punished, as long as it is not done too harshly. That is the only thing I am astonished about in the book. Otherwise I find it very beautiful. And it is true that all characters are so memorable that they stay with you.

Now my love, don't be all too lonely in that big house. All my love to you. Yours, Li.

Werner to Elisabeth

Leipzig, September 6
Dear little Li!

Outside it is banging mightily again, but this time from up in the highest, not from the antiaircraft ammunition; it also is raining, and the air is like in a greenhouse. Now I have another week of solitude behind me, made tolerable by doing a great deal of work. But in reality, it is a situation that does not make any sense; having a wife and four children without hearing them around you or being aware of them. One has to get over it by recognizing that others have it so much worse.— . . .

Today I got, as they put it, a final notification that our coal ration for the coming winter would be set at 155 zentner coke and 19 zentner briquettes. If I would not heat at all until your return at, let's say, the end of October, and we then were rather thrifty, we could manage, basically. Last year, according to my estimates, we used 140 zentner coke and 19 zentner briquettes. We began to heat rather early and were not trying to conserve, only before Christmas we started. Perhaps we actually could heat the whole house moderately with our rations. The winter will not necessarily turn out as cold as the last one.— . . .

In the last two days I did not get any mail from you; it probably serves me right, because I have not written much from Berlin, but please don't be angry and keep writing anyway to your somewhat lonely husband. Stay healthy and say hello to the children! Yours, Werner.

Elisabeth to Werner

[Pessenbach, September 7]
My love!

Today Martin is one month old. And he now weighs nine pounds. I am delighted how he has come along. . . . My love, if only the weather will be as nice later on when you get here. It is indescribable. These soft colors, the crispness and warmth of the air, the blue of the sky. And there is a wonderful tranquility. One can really recuperate here. And that's what I am doing. . . .

Everybody here reads the newspapers all the time. I cannot get myself to do it. I find the world so much nicer without! But since Mrs. Prätorius has left, I am again all alone in my apolitical opinion and my more human feelings, because Mrs. E., as the wife of an officer, is not talking much. . . .

Love, why don't you go sit in the garden a lot so that you can experience some of this late summer beauty? You do know, don't you, the *Late Summer* by Stifter? The peace, the harmony, the otherworldly, mild calm of such a day is the realm of this book.—

Now I have nothing else left to read. But that does not matter. I can easily fill the few days here another way.

Now a thousand greetings from my heart! Yours, Li.

Werner to Elisabeth

Leipzig, Sunday afternoon [September 8]
Dear Li!

Yesterday in the afternoon two cheerful letters from you arrived at the same time; that made the loneliness here right away much more tolerable. How good that you are getting stronger and that you have a little of real summer left to enjoy. Here too the sky is cloudless, but one is in this city so infinitely removed from nature as such. Only the roses from the garden indicate that it is summer. . . .

Last night I visited the Frels family, where it was very nice and cozy. Jochen Frels is with the soldiers; he no longer wanted to attend the university and seems to feel more contented there than at home. . . . Ursula is in anticipation of a B.d.M. [Association of German Girls] trip to Italy; only Jutta seems to want to stay calmly at home. The Frelses have furnished the air-raid basement very comfortably. Since I have been here, there was no alarm yet; it seems the British just wanted to be disruptive during the [book] fair. . . . Mrs. Winkler [housekeeper] mentioned that her youngest found the service in Warsaw so tedious that he signed up for Africa. She is very sad about it.—The older people are tired of war, but the younger ones, generally, seem quite content.— . . . This afternoon I want to prepare my lecture, work, and practice. To get out of the house is not rewarding in Leipzig. So keep getting rested some more, and say hello to the whole Ötzschlössl and to the children! Yours, Werner.

Elisabeth to Werner

[Pessenbach, September 9]
My love!
Today all of the "youth" has gone to Kochel to see some kind of movie. I did not go along because it will be too late for me, especially since I frequently spend half the night hunting down mosquitoes, whirling about my room with a slipper in hand. . . . For today, I believe, I have killed them all, and am now lying cozily in bed and take a walk up to you. My love, how are you? Very lonely—yes, I know. Soon you will come to me and afterward all of us will also come to Leipzig. If you get any additional coals because of Martin—which I do believe, then we can come one day sooner for every zentner we get. Of course it all depends also on the war, but I cannot imagine that the war in its current form can last very long. I would love to talk to you again.

Here I always listen in amazement to this kind of talk. Ever since Mrs. Prätorius (called Well) is gone, Dr. Evers has risen to dominance, and she is such a strange mix of toughness, nationalism, and female illogical thought. I much prefer the somewhat cooler realism of Miss P [Penzberger]. . . .

Oh, how I look forward to getting home! I am a little fearful of the long nights when I have all the responsibility but am not able to do anything, if someone were to come. Here one is extremely anxious, so that I am often amazed. But we will be three of us women folk, it should be fine. . . . Good night, my love! All my love and my best. Yours, Li.

Elisabeth to Werner

[Pessenbach], Wednesday noon [September 11?]
Love,

Now I have really made a stupid mistake, I addressed the long letter this morning to Leipzig instead of Berlin. Now you will be without mail for several days!

From the radio we learned of an intense bombing of Berlin. It will be disastrous if the British do not soon yield. Also the "Brandplättchen" [incendiary devices dropped from planes] are a really terrible thing. And we will quite certainly fight back in terrible revenge. One must not think about what will happen in the next few weeks. And even less about what if the war is *not* decided in the next few weeks. Today I received two letters . . . , both very nice and both in the same tenor: it will likely take long, very long. I cannot really believe it. Then nothing will remain of Europe. If only one knew how strong the British still are! Our airplane losses compared to the British losses are now rather high; yesterday the radio said 21:48. If only one knew more! Dr. Evers had seen the south coast of England in the weekly show; it must look frightening: one wrecked ship next to the other and the coast itself a heap of rubble. . . . Oh, how glad am I that you are not in danger! And how well we are doing, compared to others!

My mother called just now. The car will get here tomorrow at 4:30 p.m. Lisa already announced a grand reception for me. . . . These three and a half weeks here have gone by unbelievably fast. I cannot quite grasp that we drove out of Munich so long ago already. I remember this trip very fondly. It was so nice to see nature again, to sit next to you; even though the stay in the clinic was brief, what happened there is always like a complete time change. Everything begins all new, and what happened before was long, long ago and barely is still a part of you. A little later it balances again, and only a few singular impressions remain, which are stronger and more vivid than everything else one can experience. Thus, with the twins, it was the clouds and trees which I could see through my window, . . . and then the Reger lied: "Last Evening in the Quiet Hour," which was in my head there all the time and almost intoxicated me with its balm and intimacy. Even now, as I am writing about it, I feel as if I were reliving it, so vibrant and close it is for me.

And with Jochen, it was very different. There is only one moment so brilliantly strong in my memory: the moment when I saw Jochen lying before me, after everything was over, and the little perfect body lay there before me. I imagine one can never see one's child the same way again as in that first moment. We women have this advantage, because no words can give a sense of what this experience is like. . . . You know, it is as if one were tying the bond, which was loosened at that moment, on a different level anew, as if one were surrounding the child with one's soul just as tight and close as it had been within you previously.

And with Martin it was very different again. There it was you near me, which was so precious to me, how you sat with me after the birth, and then also, how we were driving out here together. . . .

What kind of a letter this has become. I slipped into talking to you. This letter is for you to read at night before you go to bed, then it will be as if we were sitting together a while longer and talked with each other about this and that. . . . Love, enough now! A thousand greetings, my love, from your wife.

Werner to Elisabeth

[Berlin], Thursday morning around 1 o'clock
[Friday, September 13]
My dear Li!

Now I am sitting in the bunker of the Harnack House, and outside energetic shooting is going on. Last night, the Reichstag, the Brandenburg Gate, and the American embassy supposedly were hit; I read it in the paper. Now you can hear the British planes again, distinctly. I have to think of the statement Fermi made, and am slightly amused about how easily people are satisfied; who would have thought, ten years ago, that you travel matter-of-fact to Berlin for a few days, dutifully, only to get bombed there night after night. The next day you read in the rag how many houses have burned down, how many people perished, and go about your business, calmly; those who are excitable are glad that it is even worse in London.

Since one cannot get real sleep in the bunker, I took the Stendhal with me, who is difficult to put aside. Although I always get annoyed again about the times he describes, and the characters, he is a stellar writer. The fact that he writes about the times around 1830, which means the hangover of the French Revolution did last forty years, could make one very pessimistic. At least, at around 1830, one was allowed again to write about the grievances as openly as Stendhal does; in all likelihood that was already an improvement compared to the Napoleonic period. Humans always seem to have been the same throughout time; but an order, which has grown over the course of centuries, is keeping, relatively successfully, the good ones up and the bad ones down—with the occasional noteworthy exceptions. After a revolution, however, everything becomes scrambled. By the way, with Stendhal, I always find that one must not speak about things the way he does. He knows an awful lot about the passion in love; basically, love to him is just a temporary state of intoxication, not founded in anything objective, therefore not "meaningful." He does not think about the possibility that—to express it somehow—the connection of two people gets decided in heaven. I am under the impression: Stendhal does not believe in anything and finds solace when there is at least the rush of passion, during which one temporarily forgets an existence devoid of meaning. But this cannot possibly be a philosophy to live life by, at least I cannot relate to it.

—Excuse, that in my tired state of night thoughts, I am writing such general things, instead of thinking that you are getting to Urfeld today and that you all must be delighted to be together. How happy the children must be! By the way, today I have reserved sleeping compartment seats for 24/25 to Munich and 29/30 return. I hope nothing interferes. Here it has calmed down by now; hopefully one can get to sleep soon. Good night! Yours, Werner.

Elisabeth to Werner

[Urfeld, ca. September 13]
My love!

Now I am actually home again. Love—I am still finding it a bit strange in my own four walls; when I am with the three older ones, I forget that I have Martin, and when I am with him, the rest of the world seems so far.—But this will change.

There was a great excitement—of course. Maria was the most reserved; also—of course. But from time to time, her eyes were shining—like two stars; I always see that in her. Wolfgang was adorable. He moved me very deeply. He would not leave me out of his sight, and his little face appeared lit from within by the most affectionate love and devotion. Eventually, he became activated,—when I still had not finished my cake—he took the spoon and fed me one piece after the other and did this with such seriousness and concentration, as one does in a cult. And Jochen—Jochen was acting all indifferent. He was only interested in the baby. He looked and looked in the basket, and could not get enough of it, had neither eyes nor ears for his surroundings. Since he still had a nasty cold, I ended the bliss and took Martin over to our nice separate chambers. Jochen would not look at me for the longest time, and when I tried to pick him up, he screamed in protest. At night, in bed, he had accepted me a little already, but true friendship may take some more time. Well, all three have a cold, unfortunately—actually everybody in the whole house has one. It must be in the walls. I will call the doctor tomorrow and ask for an oil prescription so that I can make oil wraps for Jochen's constant coughing. But now I must end. Of course, we had to talk so much that it became 10 o'clock before you know it, and Martin is now next in line. So, more to follow tomorrow. Yours, Li.

My love! You would be angry if you knew how late it is. But in the bosom of the family you inevitably must wait your turn, even though you are much closer to my heart than all others—you do know that. But the three of us women have been chatting so terribly much—all evening long, first with Mutti, then with Edith. . . . I pulled open the deepest drawers of my heart a little, and it is so endearing to be talking with Muttchen about everything from such a different vantage point. For I can now understand the difficulties in my childhood and youth a bit differently, as a cliff, that also might appear with my own children, to be circumnavigated, requiring a great deal of strength of heart and body.

And with Edith the talks also are endless because—just think—she also is expecting a child now. I am very happy about it. This makes me feel infinitely closer to her. . . .

Now goodnight, my love! How wonderful the air is up here! I hope you have not been plagued all too much by air raids in Berlin. Love, how I am looking forward to you! All my love. Yours, Li.

Werner to Elisabeth

Leipzig, September 14
Dear good Li!

Upon my return I once again found two letters from you; you are giving me real comfort when you let me participate in everything that goes on around you. Since you are now in Urfeld back with the little ones, you will just not have as much time to write; but you might call me sometime; I myself cannot really call you there anymore. In the meantime, I put in a request for a place in the sleeper car for 24/25 and 29/30 and seem to be getting it. Whether I can free myself from the various obligations is another question. Ordinarily, I have to run a seminar in Berlin every Saturday, but I will manage to get around it somehow.—

My last time in Berlin was actually quite nice. . . . For two evenings, I was invited in the Arno-Holz Street [the Schumacher residence in Berlin], yesterday also for dinner, and I played sonatas with Ernst. A medical student and corporal . . . , who was another guest, made a fabulous impression on me. It is so reassuring, when also in the next younger generation one comes across some people, occasionally, who are striking an inner chord, as if they were related. . . .

But now I close, I am tired and cold. Do not overdo anything and sleep a lot! Say hello to the children! Yours, Werner!

Elisabeth to Werner

[Urfeld, ca. September 15]
My love!

. . . Edith is not here today, Mutti moved down to the Brackenhofers'. Now I am alone with the whole company. I am trying to keep them contained as much as possible because I am not yet quite capable, after the initial good behavior is over. Maria is becoming a little stubborn, which is usual for her, every time that people around her are switched. . . . Now goodnight, my love!

Soon you will be here—that is wonderful! Be well!

Werner to Elisabeth

Leipzig, September 16
My love!

Now you sound as if you are really comfortably back with the children, and the new nanny must also have started her job. I hope you find everything to your liking. How might it look there and how is the weather, what are the little ones doing? Here we have a nasty cold spell, I am wearing my winter suit and thick underwear and am warming myself up a little with the "sun" (unfortunately, just electric). But it appears that tomorrow it will be better. The institute is heated. Yesterday, in honor of Sunday, the Frelses also started their stove. By the way, the Frelses only receive sixty zentner briquettes and nothing else for the entire winter, because of their stove. So I have not dared to apply for an increase in our allotment; I wrote we would do our best. In case we ran out, we would hope to get consideration in retrospect, due to etc. . . .

For two days I have been very tired, I am not doing all that well, also am missing you and the children a lot; I am looking very much forward to next week in Urfeld. On Wednesday I should be in Urfeld on the afternoon bus, if nothing interferes here.—For tonight a young lieutenant has announced himself, whom I had met eight years ago as a young scout; I am curious who he is and what he looks like. I have finished with the Stendhal; the story has left a deep impression on me, but I am a little disgusted still. To not believe in anything! That is really terrible.—

. . . Say hello to the children, all four of them; and do not overwork, right? Good night for now! Yours, Werner.

Elisabeth to Werner

[*Urfeld, ca. September 16*]
My love!

Today we had our final good-byes, my parents and I. From here on in, you will be treated better, my love! But today I am too tired to write a lot. Forgive me! Saying good-bye to Mutti is rather difficult for me. Our connection is so lovely now, the relationship so close that I really find it painful to see her go. I am now happy to be her daughter.

Here everything is working exceptionally well. The twins are more cheerful than I have ever known them to be. It makes me totally happy. Jockerle is improving. And the "new one" is working out incredibly well. She takes on all my work—I feel completely free from work—is getting along well with the children, so that they are content and merry. And she has a good rapport with Lisa too.

Many thanks for your letter about Stendhal. I was especially happy about it and share your opinion exactly. Good night, my love!—

It is now midnight and I am still up, because just as I was falling asleep I heard a loud racket upstairs. Both boys were crying, and Miss Annalene was sleeping soundly. She seems to have a blessed sleep! Now I have covered the lamp upstairs in their room and am waiting for them to get back to sleep so that I can turn off their light.

Next to me the "little brother" is snoring. I must say, this tender age is the loveliest for a mother. I am feeling once more this indescribably nice calm such a child radiates.— . . . With love. Yours, Li.

Werner to Elisabeth

Leipzig, September 17
My Li!

It is late already and I am very tired. But overall I am doing much better than yesterday, so I want to send you an extra greeting. The visit from the lieutenant yesterday has revived me and I am energized for work. A while ago I studied and memorized five pages of a piano concerto—I have known it, of course, from earlier times. Now I have been sitting with the lecture and my private philosophy; my eyes gradually just won't stay open. What the lieutenant's name was, I actually still do not know, but he looked nice, I vaguely remembered his face. The childlike features had become quite manly, only the eyes occasionally betrayed a bit of insecurity. He reported to me about France, where he had been part of the crossing of the Maas River and the breach of the Maginot Line at Charleville. Today he is leaving with his battalion to Norway, possibly to Narvik. How different the world must appear to a twenty-year-old like him. He thought that sitting around and doing nothing was not good for the troops, but he also believed that the war will last a very long time yet. Up to now, none of the two main adversaries is seriously weakened, and many are expecting the entry of America into the war by springtime. Since politics are governed by higher powers, we must remain patient and try to establish our lives as reasonably as possible under the circumstances.—

The inauguration of the new nanny seems to have been a real success. It is so important to our whole family life, and I am delighted if it continues well. I hope our Jochen will soon be all well again; and do take good care of little Maria, she needs the love of the adults most of all.—

Eight days from today, I will be on my way to you all! So good night for now! Yours, Werner.

Elisabeth to Werner

[Urfeld], Tuesday, September 17
My love!

Today I really wanted to call you badly! But when I came to Bracken-hofer at 8:30 to register the call, I was told it would take *very* long for the call to get through, two to three hours; so I gave up with a heavy heart. A really heavy heart, because after such a crazy day, I needed to talk with you, my love! Yes, crazy was the day and the night before as well, and this night promises to be more of the same. Jochen and Maria are again totally out of sorts due to the changing of people. Worst is Jochen, who has the added bronchitis. He is completely beside himself, starts crying over every little thing, and has such a light sleep that he wakes up from the slightest noise, and begins to weep. He is now in the room next to mine, while I stashed Martin in the living room so he won't disturb him; later on I will get him back in here. And Maria is also a challenge, misbehaving, close to tears, and excitable. She casts furious and contemptuous glances at "Aunt Annali" who told me at night that Maria seems to dislike her. I comforted her. Maybe it helps.

Several times during the day, I nearly despaired with all the crying and misbehaving. . . . But I think in a few days it should be calmer again here at the house. Then Annalene also will be more familiar with everything, and—I do not really doubt it—win Maria over. . . . Much, much love!
Yours, Li. . . .

Werner to Elisabeth

Berlin, Thursday night [September 19]
Dear Li!

I came here yesterday afternoon again and early this morning I got a letter from you; thank you very much for it. I am glad that the big change-over is happening more or less smoothly. It can't be easy for the children to cope with the disappearance of your mother and then having another new help at the same time, but hopefully you will not have too much trouble.

I can easily imagine that the twins are overjoyed about your presence; Jockerle probably too, but he cannot yet quite understand it. . . .

This morning I had to attend a meeting of the Reich Association of Academics as the representative of the Leipzig Academy; rarely have I been so turned off by German professors as I was in this meeting. On top of it all, these Wilhelmine period luxury edifices where the meeting took place and this impertinent, arrogant tone of the Prussians—allow me to consider you for the moment a Rhineland woman—it really made you want to run. If I did not know that there also were other people here—I would believe that tact and culture actually never penetrated beyond the Roman *limes*. But of course, I am only venting my anger here, you must excuse it; in reality there surely are many nice people here, and Berlin, as a city, is infinitely more beautiful than Leipzig. At noon we were guests of President Vahlen; only around 4:30 could I get to my work at the Harnack House. At night I practiced an hour on an ancient grand piano in the auditorium, afterward talked on the telephone with your mother, who had just arrived. She told me very nicely about you and the children, tomorrow I will go over there for dinner again. Now I must still prepare a talk for the colloquium here. So good night for now! Yours, Werner.

Elisabeth to Werner

[Urfeld, ca. September 20]
My love!

Today's letter from you made me all sad. Are you seriously thinking that the war will last for a very long time? How one hates it, that war. If only it would end! I cannot think about it at all, the future will be so dark and full of terror. . . .

Tonight the rain has started. There is some hope that it will be nice again by Wednesday. How I wish it for you!—And me too. Martin is thriving on schedule. He now weighs ten pounds. Quite excellent, right? . . . Good night, my love! Yours, Li.

Wolfgang, Maria, and Jochen marvel at their new little brother, Martin

Werner to Elisabeth

Sunday afternoon [September 22]
My dear Li!

Now it only will be a few more days till I visit with you all. Your last letter sounded quite content again; I hope little Jochen keeps improving. On Friday night I was in Steglitz. Your parents seemed in good spirits, and they reported from Urfeld. . . .

I am now very excited about coming to Urfeld. In reality, I have so much work to do that it is rather impertinent to leave now; but on the other hand, I have the feeling that I am more industrious at this time than the average person, since I work both here and in Berlin; so I have a moral justification for a few days off. . . .

Last night I was at B's; we had very good schnapps there and butter cookies, and one talked about groceries and coal and such (among other things). You are probably right about us being always too decent and there-fore the dumb ones; but I find it so difficult to do it any other way. The Banks

also mentioned that the Germans were split into two classes: the undernour-
ished and the under-the-table nourished. I simply do not have any opportunity here anyway to go on any exchange-of-goods trips. But wherever I get
invited, the meal is like in peacetime.—

—Good-bye until the day after after tomorrow! Yours, Werner.

Elisabeth to Werner

[Urfeld, September 21/22]
My love!

This is the last letter before you arrive. Oh, how glad I will be when
finally you are here! It is so tiring to be around a stranger all the time. And
so often I miss you terribly. . . .

It is true what you have always said, although I always protested; the
youngest child is the closest to the mother. Jochen has become such a big boy
in the meantime; he is a small, separate world to himself. Right now, I still
prefer to withdraw into my little room, where the calm, peaceful breathing
of this helpless little being makes me wonderfully calm and peaceful as well.
Here there is not yet any dissonance and naughtiness, and there is really
nothing for me to educate. And it is splendid when a child thrives unimpeded
like Martin right now. . . .

So good-bye, till you come. If the weather is good and I am doing well,
I will pick you up in Kochel. Be well till then! Yours, Li.

Werner to Elisabeth

Leipzig, October 1
My dear Li!

The travel back here went according to schedule. Shortly before 9
o'clock I looked outside to the platform, thought I read Tutzing and was
shocked, because then I would not have been able to catch the train in
Munich. But it was Gauting already, and all went fine. Mama stood at the
sleeping compartment and seemed quite well and cheerful. I found everything in order here. Unfortunately, I also found a letter from your father that

seemed very tactless to me; I ripped it up and also will not go to the Arno-Holz Street for the time being. This letter was written out of concern for you, and is excused on these grounds; but to me there are things about which one does not write.— . . .

Last night, Mr. Hetzer presented a lecture for us about the mathematical element in art, I learned a lot from it. In addition, I noticed with satisfaction that the thoughts I have formulated over a long period of time about these very questions also have merit in a discussion with experts, at least in their basic form. Aside from this, I have ordered, in a fit of carefree planning, a whole lot of tickets for concerts in the Gewandhaus: for the 24th one for you, and for the bulk of the chamber music evenings for both of us.—

The days with you all were excellent, you all look so healthy and fresh, and it is truly a pure pleasure. . . . I hope your weather is nice with much sunshine! Yours, Werner.

Elisabeth to Werner

[Urfeld, October 2?]
My love!
It is 6 o'clock in the morning; for one and a half hours I have been on the go with the children, Jochen will not sleep anymore, is playing music on his beloved harmonica and thinking out loud, Martin is awake as well and wants feeding, the big ones are grumpy about the nighttime noise, Lisa looks sleepily out her door, only Annalene is sound asleep. How this one can sleep—it is admirable!

But as I open the window and push aside the shutters right now, there is such a wonderfully strong and cold and fragrant air streaming in—at once I am really awake and now I wish you a "good morning." Love—you have been a whole day in the city again and been working so hard. . . .

I hope that the air-raid sirens do not plague you too much! And thank you again for coming. It was so nice to be living with you again, not just getting a visit from you. And the heavens are full of music to me. Present and future are equally good and are keeping their wise balance.

Be well, my beloved heart! . . . Yours, Li.

Werner to Elisabeth

Berlin, Friday night [October 4]
Dear Li!

My intention to write letters in the air-raid bunker is not yet relevant, so I am instead writing you in advance now. My presence seems to be a deterrent to the British; yesterday, for the first time in eight days, there was no alarm. Although when I woke up from the sirens the night before, I apparently fell asleep again, because next I awoke from a big bang in the immediate vicinity. I wanted to get up then, but there were only a few more antiaircraft shots, and then everything was quiet again. The third time, I awoke from the all clear. I hope this night is quiet also.

This evening at the colloquium, I met the old Planck, who appeared to me still totally clear, mentally; at the same time, he continues to be a real mensch who is feeling and wishing—if one is aging in this manner, then getting old is actually something quite nice. Planck wants to be "remembered" to you, as he put it. About the war and its course, Planck was quite unhappy; he also talked about the intellectual life in Germany and elaborated to me on various hopes he had.

During this, he became very animated and beseeched me not to become discouraged. Which I am not, anyway. Then I met Gerlach from Munich. He told me that this certain Mr. Müller, who cannot take over Sommerfeld's lectures since he does not know the relevant field, has now taken on as an assistant a gentleman by the name of Glaser to give his lectures for him. This Glaser used to be in Würzburg and, as Döpel told me, has been mentally disabled for some time. This Mr. Glaser, P.G. [Nazi Party member], has now written an essay and published it stating that there will not be any purity in German physics until all Jewish quantum and atomic theories (and their representatives) are forever expunged. Perhaps I can motivate Mr. Schmidt with this again, but, overall, I find this whole monkey business amusing. Through my reading of Stendhal (*Charterhouse*) I am used to the stupidity and wickedness of humanity as such; the exceptions become the more enjoyable on account of this. By the way, I somewhat like this Count Moska in the *Charterhouse*, more than the

Fabrizio character. I could imagine that in twenty years similar books will
be written again.—

Just as I came home now, I received your letter; many thanks and do not
overdo anything. But see to it with every possible means that we get enough
coal. Fourteen days from now, the twins will arrive in Leipzig, and I am so
terribly looking forward to all of you. Say hello to the children and stay
healthy! Yours, Werner.

Elisabeth to Werner

[Urfeld, October 4?]
My love!

Just two weeks from today the children will come to you, love; I am so
glad you will not be alone anymore. Here, however, it still is wonderful.
Yesterday it was so nice and sunny that I let the children have another
sunbathing time. And today—it is not yet time for Martin's bath—I am
sitting in the warm, sun-drenched room. I have worked a lot yesterday, have
been sitting till 12 o'clock doing the budget numbers till my head hurt. But
now everything is looking good, and I am very pleased. . . . During this first
half of the fiscal year—i.e., since April—the income is at: 14,061.39 marks
and the expenses at 11,714.37 marks. That is a very good result so far.
Included in the expenses are all those for the Walchensee house, and on the
income side not included is any revenue from stock purchases and sales.
Doesn't this relieve your worries a little? . . .

Werner—I am extremely upset and sad about that letter from my father.
I know this nasty tactless behavior very well, this manner of intruding on the
most intimate and innermost things. When you came into our family, I was
very afraid of it, and always relieved when we were back in our own place,
and all had been fine. In the meantime, I almost had forgotten about it, and
now it did happen. Love, I know how hurtful he can be and find it terrible
that now he has hurt you too. I am at the point now that I have no other
feelings for him except the duty of a child toward her parents. Do it likewise;
he is old and not all well. But please, never infect my mother also with this.
I know that she suffers as I do, because he always has stood between her and

us. And in spite of it, she has stood by him. I love her dearly and often think what a wonderful woman she could have become if she had had a husband who did not cover up and bury her tender heart, but nurtured and unfolded it. Now you will perhaps understand me in, some sense, even better; but, love, do not love me any less for it! . . .

I am *very* excited about coming home, even when it is not easy for me to leave here. I am very happy here and so grateful to you for all the beauty we have here. You my love, love!

Your little wife.

Werner to Elisabeth

Leipzig, October 6
My dear Li!

It is almost midnight, and I am conducting my life very unreasonably—so it is time that you soon should come here again. I have studied the E-flat-major concerto for almost two hours, and within me I am quite caught up and excited by the glorious music even now. Overnight, I have mentally constructed a Corona talk about this concerto—I was not sleeping well—with an exact analysis of the architecture, the mathematics in the different motifs, a demonstration on the piano of different themes with their instrumentation and, in the end, the entire concerto ought to be performed. The work is so incredibly complete that one could not do justice to the sheer number of symmetrical interrelationships in the architecture. But unfortunately, I do not have such a Corona talk in my immediate future.—

Otherwise, I am quite busy as well. Yesterday morning, I had a colloquium talk in Berlin, in the afternoon almost three hours of discussing work with Döpel, this morning, I took measurements at the institute, in the afternoon preparation for tomorrow's lecture, then wrote a little more on the "philosophy." It has now ended up somewhat in the physics territory, seems a little more arid therefore, but is progressing well. . . .

I am so much looking forward to your arrival. . . . The air-raid basement also will be finished soon. So the house is getting festive improvements for all of you. I hope you are faring well on your trip, and also in general. Yours, Werner.

Elisabeth to Werner

[Urfeld], October 6
Love!

Today no letter from you again! Of course you must have terribly
much to do in Berlin! I hope it is the only reason. Here I have begun to pack
today. . . . Around noon, just when all three children were naked and
whirling about on my balcony, there suddenly arose a frightful sound. The
whole air was filled with it. It came from the direction of Mittenwald and
became ever more intense, until we could see way high above a large number
of planes; we counted up to fifty of them. Woi was all excited about it. It was,
of course, a great display. How unimaginably gruesome it must be, when
three hundred enemy airplanes show up. One can easily understand that man
cannot withstand this onslaught of technical power anymore!

But I must see to Martin; he is screaming his head off and needs
feeding.

Monday
. . . We had six hundred Bess Arabians [refugees] arrive here today.
Mostly women and children. The men come on foot, with their belongings
loaded onto wagons. One can tell that they are from the Balkans only
because of the large headscarves they wear. They speak a friendly German
with a Swabian inflection and have very German, wide faces. But it is a
pitiful scene. All the women have such sorrowful, silent, and subdued
faces—often they look terribly miserable and sad. There is a great horde of
children along—some of them sick. But overall, this crowd of children is,
naturally, very lively and adventurous and explores the whole area. Now it is
impractical that we have no fence. Troupes of boys or girls appear up here at
the house all the time. When I worked down in the garden today, women
and children were assembling along that fence and silently watching me, the
way one observes an animal in the zoo. The poor people also have not seen
mountains before. And sadly, this day was not one to win over their hearts.
The mountains were uncannily close, dark, and threatening. And now the
rain has been rustling around the house all evening long. . . .

Good night, my love! Yours, Li.

Werner to Elisabeth

Berlin, October 10
My dear Li!

I am longing to hear from you. The mail does not seem to be working properly; I only got one letter from you yesterday, written on Saturday, so it was four days in transit, nothing since. I hope all is well with everybody, but I assume it is.

This time I am very dissatisfied with my stay here. The people in the institute are so terribly slow, and when I arrive here on Wednesday they are usually exactly where I left them the previous Saturday. I now am developing a certain respect for Döpel, who does not usually appear to be an especially good physicist. But he is working infinitely more precisely and faster than the people here.—A while ago, by the way, I received two invitations to give talks abroad, one from Budapest, the other from Paris. In both instances I have permission to accept, if I want to. I don't know yet exactly what I should do. The thing in Budapest is more fun for me than in Paris. To Budapest, I could probably also take you along, and we could, around mid-March, combine it with an, albeit very brief, trip through Hungary. To Paris, I would have to go by myself; my French is very poor, and that bothers me, although the talk, of course, would be in German. It also is not nice to travel to an occupied enemy country. Probably I will accept Hungary and at least postpone Paris.

. . . Write to me soon, and greetings to the children! Yours, Werner.

Elisabeth to Werner

[Urfeld, ca. October 11]
Love!

Do you have any idea how nice Urfeld is? No—of course you do not know it completely. I myself have only found out today how totally wonderful it is. During the morning, the weather was stable, just barely, but the sun still came through from time to time and you could go out without getting wet. Only in the afternoon it started drizzling. . . . I was just about to fill the hour until it was Martin's time with some sewing work, when a good genie suddenly took my hand and so I followed. I did not know where I should go, because I always thought there are no walkways here to just roam aimlessly, which I always had deemed a shortfall of Urfeld, . . . and then I discovered a path leading into some bushes. I followed this path and there it opened up to a new, unexpectedly gorgeous aspect of this landscape. I came into some beech woods that were so deserted that you heard nothing but the dripping rain, the falling of the leaves. The beech trees were all yellow and brown, and it smelled of moisture, of wet, decaying leaves and freshly cut wood. And now I detected a network of little paths that cross the entire slope, and I walked a long time, always new paths, meadows, hollow ways, and woods. In between, constantly changing, surprising views of the lake and the mountain range. And on my path were the fresh imprints of deer that must have fled from me. . . . When I came home, I suddenly looked at our house with very different eyes also. Everything here has come so much more alive for me. I can see how it is nestled in nature, not as a foreign object, but as a part of it. It feels, as if I had only today understood, that we are really living in God's nature.

And yes, your letter today also has given me much joy. You will have to, even when we are there, devote yourself at times so totally to music. I will not be jealous! I do know myself how nice and how essential it is. You—I hope you have found the Stifter. He is, in every sense, the opposite of Stendhal. And you would enjoy him *very* much, I know it for sure. . . . But now, good night! It is 11 o'clock and Martin must still be getting his due.

Be well, my love! And always go in the basement. I am quite concerned, knowing you are in Berlin! Yours, Li.

Werner to Elisabeth

Leipzig, October 12
My dear Li!
I am writing on institute stationery because I have a little free time here and can use it for a letter.—My experience that my presence seems to deter

the British was confirmed again: in Berlin I could sleep uninterrupted for three nights, whereas here there was a huge air raid this last Thursday.

One bomb was dropped on the waterworks near the Bonhoeffers', but hit the field next to it. Bonhoeffers were standing at the window just then and could see the airplane right close up. A second bomb fell onto Linne Street, at the corner to Johannis Avenue. There too only a few windowpanes and a piece of wall are broken. The alarm lasted for three and a half hours. And just think what bad luck Mrs. Winkler had with our house that very night: She had been upstairs, in the ironing room, and left the lights on in the stairway to the second floor; since it was still daylight, she could not notice it from outside. Now it becomes dark, and the light shines through Gerburg's room brightly out into the street. Due to the alarm, it only gets noticed around midnight, reported, and the police show up and open our house in Mrs. Winkler's presence with the aid of a locksmith. Of course, Mrs. Winkler is called down to the police and will most likely have to pay a high fine. I feel very bad for her and tried to comfort her, since she was so very desperate, more about the fact that she left the light on than the fine. With the latter, we can, of course, help her, should it be too high. I told her this for comfort. I also find it unpleasant that our house will now be under close scrutiny for a long time to come. I will check on all the darkening installations again.

Here I found your letter, thank you so much! That you have such good weather so often is wonderful. How nicely one could arrange it, if we lived in Munich: you would stay put in the wintertime, and I would come to Urfeld every weekend. But now, it is really better that you all will come here—in spite of the attacks, which, during this winter, should still stay a rare occurrence. So, in eight days, all of you will already be completely in preparation mode, but the twins will already be here. So, my very, very, best! Yours, Werner.

1941

MANY OF ELISABETH'S *letters from this year have been lost. Surely she did not write fewer letters than Werner—as always when apart, the two shared their lives through letters—yet only half as many of Elisabeth's letters compared to Werner's survive from this period. The loss may reflect the fact that Werner, sometimes in Leipzig, sometimes in Berlin, does not have a proper home to collect the letters that reach him. It is easier for Elisabeth, in her reclusive Urfeld domicile, to keep Werner's letters safe.*

With the exception of one letter from Werner in which he reports on a trip to Budapest at the end of April, the letters begin in June. As in previous years, Elisabeth is spending the summer, from June to September, with the four children in Urfeld, with just a few days in Leipzig during the period. Living in Urfeld has become a familiar arrangement, and she is glad to be far from the events of the war, whereas Werner in Leipzig and Berlin is much more exposed to the political atmosphere and events.

Beginning with the invasion of Russia, the war takes on a new and more menacing dimension. The death notices are increasing, and the Heisenbergs suffer personal losses: Elisabeth's younger brother, Ernst, is killed in action in October, the son of their good friends, the Jacobis, perishes, and a young colleague of Werner's whom he treasured—Hans Euler—crashes while on a reconnaissance flight.

Added to war-related worries for Werner are agonizing deliberations about how to deal with the scientific findings of the uranium project. Obviously, this project was subject to the highest level of secrecy, and Werner is discreet in his letters, revealing nothing. But in retrospect much can be gleaned. The notice that Werner plans a visit with Bohr in Copenhagen reminds one that in September 1941 the now-famous conversation between the two took place. This visit embodied the hope of making contact again with the "international community of scientists" to discuss what was happening in atomic research. Werner writes directly about this twenty years later in his autobiography:

We knew that atom bombs could now be produced, in principle, and by what precise methods, but we overestimated the technical effort involved. . . . Nevertheless, we all sensed that we had ventured onto highly dangerous ground, and I would occasionally have long discussions particularly with Carl Friedrich von Weizsäcker, Karl Wirtz, Johannes Jensen and Friedrich Houtermans as to whether we were doing the right thing. I can clearly remember one conversation with Carl Friedrich in my room in the Kaiser Wilhelm Institute for Physics in Dahlem. Jensen had just left us, and Carl Friedrich said something like this: "At present, we don't have to worry about atom bombs, simply because the technical effort seems quite beyond our resources. But this could easily change. That being so, are we right to continue working here? And what may our friends in America be doing? Can they be heading full steam toward the atom bomb?" . . .

"It might be a good thing," Carl Friedrich told me, "if you could discuss the whole subject with Niels in Copenhagen." (*Physics and Beyond,* 180–81)

The talks with Niels Bohr took place between September 15 and 21, 1941, during a conference organized by the German Scientific Institute in Copenhagen, but did not yield the desired consensus: "I found it most painful to see how complete was the isolation to which our policy had brought us Germans, and to realize how war can cut into even the most long-standing friendships, at least for a time" (Physics and Beyond, *182). That Werner's personal relationship with Bohr did not fundamentally break down, however, can be seen in his letter to Elisabeth at the time.*

Many of the couple's letters from this year reflect ongoing dire conditions. They speak of health problems and lack of energy. Werner misses his family; his university activities seem fruitless and nonsensical. He prefers to retreat to the privacy of his writing on philosophy. (His "private philosophy" was published posthumously under the title Ordnung der Wirklichkeit *["Reality and Its Order"]). And he is counting the days until he can reunite with his wife and children in Urfeld. From October 1941 on, the family is together in Leipzig again.*

Werner to Elisabeth

[Budapest, April 28]
My dear Li!

A letter from here usually takes weeks to get to Germany. Therefore I will write a kind of diary for you and post the letter in a mailbox in Vienna. If I am lucky, it will reach Leipzig on Thursday.

The trip was cold and unpleasant; only south of Vienna fruit trees in bloom appeared alongside the train; in higher elevations even a few patches of snow still remained. But here around Budapest, spring is in full swing; in a little train station I came upon a hospital train from the Balkans amid red flowering peach trees; from their beds soldiers were looking out as if mesmerized, among them some marvelous faces. Throughout Budapest too German troops are moving north all the time. The city is positioned vaguely reminiscent of Dresden, but much more lavish and grand. Ships that travel on the Danube already go all the way to Africa. The western bank reaches steeply upward in several hills; up there is the most beautiful part of the city. I live halfway above the Danube, in three exquisite rooms of an old collegium; the house sits completely amid greenery, in the evening the air is filled with the fragrance of blossoms. A few steps away, there is a place from which one can overlook the Danube's course quite far. At night the two streets along the banks form a glowing chain of lights; such an image can barely be imagined anymore back home.

The first night I was the guest of Professor Ortway. On Saturday a visit to the embassy to deal with the official part. The Freyers happen to be in Leipzig just now. I was there, anyhow, as a lunch guest of his sister and the children. At night I was at the opera; though I could not understand anything, I was greatly enjoying the music (Mussorgsky) and the colorful scenery. Afterward, I went with an assistant of Freyer's to a "nightclub," where there was unbelievably much and great-tasting food. At 2 o'clock I got into bed. Today, Sunday, there was a trip by car with Ortway and another colleague out to the countryside. Walked up a mountain for the view, some kilometers west above the city; the sun came out, the sky was clear. Then a walk on the Margaret Island in the Danube. Everything there in bloom: tulip beds, pansies, primroses, almond trees; the beech trees are already in their light-green foliage. How nice it would be if you could be along for all of this.

Monday night

Today was a strenuous day; in the morning a tour of the Tungsram lightbulb factory, followed by a little excursion in the environs for lunch. I have been talking with people since 9:30 this morning without a break, working on the talk for an hour, which I gave after 6 o'clock in the large auditorium of the physics institute. The room was totally swamped, and I was celebrated like a prima donna. I cannot say that I would always want it like this, but it is really more fun to speak before four hundred people who are elated than teach a class day after day in front of six bored Saxon faces. Afterward there was a festive dinner in a hotel in the city. (I consume every day at least once, sometimes twice, one half of a roasted chicken.) It is now late; I am sitting in the warm air, filled with the fragrance of blossoms, at an open window, and have to work on my talk for tomorrow. Do not hold it against me that I only talk about me, but all this is enjoyable mostly when I can tell you about it. Good night for today!

Tuesday night

Now the time in Budapest is nearing its end. This morning we visited the institutes, at noon a breakfast at the Countess Zichy's, in an ancient little palais beautifully situated atop the Burg mountain, in the afternoon a stroll through the city and a few purchases. In the evening the second talk, which dealt with a physics topic this time. Regardless, the auditorium was overflowing again. Following, a banquet in the fanciest hotel in Budapest. It is now 11:15 and I still must pack my suitcase, my train leaves at 7 for Vienna. The days in Vienna after this festive time will likely be even more sobering. Right now I am most excited about coming back to you and the children. I hope to hear a little bit from you in Vienna. Yours, Werner.

Werner to Elisabeth

Leipzig, Wednesday noon [June 11?]
Dear Li!

Before I leave, I quickly want to write a greeting and include mail that came for you. The departure this morning was truly very rushed, a sheer wonder that you still made it to the train in time; afterward I was a little mad at myself that I called for the car too late, also was sad that I could not say a proper good-bye. But it is a good thing that the train did not leave us behind, otherwise we would have had to trek back home with kit and caboodle.—The house still looks like a vacated battlefield, despite Gila Frels, but gradually

Water play in the Leipzig garden: Wolfgang,
Jochen, and Maria

it will get back in order. Suitcase and playpen are on their way; the latter created problems at first, since it is forbidden to send such things these days. I then declared it "canvas with wood pieces."—Hopefully you were able to get proper seating; it did not appear too terribly crowded. When I leave here, you should soon be in Munich already.

I hope you are not finding Urfeld too lonely; I myself really do like our little house very much, and I actually like thinking that you are there. I hope you will have much sunshine up there.

Be well for now! Yours, Werner.

Werner to Elisabeth

Berlin, Friday night [June 13?]

It is terribly late already, because I just now returned from your parents, but I would like you to get mail from me on Sunday. I will post the letter tomorrow in the mailbox for the Munich train. . . .

There is very little to report from here. Last evening I played tennis with Wirtz, his wife, and Weizsäcker in spite of the cold temperature. That was a great deal of fun. You can feel, while playing, how the body gradually becomes lighter and more flexible, my game too was already a little more assured than last time. I really needed such rejuvenation after such a long period of rusting. Work at the institute is going as usual. In September, i.e., toward the end, a small conference is planned in Copenhagen, to which Weizsäcker and I have also been invited. It now looks as though I could soon speak with Bohr again, after all. From Krakow I got the notice to speak there in late July. I can apply for it and it will suit me just fine if the trip is scheduled before the summer break.—

When I return to Leipzig tomorrow, only half of me will feel I am coming home. I will miss you very much there. I hope that, at least, a letter from you will be there. . . .

Now say hello to the children, tell me about them, how they like it up there, and take good care of yourself! Yours, Werner.

Werner to Elisabeth

[Leipzig], Sunday afternoon [June 15?]
My dear Li!

Now at least one letter from you has arrived and I know that you got safely to Urfeld. . . .

Upon my return, I found the house in good shape. Gila had tried very hard. . . . In the afternoon I drove to the institute, became a little angry about Döpel, who did not conduct the experiments as I had wanted; we will probably lose time on account of it. Döpel can at times be rather obstinate. Then Erwin called, he wanted to come to dinner, I only got home around 8 o'clock after the meeting at the academy. And imagine, Erwin is at the moment in political difficulties: the anthroposophical societies and schools had, actually, only been protected by Hess from ruin. Now, after Hess has departed, the battle was executed radically: the society and schools were shut down, the head of the society arrested after his home was searched. Marianne [Heisenberg], in Dresden, also had the house searched. So Erwin thought it wiser to not travel to Dresden, and he stayed the night. Of course he will go back to Wolfen tomorrow and work again; he really has no reason to go into hiding. But, naturally, he is very upset about the forcible end to the formal framework of his social circle. By the way, Weizsäcker's acquaintance, the young Haushofer, has also been arrested after the Hess affair. Supposedly, Hitler himself is in charge of the whole investigation; although I do not think that Haushofer is really involved in the matter.—In Berlin, all are waiting with excitement for the continued progress in the war; the most contradictory and senseless rumors get spread and, what is even stranger, are believed by many fools.— . . .

It is so quiet in the house, almost eerie, I feel a little alien in it. I will use the free time to do much work. Say hello to the little ones and be well! Yours, Werner.

Elisabeth to Werner

[Urfeld, June 15?]

A week ago today, we had this lovely warm summer evening—do you still remember? We were walking through the park, and this song by Matthias Claudius came to mind. "And from the meadows is arising, wonderfully, the white mist." And we then dug up so many beautiful things. That evening, love, is as dear to me as little else is.

But imagine this, I wanted so much to bring my favorite pictures from my room; now they are lying in the desk drawer and I do not want to take them out. They do not fit here; I do not quite know why. Everything up here is so pagan. The world in which one lives is so bountiful, so sensuous with the intensity of colors and variety of shapes, that for this whole spiritual-mystical world there is no more room. I myself am quite astonished; I take the pictures out occasionally and lock them up again, a little later on, quite as unresolved as before.

How might you have spent your Sunday? This morning I thought a lot about how we might be walking through the garden and inspecting the flowers. Might roses be already in bloom? Do you know that I first became aware of the beauty of the rose in your garden? Since then I have always been a little sad when I miss out on their flowering time. I listened this morning to the very beautiful music of the morning service. In reality, though, the children were making quite a ruckus throughout; only Woi was listening for a while, all attentive. Then he involved himself with his pencils and presented me a short time later, mightily proud and excited, with his "pear." He had drawn it recognizably and quite distinctly with a stem and the bloom at the top. I was at least as proud as he was.

Love, I have a big, big wish list: first, could Gila please send Ria's doll and two bears for Jochen and Woi . . . but most of all much, much *good* typing paper. I am making quite a lot of progress with your work [typing the manuscript of *Reality and Its Order*]. It gives me incredible joy. More about that tomorrow. Now I am so dead tired!

Much, much love. Yours, Li.

Werner to Elisabeth

[Leipzig], Tuesday night [June 17?]
Dear Li!

Downstairs, in the living room, are Erwin and Marianne, and since I am not needed in their negotiations, I have absented myself briefly up here. I was very glad about your two letters; by what you write, I can take part in your lives in Urfeld, and I dream myself into a quiet rural withdrawal in which one can pass the time calmly until the end of the war. But, of course, it is slightly different where you are as well. . . . The immense quiet and emptiness of the house tells me more distinctly than before how rarely now I am actually producing or working. My time gets wasted with small irrelevant things; there is also no object on which one could focus all of one's energy. Only music is getting its due now more than before. The private philosophy gives me joy, but it too is not always progressing on its own, and one cannot hurry it.—

Father and son conversation: Werner with Martin

. . . Tomorrow it is back to Berlin; there too I will just sit around again and not work on anything useful. But forgive me that I am writing this to you; I am just not pleased with myself.

I hope you and the children are in good spirits. My best to you, love! Yours, Werner.

Werner to Elisabeth

[Berlin], Friday morning [June 20?], at the institute
Dear good Li!

Now I have gotten two such nice letters from you since I came to Berlin. I am so reassured when I know that all of you are enjoying life in Urfeld. Often I long for our peaceful communal days up there; particularly ever since I have been in a somewhat miserable state myself. The hay fever is plaguing me right now quite a lot, mostly caused by the travel, after which I was very sick; the medication I take for it has put me in some kind of anxiety state at times. The latter I have never known in all my life. But it should soon rectify itself. Since the start of the week, the weather has been unbelievably nice, so that I can enjoy the atmosphere of life outside, although I know that it will make me miserable. . . .

I am just getting a phone call and have to go to a meeting before the colloquium. So be well for now, tomorrow in Leipzig I probably will have more time to write. Say hello to the children and to Aunt Gisela! Yours, Werner.

Werner to Elisabeth

Leipzig, Sunday afternoon [June 22?]
My dear Li!

Now that we cannot sit together in the garden as we would on a Sunday afternoon, I will chat with you a bit in a letter. Today I am feeling much better already than on the last days in Berlin, apparently out in Dahlem there are especially many trees in bloom; here I am now able to work, sitting in the garden, without feeling really bad. Besides, the roses are now in bloom for real; on my desk I have, in the small Japanese vase, three very different, wide-open roses; one is deep red and feels like velvet, the second is more modest, a lighter, somewhat bluish red, and the third a light, somewhat yellowy tinted red. . . .

The household here is functioning quite well, by the way. Gila is trying very hard and is proud of her accomplishments at shopping. Yesterday she brought home ten oranges. The amounts she is putting in front of me do make me feel guilty, though, about all of you; you are spoiling me too much when you pass on so many coupons for my nourishment. At least I would feel terrible, if instead you or the children had less to eat. . . .

Today you are probably listening to the radio a lot, since the long-awaited war with Russia has begun. Overall, this turn of the war makes me more optimistic, although we will, of course, go hungrier in the winter. But maybe it will make for an easier understanding with the Anglo-Saxon part of the world.—I regret not being able to talk with you some evenings via telephone in Urfeld. Have you inquired about an installation at the post office?—Tonight I am at the Jacobis' to play the César Franck sonata. So, be well for now, I hope you have a nice Sunday! Yours, Werner.

Werner to Elisabeth

[Leipzig], Tuesday night [June 24?]
Dear good Li!

You seem to be really jolly in Urfeld; I can imagine it so well, those glorious days now, and the Urfeld colors, as well as the children with a healthy tan. . . .

Today was a very full day: first thing in the morning, some gardening. . . . Then at the institute, conferring on a talk, dictation of six letters, afternoon seminar, colloquium, followed immediately by a Brahms concert of the radio youth music group at the invitation of the Frelses, whose daughter, Ursel, is singing there. I truly enjoyed the concert; such a group of young people does everything much more decently than we grown-ups do. A sixteen-year-old played the piano enviably well; a girl of similar age sang a lot of Brahms lieder, though not the ones you and I know. Only at the

A-major violin sonata could one see that the young people had overreached. Best of all were the choruses; I can imagine why Ernst is attached to his chorus with all his soul. Mrs. Frels says that Ursel Frels also considers the time in the chorus the happiest time in her life. When I hear music played by such young people, old memories begin to resonate in me too. I projected a little, how later on Ria and Woi will make music in such a circle, and that someday a bunch of nice young people will be standing on our terrace in Urfeld and sing for us. Overall, I think we must connect much more with the youth, among the grown-ups most are boring, and the few who would not be tend to be lonely by nature.

. . . If you were to come for your birthday, it would of course be very nice, but I am afraid you would not like it here; I am not quite at my best. But surely it would be nice. Please write back quickly so that I do not send you the packet. Or better yet: call me on Sunday night! Many greetings to you all! Yours, Werner.

Elisabeth to Werner

[Urfeld, June]
Love!

Just a quick note! Oh, we are doing so well. With Aunt Gi the entire heaven has opened, and it works out superbly. We make music together and can talk endlessly with each other. Today the Everses came here to pick me up for a bicycle trip through the Jachenau. It was just magical. The Jachenau is simply the loveliest sliver of land imaginable, with its grand, white, well-to-do farm houses—hard to find something as untouched and genuine. But the high point was the visit with the great aunt of Mrs. Evers, an eighty-seven-year-old farm woman. I could not dream up something so wonderful. We found her in the stables, feeding the pigs. A delightful, barely stooped old woman, snow-white hair, wonderful bright eyes, red cheeks—the picture of grace and loveliness—just think, at eighty-seven years! "My head," she said, "is the best thing about me; it is not old." She exuded mental sharpness and joy, a tender and mature wisdom, and kindness. It was delightful and I shall never forget it, I hope.

So, love! I will call you on Saturday—tomorrow. Meanwhile, a thousand greetings to you, love! How good to see you again, especially when you are not doing so well. Do not worry about me not "liking it." I am doing so well now, nothing is missing but you! And you, just as you are,—you simply are my life. You love! Yours, Li.

Werner to Elisabeth

Leipzig, Monday night [July 7]
My dear Li!
Now you are back with our little ones; I have mentally come along on the whole trip, imagined how the three big ones got up from their nap and ran down to the mail bus to pick you up, and how then you all sat together, probably munching on some cake or such. Now you must be sitting by yourself in the large room or on the terrace, and can look out on the mountains and the lake. I am back at my desk, next to me a large bouquet of roses, among them a few wonderfully big white ones. The days with you here were very fine, genuinely festive, even while working, it seemed to me as if we were again young and newlyweds. So my thanks for these days!

. . . —In the afternoon I practiced, then had an academy meeting; in the Augustus Square I watched how they deal with English firebombs. That is now the kind of daily life here.

So, enjoy everything with the little ones in Urfeld! Be well! Yours, Werner.

Elisabeth to Werner

[Urfeld, July]
My love!
. . . Today I was in Pessenbach at Mrs. Evers's house and picked up my bicycle. . . . The way to Pessenbach was beautiful. The heat was glimmering above the meadows; the scent of the freshly mown grass was intoxicating. All was quiet—nature was asleep; just the crickets were chirping and the strange dragonflies, which appear so prehistoric, were swaying above the

sleepy brook by the wayside. How weird the dragonflies are with their protruding eyes and these magnificent colors: darkish blue green and deeply black wings. I met no human—just saw the mowers on the fields as they were turning the fragrant hay. I was undisturbed in all my thoughts—was thinking of you—you! That you are so far away and cannot experience this with me; that these days just now were way too short, well, and much more about you and me. I came home late, so that I could only put the children to bed. I will engage with them more over these next days, they are now so distant. I cannot get closer at all. Good night, my love! I am very tired; otherwise I would keep on writing, because there is so much I want to tell you.

    Yours, Li.

Werner to Elisabeth

Leipzig, Wednesday afternoon [July 9?]
Dear Li!

    Before I depart for Berlin, I want to write to you briefly. . . . Yesterday I was at the Office for Requisition Coupons about the bicycle. On their advice, I turned again to a repair shop that *might* repair my bicycle. If I am successful, I can come to Urfeld together with my bicycle after all. . . .

    Otherwise, there is little to report. I find the course of the war very depressing. Newspapers in Leipzig are now full of obituaries. A few acquaintances of acquaintances have received letters from the east, but they do sound very downcast as well. Of Jochen Frels and Gila's fiancé there is no news yet. An acquaintance from Gila's dance class is listed in today's paper among those killed in action. Thus the war is suddenly becoming serious. And as far as everything else is concerned: since you are gone, I do not like it here anymore at all. I hope to find a letter from you today in Berlin. Say hello to the children—and all my best! Yours, Werner.

Werner to Elisabeth

Berlin, Thursday night, July 10

My dear Li!

When I arrived in Berlin, I did find your letter. How nice that the children are so well and happy. I myself am already excited about seeing them again. . . .

Since I wrote to you yesterday, I have read the book by Huizinga *In the Shadow of Tomorrow*. Actually, I have not enjoyed it much. It is the lament about a cultured world that is severely diseased, and with whose salvation the author is so deeply preoccupied. We know meanwhile that this world is dead and that, at least in Europe, a perhaps younger one but at any rate a more barbarian one is in ascendance. The thoughts of Huizinga are, most likely, not new to anyone in Germany who can think. But we do not share the hopes and fears, because we already know the next chapter. For us, the problem is much rather how in this cruder world one can preserve and pass on those values that make life worth living.—

This morning there were a series of meetings, in the afternoon tennis and swimming. Toward evening I wrote on the private philosophy, and started the passage about the roses. I now write on these things with great enjoyment. Not always with a clear conscience because, basically, I understand almost nothing of all these things. But since Bohr probably will not write down his thoughts, it is good that anyone who knows them is writing down what he makes of it. In Urfeld I could maybe seat myself at the little table in the bushes and also continue pursuing these thoughts. I am now looking forward to this time so very much; mostly to that which I need the most of: the calm of the external life. Your proximity and that of the children count there above all, and the mountains with the lake will do the rest. Now be well for today! Yours, Werner.

Elisabeth to Werner

[Urfeld, ca. July 12]
My love!

Your letter yesterday was a great joy for me. Thank you, love! I had
wanted to write back last night, but I could not keep my eyes open; I did not
get past the first two sentences. Well, that you did not enjoy Huizinga makes
sense to me. It is more or less the same that Klingners also always bemoan
and lament on. I find it so wonderful here, that all these things do not need
discussing. You live life as it is presented to you and try to emphasize in
action all those things you do love. Everything else happens outside our
influence and you take it, like the rain or sunshine, as any other fate. To me it
seems the most sensible and best way to live. I can hardly think about what
the end of the war will be like. To me the war is real only through the fates
of individual people; I look on the rest as if it were a huge event, similar to
nature—but largely with a detached attitude.—

How beautiful this world could be if people could live peaceably with
one another!

This summer displays its glory and beauty unlike any other I have
experienced. Every day we go splashing in the lake, all day long the children
run around in their short pants or all naked up here—we are eating the
wonderfully fragrant wild strawberries, the meadows are in full bloom and
in the warm wind they undulate like the ocean; the earth is steaming in the
heat, but toward evening there blows "the cool evening breath," which I now
must sing to the children every night. . . .

Now I must go to sleep. More tomorrow! Yours, Li.

Werner to Elisabeth

Leipzig, Sunday afternoon [July 13?]
My dear Li!

Today I am staying put in my den; the whole house is quiet, the summer
outside unbearably hot. I have not done much today: read the paper, sat
down with my calculations a bit, and then wrote more on the philosophy.

Once it cools down, I want to work a little in the garden. But that gave me yesterday another bout of hay fever, so I have to be careful. I much prefer it here in Leipzig compared to Berlin. Here I am at least able to pursue my own thoughts calmly; there I have to do fruitless busywork all day.

. . . —Basically, we do have it indecently good in this war. For your summer in Urfeld I am a little envious; but in three weeks, I will get out to you and the children. Just make sure that until then there still is some nice weather left over. To you and the children my best! Yours, Werner.

Elisabeth to Werner

[Urfeld, ca. July 13]
My love!
Now I was out picking strawberries—I found a wonderful place in the Jachenau, and we had a gourmet evening meal—all six of us, and some left over for Martin tomorrow. I will go there every year now. . . . When I returned home—completely exhausted and blue red—I found the children in very high spirits. They had been at the lake, splashing around with great exuberance. They are not at all afraid of the water—in like lightning. And they cannot get enough of it. Actually, it is Woi's doing that all three are so eager—because he is so passionate and without a hint of hesitation. Maria and Jochen are only following his example, albeit with a bit of anxiety in their faces. Woi is a droll little guy anyway. He is now already living his own life. When I was preparing tonight's evening meal, he stood beside me with his little suitcase and was patting it affectionately from time to time. Suddenly he told me: "Woi big frog touched. Put into suitcase." I could not really believe it. I was not allowed, though, to open it: "Frog always jump away." After a while—I had almost forgotten about it—he gingerly opened the suitcase and, sure enough, a huge brown toad is sitting inside, which he then matter-of-factly and deftly picked up. With his permission we then maneuvered it back outside. But he is like this with everything he can get his hands on now. Everything is studied intensely, touched, possibly taken apart. He really is a sweet little kid.

The toil of picking strawberries was not enough, though, to prevent me from planing wood very busily. Please bring along a "simple" or "basic" plane. Without it, almost nothing can be accomplished. . . .

Now a thousand greetings to you! Yours, Li.

Werner to Elisabeth

Leipzig, July 15
Love!

Your two letters with their descriptions have given me much joy. Such an intense summer has not happened in a long time, really; sometimes it almost seems to me as if there were a connection between the wildness of mankind in these years and the stronger breath in nature. In the city it is not easy to bear such a summer, but for you there it must be glorious. I am glad about the splashing in water of the children, but am a bit anxious too. With such little kids one has to really pay close attention.—

By the way, I think that you are working almost too hard. Especially the planing is no work for women, but heavy work for men. Why don't you get a Bess Arabian man for it? Or let a carpenter come for a day. . . . Also, you might as well save the heavy work for me. The only thing I am not good at is making a fence and similar things. . . .

Life here is on a steady, quiet course. On Sunday night Mama arrived. I do not find her in a good state, so confused within, and distraught about politics. It is not so easy to have a conversation between the three of us (Mama, Gila, and I) and do it "right," but it should improve. . . . Heimpel was telling me yesterday, he had a student in his seminar who had received a letter from Wolfgang Jaeger. The latter had fought in Lemberg and had written that the atrocities of the Russians there had been more terrible than what was reported in the papers. . . .

It is almost evening now and I must finish the letter, because I want to keep Mama company. In three weeks, I should already be with all of you up there, I am terribly excited about that time. Say hello to the children! Yours, Werner.

Werner to Elisabeth

Berlin, Thursday night [July 17?]
Dear Li!

This time I had many of your letters awaiting me here, thank you so much! . . .

Last night after my arrival, I paid visits to the Wirtz family and Weizsäcker. It so happened that the son of General Haushofer was there, who had interesting things to tell. On the whole, I find the species of homo politicus not very likeable, but this one, at least, was cultured and humorous.—The reports of the Wehrmacht from the east sound somewhat worrisome, the resistance of the Russians seems much stronger than anyone had expected initially. What would happen if the German push were to come to a standstill somewhere is barely imaginable. How good it is to have our house on the Walchensee.

My main activity at this time is to look forward to taking a vacation where you are. Work is not going well anymore, and it is time for me to get away from this daily grind. Experiments in Leipzig have to be completed before, however. These seem to go rather well at this time. We are discontinuing our colloquium for now, to be continued in September.

Today I am quite tired, my thinking is criss-crossing and can no longer stay focused. So I better close this letter and write more again tomorrow, or the day after. Good night! Yours, Werner.

Werner to Elisabeth

Leipzig, Saturday night, July 19
My dear Li!

Now I am back here, Mama also has returned from Wolfen, and everyone is busily writing letters. In the afternoon, I cut the grass underneath the fruit trees, and then I practiced the piano. I am quite tired. . . .

Mama and I will be at the Schweiters' this afternoon. To this end I have been studying the piano part of the C-minor sonata by Reger; but with Reger, I am on strange footing. As much as I like the Mozart variations, I cannot relate well to the sonatas. His music appears to me so without form; when I play, it all diffuses under my fingers, and I keep asking myself a lot what this heaving of sounds is good for. Of course, I am also playing the Reger poorly, partly due to its technical difficulty, partly because he is just implausible to me.—Later on I will attend, without Mama, an evening invitation at the Tiemanns'. Too bad that you are not also there. You would have a good time talking with Mrs. Tiemann, and he would be acting all charming around you. . . .

Weizsäcker's prospects seem to be poor. Although he has heard from both Rust and Mentzel he should go to Strasbourg, the state authority, Dr. Führer, informed the University of Strasbourg that Weitzsäcker's candidacy would be out of the question. I find it perhaps instructive for Weizsäcker to get a taste of the games and intrigues himself, but I would very much hope that he can prevail. I fear they will make sure that he now gets drafted for military service, so that one can have a pretext to fill the position with a gentleman of Thüring's caliber. Inside Germany all things are going poorly; against Russia, at least, it looks now as if it is going better again.— . . . Such sad things are happening in the world; we have to hold onto each other firmly, so as not to become discouraged.

—Now I have written almost all morning long this Sunday, I have to get back to work for a little. Be well for now, and say hello to the children! Yours, Werner.

Werner to Elisabeth

Leipzig, July 21
My dear Li!

I have such a bad conscience for not being able to write you the kind of letter you would enjoy. But I myself am often so sad and downcast about everything that is happening, without you I would not quite be able to cope. I just got news from Bonhoeffer that the young Geltzer was killed in action in Russia. You may remember him—he had played a long time in our quartet, but that may have been before your time.—But he was also, after the war began, at our house once, when you must have seen him. He was such a nice, gifted, and always cheerful person, so through and through all right. And how many people of his kind will yet perish this way!

Love, but I do not always want to think of these things; I am so happy about coming to you all soon. . . . All my best to you all! Yours, Werner.

Werner to Elisabeth

[Leipzig], Wednesday afternoon [July 23?]

Now I have not heard from you in a while; but I will likely get a letter from you at the Harnack House. Here everything is going along as always. Last night Erwin was here, it was quite comfortable, even though almost all the talk was about politics. Mama has just left for Dresden.

I have to ask you about a few things regarding our trip: first the issue with the bicycles. My bicycle is repaired and looks almost new. Unfortunately, there is a decree that bicycles are only allowed on express or regular trains, and only for a hundred kilometers. So we either have to leave the bicycles here (Gila also wanted to take hers) or take them apart to pack in crates (??) or cut the trip into sections, where one travels a hundred kilometers, then rides the bike to catch the next train, again for hundred kilometers, etc. This procedure would probably take one and a half to two days. (I just see: it might be accomplished in one day.) . . .

Tonight I want to visit with Werner Marwede in Berlin. My work there and here is really getting to me, I so want to travel soon to see you all. But I must bide my time until the end of next week. Being alone, especially during this time of war, is hard on me. But it is for only ten or so more days! Be well for now, yours, Werner.

Werner to Elisabeth

Berlin, Thursday afternoon [July 24?]
My dear Li!

This afternoon there is relatively little work to do, so I want to start a letter to you. I will also play some tennis later. Thank you so much for your letter; I enjoyed your report a lot, only the dream at the end made me a little sad. You must know that, aside from you, there is not a single person who is close to me and with whom I have a total understanding—the children are still little and must first become persons, and Mama is really of the old generation. So my entire life is focused on you and—unless it concerns strictly thinking—circles around the question all the time, what you would say, whether what I am thinking is fine with you. You must believe me that I hold you dear, even if this sometimes is hidden under a veil of weariness.

—Meanwhile, we have played tennis and I am feeling quite refreshed and alive. Now I must again ask about the question of the bicycles. . . .

Yesterday I was at Werner Marwede's. He had very interesting things about Russia to report, of the poverty in the population and the life of luxury among the "elite," counting just about a few hundred thousand only. Also about the drinking orgies of the German trade delegates where, in the end, plates and glasses were thrown against the walls, and finally everyone was lying really drunk on the ground. He was presented by some others of the delegation with a huge chocolate cake (the value of which was equivalent to several months' wages of the workers) with the inscription: "To the master of guzzling, from his students."

Until we meet again! Yours, Werner.

Elisabeth to Werner

[Urfeld, ca. July 28]

Now I have just registered for the phone call to you. Your letter only arrived today, so I could not yet call on Saturday. I hope you did not wait too much. Love, you must forget the stupid dream again. You know, it did not arise from the source you think. It arose from a great insecurity and unhappiness with myself, with this stormy "me" that time and again comes over me unbidden, and has brought on everything bad that has happened to me. And here in the solitude, where I am my only company, I am often overcome by this dark notion that this bad power might take from me the dearest and best that is mine. Long solitude may only be suitable for people who are well grounded in themselves, not doubtful. I myself am still finding it painful—at times. But I believe in a few years it will be over. . . . How much I am looking forward to both of you, mostly to you, my dear heart. Yours, Li.

Werner to Elisabeth

Sunday night, July 27
My dear Li!

Now it will only be one more week until I come to you all. The travel plans are getting cleared up gradually; even without your call, I now know how we will do it. The trip with a bicycle is too complicated; I have found out meanwhile that on Saturdays and Sundays bicycles no longer are transported at all. So we will take the rapid train 7:18 a.m. on Saturday to Munich. Arrival there at 5:27 p.m. Since there is no mail bus on Sunday, I suggest the following: you take the bicycle a few days in advance down to Kochel and park it there for me to pick it up (at the Schmied [the Schmied von Kochel hotel] or at the station, e.g.; you only have to let me know in time where). I then come by myself with the noon train to Kochel and will be with you all around 4:30 p.m. . . .

Today I worked all day on physics and am no longer capable of a sensible letter. So enough for now, soon I will write more and, besides, I will come up to see you, I am looking forward to it so terribly much. My best! Yours, Werner.

Werner spends August with his family in Urfeld. On September 1 he must be back in Leipzig and resume commuting to Berlin, where he lives in the house of his parents-in-law. His mother accompanies him to Leipzig to take care of the household. Elisabeth remains in Urfeld with the four children, but two days later Gila Frels, daughter of their neighbors in Leipzig, comes to assist her. She has quite often helped out before, and Elisabeth is hoping to manage the household with her and the occasional help of Mrs. Winkler, an older family acquaintance. Only in Leipzig can Elisabeth expect to find a permanent new nanny for the children.

Elisabeth to Werner

Monday, September 1
My love!

Now it's not yet late, and I am all cozy here. Nothing of the dreadful mess all over the house at 7 o'clock can be detected anymore. I have closed the curtains at the windows, there is still a little warmth in the stove, and the rain is making a constant sound while it also splashes thickly from the downspout. I am sitting at the big table, the carafe I so like next to me, and also a small glass for the nice red wine, and then I have just lit the last cigarette. You do know my weaknesses! But after such a day, one ought to be able to spoil oneself quite properly!

Oh, the day was not all that bad. Just the morning! Work is piling up and so much has to be done simultaneously. But in the afternoon I dedicated myself exclusively to the children. . . . —I have today—perhaps for the first time in my life—felt what it is like to put yourself completely aside and live only for the well-being of others. It fills you with a great peace, and transmits calm and peace also to the whole circle you live in. It's just that it should be available more often! It makes the haste and unrest that dominate me so frequently otherwise disappear.

Love, now you soon will be home. I hope you have it quiet and no airplanes interrupting. Oh, how I fear these planes on your behalf, and later on also for the children and me; I am so afraid of my not getting enough sleep! If only that is all there will be, that lack of sleep! Love, right, you will go into the basement! Do not be careless, you!

Last night I tried to write to you, my heart was so overly full. But nothing right came of it. With me, it does not work like this: what overly fills your heart will come flowing out of your mouth! No, then nothing comes out of me, no matter how much I want to tell you everything that your stay here has meant to me; want to tell you how the world changes, how everything wakes up and becomes warm and meaningful when I sense you near, my love. So then, when the letter did not work, I got out this little book from Gila and leafed through it. You were right, you much-loved man! It is the

Goethe poem ["Closeness of the Lover"] you had in mind. And it is the most beautiful poem in the book:

> I think of you, when shimmering sea reflects the sun to me,
> I think of you, when quivering moonlight paints the springs.
>
> I see you, when the dust is clearing far down the road;
> In deepest night, when on the narrow plank the wanderer shakes.
>
> I hear you, when afar in muffled swells the waves are rising.
> In tranquil bower I will often listen, when all is quiet.
>
> I am with you, though you be far away, you are near me!
> The sun is setting, the stars soon shine for me. If only you were here!

Didn't the Pitzinger sing this? It seems to me she did. But through this human connection, the poem has become new to me now. These must be the first Goethe verses that reached my heart.— . . .

Good night! My love, you! Yours, Li. . . .

Werner to Elisabeth

[Leipzig], Tuesday noon [September 2?]
My dear Li!

Now I am back here, and Gila will come to you in about two hours, I believe. . . . The garden is in a bad state; many of the dahlias have keeled over onto the large bed, the walkways are green, all the beds full of weeds, and the grass on the lawn is knee high. As soon as I come home from the institute in a while, I will work in the garden. But of course, a stack of work is at the institute too, I barely know where to begin. . . .

Mrs. Frels, to her credit, has been conserving unbelievable amounts of applesauce, also plums; I can barely believe that she herself has got an equal amount, it is so much. She looks somewhat tired and worried, whether that is due to so much work or the anguish about the war, I do not know. Probably both.—The city is overflowing with people. Yesterday's paper had the large headline: "1,000,000 Shoppers in Leipzig." No word in the paper about the number of sellers. But there is lots of commotion, perhaps I can buy a few things when the fair is over, maybe tomorrow.—

But enough of the practical issues. The time in Urfeld was particularly good, so calm and harmonious, although you had more work. I was so fully happy there—in the way I can never be in Leipzig with its hectic workload, not even when you are here. All the same, I am now thinking at times: you could really come back here a little sooner. The airplanes do not seem to be all that bad, at least not so far. And it would be so nice to have you all here together. What do you think of that? . . .

Many, many thanks to you for the time in Urfeld, and try to get some rest when Gila is there. Greetings to our little ones! Yours, Werner.

Werner to Elisabeth

Berlin, Thursday night [September 4?]
Love—,

Now I am sitting in the large room with the balcony in your former house; the atmosphere of the house is not yet very familiar to me, but I can sense a little how it is connected to you. That you grew up here is only a mental concept, not an internal sense; but it pleases me to get to know all this better. My thanks for your two loving letters. The children are really nice to make your work so much easier while you are alone. But I myself am thinking that you have become unbelievably expert over time. Now it all is done swiftly and easily, and you are remaining upbeat even when not everything goes well. I am looking forward so much to the time when soon we can live together again for a long time. However—the air raids, I am just not sure about how much we should consider them after all. During the second night in Leipzig, we had alarm from 1 to 3 a.m. An hour ago, here in Berlin, the sirens also went off, but no shooting so far. . . .

Meanwhile, we have moved down to the basement, the other housemates are sleeping nearby; I am seated at a small table in the center space of the basement. For a time there was a lot of shooting, but now it is all quiet again. I will go up to get my work and then hope to get more done; it is only

11 p.m., the alarm may yet keep going for a long time. So good night for today! Yours, Werner.

Elisabeth to Werner

[Urfeld], September 9
My love,
A thousand thanks for your letter. I will immediately send you all the food coupons. . . .

How nice that you are now really getting to go to Copenhagen! Should I be writing to you at all there? And to which address? And from when on?

You know, I am actually quite glad to do the household over the winter just with Mrs. Winkler. I believe it will go quite well. The cooking is much fun, and to ration and determine everything yourself is probably preferable this winter. . . .

—You know, I don't quite know how to say it, for it is a very immodest wish: I would so love to travel for a couple of days when we are back in Leipzig and Traute [Mrs. Winkler?] is familiar with her work, and Gila is still available: to Irmgard [Schumacher] in Potsdam, to the Westphals' in Freiburg, and to Edith in Überlingen. I would go with you to Berlin on a Wednesday and then return on Saturday eight days later. What do you think about it?

Love, it will surely cost a lot of money, the trip and everything; but, you know, once in five years, I would like to go by myself on furlough. Every five years, right?

Next time I do it, I will take Woi or Ria with me! All my love to you. Yours, Li.

Werner to Elisabeth

[Leipzig], Tuesday afternoon [September 9?]
My dear Li!
Three days have already gone by since your last letter, and I am longing to hear from you and to chat with you. I do know that you are all doing well

from the telephone call, but I still would like to take part in your life mentally.

Life here is running its course with much work, and not much calm. Mama too has much work with the household, but fortunately, she is calmer inside than earlier. In general, I get the impression that she is gradually accepting becoming old; her face too is now more relaxed. . . . All of us are nowadays somewhat tired, there are many air raids. Since I have returned from Urfeld, I have been through four, three here, one in Berlin. . . .

The trip to Copenhagen was granted, by the way, the organization is still a bit complicated. I will probably leave on Sunday night or Monday. I am looking forward to seeing Bohr very much, also the city that I am so fond of. I am a little bit at home there as well. Perhaps I can bring back something from there. . . .

Be well for now, in a little over fourteen days I may be able to travel south again! Yours, Werner.

Werner to Elisabeth

Berlin, Friday afternoon [September 12?]
My dear Li!
This time I can only write to you in great haste because I have to catch the train to Leipzig afterward. I have a bad conscience that I have not written to you since Tuesday, but it was indescribably busy here: last night I was about to write when your cousin Dieter Pütter came; I stayed up talking with him till 1 in the morning. It was quite nice—but how vastly different the world of a young lieutenant is from that of a professor. Dieter was talking in all seriousness that we would, during the course of this war, also be landing in America. He is of the fortunate age when nothing appears impossible and everything also will turn out well.—This morning I was running about for my passport but have not yet gotten it. Now I am off to Leipzig, return here the day after tomorrow, and then continue on to Copenhagen on Monday. The passport will get here on Sunday.

You have written me two lovely letters. Of course, I totally agree with your wish to go "on furlough." You do need such a time of rest, and I am glad that you are enterprising, even if I have to make do with another period of solitude in Leipzig, which will be sad. I hope you can arrange it all to your liking.— . . . So, it is now 5:30 p.m., I have to get to the station. Before I leave, I will write you once more. My address in Copenhagen is: Tourist-hotel, Westre Boulevard.

However, letters will probably take a long time.—All my best to all of you! Yours, Werner.

Elisabeth to Werner

[Urfeld, ca. September 16]
My love!

How far away you are now. I just looked it up on the atlas again. Since it is exactly as far as Elbing, that makes it twelve hundred kilometers! And one cannot really reach you at all. This here is now a veritable collection of letters. But I will send it tomorrow, so you will find something when you come home.

Love—Mama wrote me today of the sad news about Euler. How hard it will hit you, when it is ripping even me apart. And the poor, poor mother. How can she live now? Can't we do something for her? If only one knew what happened to him. Missing—that is worse than killed in action. The news about Mrs. Oboussier [a friend of Elisabeth's mother]—well, you know, that does not hit so hard. When a person is old, then dying is natural; their life is like a filled vessel, one cannot be so sad about it. But the death of this young man—this horrible strength of Russia, which I have always sensed and which had fascinated me completely for years, it makes me wonder now whether it will siphon off all our youth, our strength, and our fortune. But about Euler—he himself wanted it, and maybe, in some sense, it may be good. He was too tender, too good, too sensitive for the world, and in a certain way he was now happy; maybe he could not have died any happier, assuming he did die—been missing already for so long! Perhaps his life *also* is a full vessel, because everything later on would have grated on him again, and made him unhappy. All things in him were so warm and mature and pure, as this wonderful letter he had written at the time in March showed you.—

. . . I am so terribly looking forward to seeing you! The children also are talking a lot about all the nice things they have in Leipzig. All my love to you! Yours, Li.

Werner to Elisabeth

Copenhagen, Tuesday night [September 16]
My dear Li!

Here I am once again in the city that is so familiar to me and where a part of my heart has stayed stuck ever since that time fifteen years ago. When I heard the bells from the tower of city hall for the first time again, close to the window of my hotel room, it gripped me tight inside, and everything has stayed so much the same, as if nothing out there in the world had changed. It is so strange when suddenly you encounter a piece of your own youth, just as if you were meeting yourself. I liked the trip coming over here too: in Berlin we had pouring rain, over Neustrelitz storm and rain showers as if from buckets, in Rostock it cleared up, from Wenemünde on the sky was scrubbed clean, almost cloudless, but still a stiff north wind; so it remained until I arrived here. Late at night I walked under a clear and starry sky through the city, darkened, to Bohr.

Bohr and his family are doing fine; he himself has aged a little, his sons are all fully grown now. The conversation quickly veered to the human concerns and unhappy events of these times; about the human affairs the consensus is a given; in questions of politics I find it difficult that even a great man like Bohr cannot separate out thinking, feeling, and hating entirely. But probably one ought not to separate these ever. Mrs. Bohr too was well, she asked me a lot about you and the children, especially about Maria. I will show her pictures tomorrow night, I have a nice enlarged photo of Maria that I had made for Mama. Later I was sitting for a long time with Bohr alone; it was after mid-night when he accompanied me to the streetcar, together with Hans [Bohr].

Thursday night [September 18]
I will take this letter with me to Germany after all and send it from there. From everything I have heard the censorship would delay the arrival

several days as well, so it makes no sense to me that a censor should read this letter. Unfortunately, you then have to wait for my letter for almost eight days. I, for my part, have not received any mail here either.—

Yesterday I was again with Bohr for the whole evening; aside from Mrs. Bohr and the children, there was a young Englishwoman taken in by the Bohrs because she cannot return to England. It is somewhat weird to talk with an Englishwoman these days. During the unavoidable political conversations, where it naturally and automatically became my assigned part to defend our system, she retired, and I thought that was actually quite nice of her.—

This morning I was at the pier with Weizsäcker, you know, there along the harbor, where the Langelinie is. Now German warships are anchored there, torpedo boats, auxiliary cruisers, and the like. It was the first warm day, the harbor and the sky above it tinted in a very bright, light blue. At the first light buoy, near the end of the pier, we stayed and looked for a long time at life in the harbor. Two large freighters departed in the direction of Helsinor; a coal ship arrived, probably from Germany, two sailboats, about the size of the one we used for sailing here in the past, were leaving the harbor, apparently on an afternoon excursion. At the pavilion on the Langelinie we ate a meal, all around us there were actually only happy, cheerful people, at least it appeared that way to us. In general, people do look so happy here. At night one sees all these radiantly happy young couples in the streets, probably going out for a night of dancing, not thinking of anything else. It is difficult to imagine anything more different than the street life over here and in Leipzig.—

In Bohr's institute we had some scientific discussions, the Copenhagen group, however, does not know much more than we do either. Tomorrow begin the talks in the German Scientific Institute; the first official talk is mine, tomorrow night. Sadly, the members of Bohr's institute will not attend for political reasons. It is amazing, given that the Danes are living totally unrestricted and are doing so well, how much hatred or fear has been galvanized here, so that even a rapprochement in the cultural arena—where it used to be automatic in earlier times—has become almost impossible. In Bohr's institute I gave a short talk in Danish, of course this was just like in the olden days (the people from the German Scientific Institute had explicitly approved), but nobody wants to go to the German Institute on principle, because during and after its founding a number of brisk militarist speeches on the New Order in Europe were given.—With Kienle and Biermann I have spoken briefly, they were, however, for the most part busy at the observatory.

Saturday night [September 20]

Now there is only this one night left in Copenhagen. How will the world have changed, I wonder, when I come back here? That everything, in the meantime, will continue just the same, that the bells in the tower of city hall will toll every hour and play the little melody at noon and at midnight, appears so strange to me. Yet the people, when I return, will be older, the fate of each one will have changed, and I do not know how I myself will fare.

Last night I gave my talk, made a nice acquaintance too. The architect March, who had built the Reich Sports Arena in Berlin, is slated to build a new German school here in Copenhagen, and he came to my talk. On a joint trip aboard the streetcar we had a pretty good time conversing. I always enjoy people who are especially good at something.—

Today at noon there was a big reception at the German embassy, with the meal being by far the best part of it. The ambassador was talking animatedly in English to the lady seated next to him, the American ambassador. When she left, I believe I heard her say to somebody: "We will meet again, definitely at Christmas, unless something quite unexpected comes up." One has to take these diplomatic dinners with a sense of humor.

Today I was once more, with Weizsäcker, at Bohr's. In many ways this was especially nice, the conversation revolved for a large part of the evening around purely human concerns, Bohr was reading aloud, I played a Mozart sonata (A-Major). On the way home the night sky was again star studded.—By the way: two nights ago the wonderful northern lights were visible; the whole sky was covered with green, rapidly changing veils.

It is now a quarter of 1 a.m. and I am rather tired. Tomorrow I will post this letter in Berlin, so you will receive it on Monday, most likely. In one week, I will be with you again and tell you everything that happened to me. And then we all will be together for the winter in Leipzig.

Good night for now! Yours, Werner.

Elisabeth to Werner

[Urfeld], September 18
My love, you!

Where might you be now? Are you sitting in the beautiful big room at
the Bohrs', or in Bohr's study to discuss everything with him? How happy
I am for you that you can have all of this! You probably also have this
wonderful September weather we have here; and that is so extra nice at the
sea. Those days make me homesick for the sea, for the woods on the island of
Rügen. I do have a North German soul after all—it is in my blood somehow,
let Bohr say about it what he may. But you know, we also had a glorious day
here, I enjoyed it wholeheartedly. It was a thoroughly happy day as well. . . .
In the afternoon I rode by bicycle down to Kochel and, when I had finished
my errands, also to Pessenbach. . . . Then, at dusk, I pushed my bicycle up
the hill on the old road, and I felt once again so happy through and through
that I walked along singing out loud. Not another soul was there, so that I
could allow myself this carefree singing. . . .

Werner to Elisabeth

Leipzig, Tuesday night [September 22?]
My dear Li!

How good of you to call me today. It was nice to sort of feel you right
nearby again. The news about the younger Jacobi makes me terribly sad.
How much these two people will now suffer. . . .

Euler's mother sent me detailed news; she included a copy of the letter that
the chief of the air battalion had written her. Euler was leading a flight across
the Black Sea. His last location message was "Northeast of the Asow Sea." The
battalion chief believes an emergency landing is the likeliest event, but no
further news of his fate. Our acquaintance from Sweden is supposed to contact
a Russian physicist via England, who should inquire after Euler. Of course, the
question is whether the Russians are keeping proper lists of detainees. But one
must not give up hope that he is still alive. Euler's older brother, an officer, was
killed in action four weeks ago. Euler's sister lives with the mother.

The return to Germany from the free Denmark made me quite gloomy. There people's lives are still so carefree; here it is all tense in the utmost.— . . .

I now feel as if I have been away from Urfeld and from you all for many months, so much has happened during this time. But we will see each other on Saturday afternoon.

. . . Yours, Werner.

Werner to Elisabeth

Berlin, Wednesday night [October 15?]
Love!

To this announcement I want to add only a few words. You will be here yourself the day after tomorrow. I had bad news from Mama: she fell down in the street, broke her left upper arm, and is now in the Decker Clinic, Munich 23, Seestrasse. I want to write to her next: she may not yet have heard the news of Ernst's death. Aunt Gisela is still here but will travel with Edith Pütter to Bonn tomorrow. Edith will stay here for a while longer; her husband is back for a holiday. Betty [help in the Schumacher household] is not here right now because her father died suddenly. Therefore Mutti has much work to do. But your mother is really the bravest of all; I admire her so much at this time. I am supposed to send you greetings from your parents; they are looking forward to your arrival on Friday.

Much love! Yours, Werner.

1942

Only two of Elisabeth's letters, *written from Urfeld in June, are extant, so that the reconstruction of events in 1942 is based almost solely on Werner's letters. These reveal that daily life is increasingly dominated by the problem of securing provisions. Food is becoming scarce; only by canning fruit and vegetables from one's own garden is a relatively healthy meal possible. Moreover, the need to maintain two separate households is a drain on the family's resources. Undeterred, however, the couple is determined that the children should be in Urfeld over the summer.*

So Werner brings his wife and the twins as well as the new household helper, Lore, to Urfeld at the end of May, where Elisabeth gets the house ready for summer. Meanwhile in Leipzig, "little Omi," Werner's mother, and the nanny, Trautl, are taking care of the two younger boys, Jochen and Martin.

Maria Oertel's Ferntrauung [long-distance wedding, a possible choice during the war] is described in detail by Werner in his letter of June 16. Maria Oertel, recommended as a nanny to the Heisenbergs by their friends the Jacobis, had assisted Elisabeth after the birth of the twins for a year and a half. Afterward she had found a job in a nursery school and lived independently. At that time she had an affair with her patron, Professor Erwin Jacobi, resulting in a child born in 1940. Since Jacobi was married and of Jewish ancestry, this paternity had to be kept secret. One year later, Maria met a young officer stationed in Norway who wanted to marry her, provided she give the child up to a foster family. Already living under constant fear that the paternity of the child would become known and she would be convicted on the grounds of racial impurity [Rassenschande], she consented to this condition. Under these auspices, the wedding took place.

In late June Elisabeth returns to Leipzig, while Trautl takes little Martin with her back to Urfeld, where she and Leipzig neighbor Mrs. Frels and her niece will be taking care of all the children. Thus, from July onward Elisabeth is in Leipzig to take care of house and garden and to support her husband, who has now officially become the deputy director of the Kaiser Wilhelm Institute for Physics in Berlin. There is an expectation now that Werner and the family will relocate to Berlin, something not so easily done.

During this summer the prospect of an atomic bomb becomes pertinent, a fact that comes through, very obliquely, in the letters. It is easy to imagine what a treacherous path atomic physicists now walked—on the one hand hoping to convince the powers in charge that building an atomic bomb within the given time frame was not possible, and on the other attempting to continue atomic research on a smaller scale, with the end goal of a nuclear reactor. Success in this endeavor would allow them to stay in control of the entire project.

Perhaps it is not coincidental that in September Werner comes down with a nerve inflammation and needs to stay in bed for several weeks. His mother-in-law takes care of him in Berlin, while he takes pleasure in this opportunity to get back to "his physics."

At the end of September the whole family returns to Leipzig. In November Elisabeth gives birth to her fifth child, Barbara. Werner's lecture tour in Switzerland at year's end provides an occasion for a further exchange of letters.

Werner to Elisabeth

[Leipzig], Tuesday night [June 2?]
Love—

I am rather tired and must set out again to Berlin tomorrow on the early train. So do not be dismayed if this letter is only brief. I found the house and children in perfect condition. Trautl has been quite busy. Only the garden has turned into a wilderness in these few days; there must have been lots of sun and warm rain. I weeded four hours today in just one bed, on Saturday I will continue to work. The cherry tree is incredibly loaded; it will be a very good harvest. The roses are starting to bloom. Jochen and Nüsslein [Martin] are playing outside all day long, but oddly independent of each other, for the most part. . . . The days in Urfeld were a wonderful quiet before the storm of the next days. Tomorrow morning there is a meeting in Berlin, colloquium in the evening, Thursday night presentation to Speer, Friday with Milch.

How nice that you are away from the turbulent life now; enjoy the stay in our little paradise! Good night for now. Yours, Werner.

Werner to Elisabeth

[Berlin], June 5

Love—

I am sitting in the train to Leipzig before its departure and will try, in peace, to write a little, as far as the many people around me will allow. Those were eventful days in Berlin. In the Harnack House truly every preeminent person of the Reich was assembled—essentially the entire armaments council and many others in power. It went far better than expected, my own and Bothe's presentations left, apparently, a strong impression; at any rate, we were treated fabulously afterward, both personally and in terms of the facts. To me all this is exceedingly strange and unnerving; suddenly, I will no longer have to concern myself at all with the whole Lenard-Stark clique, and can push through almost anything I find important. I led the secretary through our institute; strangely, all the scheduled experiments were functioning without a glitch, and afterward one sat together at dinner and on the terrace of the Harnack House until midnight with some wine. At dinner I sat next to General Field Marshal Milch, with whom I had an excellent conversation. He completely shared my opinion on the policy regarding professors that the Reich Ministry of Education promulgated, and he voiced it with a drastic directness—which I myself would never have dared. I was very interested in the human level of the whole assembly: all of them were unusual people, of course, many really unusually smart, I suppose, all of them good diplomats, used to prevailing in a hostile situation of intrigues with decorum (and, I suppose, occasionally with stronger methods as well). Intermingled were a few strange characters who at first repel you, and during conversation exude something disarming, which can leave you quite confused.

On the whole, the circle was much more interesting but also somewhat more dangerous than the diplomats' circles that I have known from the Weizsäcker home. The politics at large were sometimes addressed; I am glad to be only an observer there. In the small politics of physics, I have to participate for better or for worse; it is unnerving for me that here large building projects, values, and works are subject to my word. Speer, by the way, bears some physical resemblance to Erwin, only younger and sturdier; the face is mostly a mask, only occasionally it becomes lively for a moment. I do not envy him the fact that his words decide the work of many millions of people, the care for the hundred thousand homeless from Cologne and the whole human misery.

But now enough of the festivities at court. When I reach Leipzig, I will meet Mama and am hoping for mail from you. . . . Our relocation to Berlin is still troubling me, mostly because of the expected air raids. The tragedy in Cologne was apparently much worse than the ones in Rostock or Lübeck.— How nice that you are in Urfeld and safe. To you and the little ones my best! Yours, Werner.

Elisabeth to Werner

[Urfeld], Friday night [ca. June 10]
My love!

Today I totally misjudged the strength of the June sun. The way to Kochel was a veritable walk through purgatory. But the children were precious. Even just to look at them in their cute summer outfits, and how delicately and easily they stepped. And I was astounded how well they held up. Only tonight they were easily in tears. I was rather more affected, and twice I felt all weak and near blackouts. Therefore I went to bed very early, hoping that by tomorrow I will be all well again. You know, I am so glad to have the twins all by themselves for once. Maria is becoming close as never before. Her shy little soul is opening up like a flower in the sun, when you are gentle and friendly with her. Oh, if only I could be there for her like this all the time. And little Woi—he is much like me, my vehement, impatient way, the sound of anger and irritation in the voice when something does not work; he is not agreeable—but the look of his sweet, soulful eyes goes straight to my heart.

Love, I have finished the English book by Galsworthy. But I really cannot appreciate these novels very much. At first I long a little for this kind of book, but very quickly I become terribly bored by them: they always seem to pass over the essence. They always equate love with passion and talk about beautiful, sensuous women in a pale and unhappy marriage, and about marriages that make you wonder whether they ought to be dissolved or not. Say, is this high-flying seductive passion really the utmost a person can achieve or experience? It seems to me this potent, fateful interface that should follow after passion is even more, and the genuine meaning of passion.—

Love me, whatever may be ahead; that is the beginning and the end, and the key to our happiness.

Yours, Li. . . .

Werner to Elisabeth

[Berlin], Thursday afternoon [June 11?]
Love!

I am sitting here in my institute and the surroundings are not quite conducive to writing letters; but I do not know when else I could find the time. Your letter recounting the Sunday excursion to Sachenbach has again made me very happy. I can participate through your letters in the carefree life of the children and am then transported into a tranquil and happier world. Here everything is so busy, constant meetings with so many different people, and I have no room at all to do the things I am actually meant to do, namely, the undisturbed inquiry into nature. Tonight is colloquium, so that I will only be home at 10:30, not able to do something else. The K[aiser] W[ilhelm] G[esellschaft] [Society] has mailed my employment contract, and I will sign it today or tomorrow. That means the dice are cast, hopefully for our common good. The KWG will take care of housing, as I made it a precondition for acceptance.—By the way, did you receive my letter from last Friday that I had written on the train? It would make me uncomfortable if it were lost and had fallen into the wrong hands.

. . . Meanwhile, it is evening, and the colloquium is behind me. . . . Now I am sitting by myself in the large room up on top and let the events of the day pass through my thoughts. When will this life, which constantly reaches the limits of endurance, turn around again to something better? I think we will know more about it in the winter. When you come to Leipzig, I will have much to tell you. Meanwhile, take care of yourself and say hello to the twins. Good night for now!

Yours, Werner.

Elisabeth to Werner

[Urfeld], June 14
My love!

It was so good of you to call; I did not feel the "Sunday loneliness" at all with your voice still in my ear and in my heart. . . . Here too there is a great deal of work waiting: I was very industrious today. All morning long, I was at the typewriter, and then weeded three vegetable beds; then spent the afternoon with the children, and in the evening knitted like crazy one half pair of baby pants while finishing the novel by Stefan Zweig, although only peripherally—I have to admit, as smart and insightful as he is, he is indescribably lengthy. With his artful phrasing, it would be an exceptional book, if only it were half as long. . . . Love, I am terribly much looking forward to tomorrow. Your promised letter will arrive.

Good night, you loveable you! Yours, Li.

Werner to Elisabeth

[Leipzig], Tuesday afternoon [June 16?]
My love—

Every moment is precious, sometimes I could cry about my lack of time; since my last letter to you, I have hardly been able to get to my own work; a half-begun math problem is written on the pad, and when I begin with it again, I need a few hours first to rethink the problem—and meanwhile, surely, the telephone will ring, or the children need me, or Mrs. Frels has a question, or the cherries have to be picked, the garden hose repaired, a venetian blind tackled, the carpenter called on the telephone, etc. But it is war, after all.

This morning the "festive" wedding ceremony by proxy of Miss Oertel took place; Mrs. Jacobi and I were witnesses. Miss Oertel let the whole thing happen bravely; it was not pretty. On the table in the designated room of the town hall some paper flowers were spread out, the officiate spoke a military Saxon dialect and did everything right: a few words too many, none too few. On the wall the Führer in a black suit; the windows were painted art nouveau style with heraldry and flowers and hearts; the pillars in the room appeared to me painted gypsum. Miss Oertel also got Hitler's *Mein Kampf,* and for the wedding festivities food coupons for four pounds of meat, twelve eggs, one pound butter. This will make for a little party at Jacobis'. Tonight we will play music there. Then I will properly congratulate Miss Oertel, or rather Mrs. Linder. We will bring her roses from the garden; a few glorious ones, pale red, have just opened, and I managed with much luck to get a lace tablecloth in town at noon; you would like it a lot, I think. Whether Miss Oertel will, I do not know, but I hope so. Any such gift that still is available for purchase should make people happy. Miss Oertel has requested from Jacobi that he play the Schubert fantasy with me tonight. Jacobi will surely play superbly, and I have just now practiced it a little. But how will it be for Jacobi to play tonight? Of all things the subject: "Oh, you! Having been snatched from me!"—I am almost afraid of the evening. At first we will probably play the Schumann quintet, the fantasy last.—

Love, I must close now, Mama has made some tea, and it is already ten minutes to 4 o'clock.

Keep up your love for me; I am so looking forward to your arrival in eight days! Yours, Werner.

Werner to Elisabeth

Berlin, Sunday afternoon [September 13?]
My love—
Today I am playing at being sick and letting your mother take care of me, which she does so tenderly. The whole thing went like this: during the trip my right thigh got much worse, the lymph nodes swelled up a lot, and a

kind of rash appeared that was very painful, and I developed a fever too. In Berlin it got better initially, and I assumed the thing would take care of itself. But yesterday morning, it became much worse again, and I saw the doctor to be on the safe side. . . . He diagnosed: local septic infection with accompanying nerve inflammation, early stage. He prescribed, above all, bed rest and not going to work. If I did not keep resting, the thing could affect other glands and become a general sepsis plus shingles, which would mean months in bed. It shouldn't, I hope, be that bad, and so I will take it easy as much as work allows. . . .

—Your parents are well, only they both look very skinny. It is quite striking these days how everybody becomes thinner; several people in the KWG, whom I had last seen before vacation, shocked me when I saw them again. . . . You hardly see anyone looking totally healthy and well nourished. And the state of war does not contribute to making people more optimistic. Aside from that, I very much enjoy the fall days. Day by day, we have sunshine gilding the treetops in your garden. . . . It may not be to my detriment that I should lie down a lot. It lets me work in peace and quiet, and maybe the work I am doing for myself is more important than the one at the institute. Enjoy these last weeks of summer in Urfeld. Stay well and say hello to the children! All my best! Yours, Werner.

Werner to Elisabeth

[Berlin], Tuesday night [September 22?]
My love—
Now I have sat way too long downstairs with your parents and talked about economic policy—one can learn much from your father there, but I believe he gets annoyed with the stupid questions I ask. I really had intended to write to you instead. . . . I sometimes feel so strangely alone here, so totally removed from the real world, and it is good when you are nearby again. Maybe it all is connected to the illness: I still have the occasional slight fever and am tired. However, inside I am strangely animated; I am working on my physics all day long, almost for all of this week already, and am making wonderful progress. Mathematics is a glorious science: a problem

that seemed to me almost insolvably difficult eight days ago I now have fought through to the solution completely; a few minor things are still missing, but I may get ahead some more in a while.

. . . —Now say hello to the children, I am looking forward to all of you! Yours, Werner.

Werner to Elisabeth

Zurich, Tuesday night [November 17?]
My dear Li!

Now I have been in Zurich only for a few hours, but already there is so much to report. In terms of the travel, you have been unnecessarily worried: eventually I got a sleeping compartment after all, and I used the opportunity for a good night's rest, the first in a long time; went to sleep at 9 o'clock and only got up after 9 o'clock. In the vicinity of Freiburg, the train traversed a totally wintry landscape; the foothills of the Black Forest were covered in snow all the way down and partly obscured by heavy drifting snow. From Basel to Zurich, though, there is not much snow yet, the woods are brilliant in their beautiful fall foliage. I often was reminded of the slopes on our Walchensee.—Then the introduction to Switzerland: you had feared that, as a German, I would encounter much hatred. But the first impression, which is so deeply moving, is just the opposite: a measure of friendliness we have not seen in years. And this comes not just from the people, who were friends from way back in peacetime. In Basel, through my own fault, I ended up last going through inspections and was standing, a little unsure, with my suitcase at the customs counter when a friendly-looking taxi driver came up: could he perhaps carry my suitcase and transport me to the Swiss train station (trains are no longer crossing the border). I spent a moment counting my modest foreign currency; he understood and smiled at once, offering that he could take a second gentleman along, which would make it "a *bitzeli* cheaper"; all together it would cost only 3.80. It ended up costing even less at 3.70. At the Swiss station I ate dinner, since the first train had left already and the next one was only scheduled for 1:45 p.m. There too it was like a fairytale: as soon as one sits down, the waitress comes over, asking your wishes; five minutes later the meal was on the table. I had placed my suitcase somewhat awkwardly in the way; the waitress asked if she might find a better place for it. When I, in my regret, quickly put it there myself, she looked at me as if to say: are you the lowly baggage handler, having to do this kind of work yourself? Although I had arrived later than anticipated, the head of the student body was there to pick me up and take care of me in the nicest fashion. I have a nice little hotel room with bath and all other conveniences. The gentleman who had picked me up had already placed a gift package of wonderful cookies, confections, and such in my room. Next I walked through the streets a little, looked at the stores, and bought a few little things. Although I am immediately recognizable as a German when I speak, I encountered only friendly and happy faces, no hint at all of any hatred toward the individual German.

However, I do not want to describe only the good traits but also the bad. I might mention that newspapers are formally loyal, but their sympathies seem to be on the side of our adversaries.— . . .

In everything I see here and experience, my only regret is that you cannot be here too. How much enjoyment would you have, strolling through the streets with their loaded display windows, and also about the serenity of the people. But even if you had been free right now, I would still not have been allowed to take you along. . . .

Now do take very good care of yourself; I will call you from Munich, maybe on Thursday morning. Be well! Yours, Werner.

Werner to Elisabeth

Zurich, Thursday noon [November 19?]
My love—
After the first surprise, I am gradually getting used to life among calm, always friendly and contented people; how strange it is to walk about the streets; life is so smooth—, even the apparently hard-fought election campaign, about some kind of tax issues, appears more like a silly secondary event that nobody takes all that seriously. Everybody seems to have work without too many concerns; they can live off it, even if it may not always be a

lot, and the fact that in the hotels there still are gluttons is of no concern to anybody.

The physicists, the Wentzels and the Scherrers, are so gracious to me, I get spoiled like I almost can no longer imagine; and I have a really bad conscience that you cannot partake in all this abundance. If you were here, one could relish it altogether so much more. But there is war, and one must not get carried away in one's thoughts.

Last night I gave my first talk, about my theoretical work, which had to challenge the audience the most. The people listened so intensely and I had such hearty, demonstrative applause afterward that our official offices will be reasonably satisfied too. Tonight the "Cosmic Rays" will be next, I have worked on it this morning, so I think everything will go well. After the talk last night, we sat together till 12:45 at the Scherrers'. In a long discussion about modern art—Picasso and more degenerate—I stood my ground courageously. I genuinely liked some paintings a lot, so that I could then, in good conscience, declare others dreadful. . . . Fortunately, politics were no longer discussed much; the night before we had come to the friendliest agreement to not agree about everything. I am glad that here, with these kinds of debates, one does not offend sanctioned feelings.—

And how are you and little Barbara doing? I have so many questions, and yet I can only hear from you in eight days. Till then my very, very best! Yours, Werner.

Werner to Elisabeth

Monday night [November 23?]
My dear Li!
I know this letter will only reach you after our telephone conversation. But that does not matter, I like chatting with you; besides I am somewhat anxious about the talk tonight, which is a very difficult one; so it is reassuring to report to you. Since my last letter, I have given talks in Zurich once more and in Basel. In Basel, I was the guest at the v. Wartburgs', who are just as nice as in earlier times. Wartburg stands behind the collaboration and friendship with Germany in such a decisive way, yet not at all in direct

opposition to the Swiss views, that it is pure joy. . . . Tonight will be my last talk in Zurich; the head of the student body just told me that the whole Auditorium Maximum is sold out; I hope I can reach that many people. Tomorrow morning I will travel to Bern, am invited for noontime dinner at the delegate's, and at night present a talk to the students. That talk will be about physics and is thus much easier than tonight's. . . .

In the meantime, it has become dark; I will walk a little along the lake to get dinner, then to the lecture. Be well for now! Yours, Werner.

Werner to Elisabeth

Berlin, December 9
My dear Li:
For the time being, I cannot yet call you from here, since private calls are not allowed. I will try again in a few days. . . .

I was in the city today, it looks disastrous. But in between the rubble, there is an occasional store with a few things still available for sale.—From Leipzig I had bad news: Hoffmann's and Döpel's homes burned out, the entire Bonhoeffer institute as well. Also, the whole edition of our new book on Cosmic Rays, dedicated to Sommerfeld, seems to have been destroyed. In general, all the large printing facilities are destroyed. In the Gewandhaus quarter and the Markkleeberg it appears to be better, one need not be all too worried about our closest friends.—Here, the war is so close that it is difficult to free one's thoughts from it. So I am doubly looking forward to Christmas and to you all.—Maybe next week I will travel to Krakow for two nights and one day.—

Be well! Yours, Werner.

1943

THE LETTERS *Elisabeth wrote to her husband in 1943 have also gone missing. Considering the complicated circumstances of that year, one can be grateful that at least Werner's letters have survived. The rapidly progressing destruction of the major cities through air raids results in evacuation and a dire scarcity of living space. Any empty dwelling is confiscated and made available to citizens who were bombed out of their homes. Werner and Elisabeth decide to close down the Leipzig household and move the family to Urfeld permanently. This obviates the plan to move to Berlin, no longer a city one would live in by choice. The house in Leipzig is rented out to a family named Weber. Also at this time portions of the institute are relocated to the Swabian Alb, to Hechingen.*

There is no thought of vacationing this year. Werner's life consists of relentless travel between Berlin and Leipzig, Urfeld and Hechingen. Hectic activity so dominates daily life, his letters tell us, that it is impossible to stay focused on scientific work. A discouraged and depleted frame of mind is taking over. Meanwhile, it becomes ever more complicated for the couple to stay in contact: letters and packages are often lost, and telephone connections become more difficult to obtain. Hopes of finding housing for the family in Hechingen are dashed because of the crowds of refugees arriving there daily. However, leaving Leipzig proves to have been the right decision: in December the house on Bozener Weg is bombed and destroyed.

Werner to Elisabeth

[Berlin], May 16, Sunday afternoon
My dear Li!

Today is Sunday and Jochen's birthday, and it is not easy for me to be so far away from you. I am so very aware of my loneliness these first days in Berlin; in addition, two of the three nights that I have slept here were interrupted by air raids. The first time a few bombs hit Steglitz without causing much damage, the second time all was quiet—the attack must have hit some cities nearby. Since the first of March, these attacks or alarms do shake me up more than earlier on, and I have trouble falling back asleep afterward; but I will get used to it, I suppose.—You will be celebrating little Jochen in full measure, he will be proud to be really four years old now, and besides, there will be the usual cake and candles. I hope your concerns about money may have lessened by now so that you can enjoy everything, especially the children, a little more.

I want to use the time alone here for intense work and believe that, in this respect, those weekends on which I cannot drive to you will have a favorable effect. I have now turned to the philosophical manuscript, since I did not really make progress in physics; since yesterday, I have almost completed a sizeable portion. Next up is the most difficult section of it all, but I believe that I can now dare to tackle it. . . .

Every, every good wish! Yours, Werner.

Werner to Elisabeth

[Berlin], May 20
My love!

Now I am coming home, rather tired from a full day's work; and since your letter yesterday told me so nicely about everything, I too will tell you something about my existence here.

It is so strange to be in this city now; one day is more beautiful than the last, a cloudless blue above flowering trees and bushes; only, in between, the ruins and the charred roof rafters remind you of war, then the constant

Barbara's baptism in Urfeld in the spring of 1943: (*back row, from left*)
Wolfgang Rüdel, Elisabeth with Barbara, Werner, Mama, Wolfgang
Jaeger; (*front, from left*) Jochen, Wolfgang, Maria, and Martin

alarms, day and night; since I have been here, we must have had at least six
alarms, but only once a few bombs were dropped in our vicinity. The resulting anxious state of mind is not good for me, the inflammation of nerves is
announcing itself again; but I get relief occasionally from the notion that
this, actually, is a section of the front, and not the homeland. An especially
quiet, comfortable section to boot, on which there are many houses left

where one can sleep in beds, and which only rarely has any shooting going on. . . .

Last night we had Wednesday Roundtable at Sauerbruch's house. It was just as in the old days: an aristocratic house, the terrace in the garden, three to four servants, and the best wines. It also was really nice: Sauerbruch is really quite a guy. Next to the Sauerbruchs' there is the Ley's villa, possibly even bigger and more luxurious. Ley had himself built a large bunker of concrete in the garden.—The topics at night were about all kinds of things, including the catastrophes at the Eder Dam and the Möhne Dam. The old city center in Kassel is underwater, supposedly. The losses seem to be less than originally feared, depending on what paper you believe. But one cannot really think about all these calamities in detail. . . .

. . . Best to you! Yours, Werner.

Werner to Elisabeth

Berlin, Monday evening [May 24?]
Love—

I have a bad conscience that I am writing you so little, and your letter today makes me realize that you are sad about it. But I was so tired from the many alarms last week, I hardly could get to sleep at night before 2:30 a.m., and in advance of an alarm I could not sleep, because one knew "soon it will start." On Saturday, I came to the Nielandses' [next-door neighbors] late at night, was received very kindly, and since they had guests, the evening stretched until 1:30 a.m. Nielands were quite upbeat, he will probably be recruited to a post as judge in Plauen, and she has not been recruited as yet. Both looked well. Sunday morning we had breakfast in the garden. It was no minor feat for me to look over into our garden, in which I myself have planted just about every flower; at times I deceived myself into hearing Woi's voice from way back in the sandbox—I really had to struggle not to let on. Of the Webers I saw nothing, also did not feel like going over there. . . .

Greetings to all the children from me. Do not worry about me; I will manage to get through this. . . . So, all the best to you! Yours, Werner.

Werner to Elisabeth

[Berlin], May 29

Dear Li,

Ever since our talk this morning, I know at least why you were cross with me; I had sensed it clearly in your letters already and more so from the telegram; . . . I do not understand that you have only received two letters. . . .

That Mrs. Schlittgen [occasional household help] wants to come only on June 8 is a great catastrophe. First because it is too much work for you anyway, and then, especially, because of the whole canning process. It so happens that the fruit will soon be ripe, at least some of it. . . . For your sake it would be best if you could catch up on some rest here. Naturally, for me too; but you just have to see how far you can trust her with the children. I will attempt to reach Mrs. Schlittgen from here by telephone and ask if she might not travel sooner.—

If nothing else works out, and that, unfortunately, is the most likely case these days, I will just have to do the canning myself here at night. You only need to write me what I should preserve and how.

Mutti could instruct me on the mere technical part. Mainly you would have to send some containers—bottles and glasses.—Over Pentecost I should have some time for it, and with my hay fever, it is more reasonable not to drive to Urfeld.

Greetings to the children and be well for today! Yours, Werner.

Werner to Elisabeth

[Berlin], May 30

My dear Li—

It may be useful to follow up on yesterday's letter with this one. I have given a lot more thought once more to these difficulties. I believe one has to simply see things the way they are: you and I will probably have, for the most part, bad times until the end of the war. You because the workload cannot be handled, and I because I am alone and have to do mostly the kinds of work that make no sense. Then too, the possibility to help each other through writing letters will of course be less over time, because for one, everybody is eventually too tired to write, and then the letters do not get there. Maybe the connection will one day be interrupted altogether for a longer period of time. So it is regrettable that I can only help you so little; the only thing left is that in case of emergency I can come to Urfeld. In that case, I would without hesitation drop all work here—basically, it is completely inconsequential anyway—and drive down to you. You may always resort to that: you need only send me a telegram or use another way to notify me, however it may work.

. . . My attempt to reach you this morning by telephone did not succeed.—To you and the children every good wish! Yours, Werner.

Werner to Elisabeth

[Berlin], Thursday evening [June 3?]
My dear Li—

It is almost midnight and I have just now canned four glasses of cherries. Now I still want to chat a little with you; in front of me on the table there is a big bouquet of roses from the garden at the institute. Today came your long letter about the clash with Edith, I have had a long talk with Mutti about it all, and we understand it so well. You are feeling the incessant work and effort, all the household hardship, and the fact that even when I am in Urfeld there is barely a moment for a quiet conversation with me—and there is Edith who has the leisure to travel about Germany and construct nice theories. Edith, in turn, is feeling the dead end down the road, the problems in her marriage and all the reproach we had heaped on her at the time; probably our earlier criticism of her husband too, and sees you, barring great disasters, headed into a happy future, with relative security, with a house, position, and possessions, etc. So both of you have vulnerable spots, where your lives do not suit you at all; besides, both of you are still very young and are not all that careful with your words and think being right is all important. But I assume that Edith is just as unhappy as you are about what happened here. To both of us, Mutti and me, it seemed as if there had not been a real reason for this dispute, just the overly stressed you and perhaps some leftover bitterness from earlier times for Edith; and it strikes me as quite absurd to think that this accidental collision of unhappy circumstances should lead to a distancing in the long run. At any rate, I will find it nice when soon you come here. . . .

Good night for today and best wishes! Yours, Werner.

My best to the children, and do tell me about them.

Werner to Elisabeth

[Berlin], June 6, Sunday evening
My love,

I was very glad about your last letter; it seems that things are on the up with all of you. . . . Very little to report to you from here. That I preserved four jars of cherries I must have written already; one of the cherry trees is now harvested completely; but we have a second one that may be ripe by the end of next week. . . .

From Königsberg I received notification that the Kopernikus Award will be 20,000 marks this time (the wheelbarrow, however, will not be delivered as well). I do not quite know what to do with it; possibly pay up the last portion of the Leipzig mortgage. Or do you have some good plan for it? I want to also bring it up with the Dresdner Bank.—

This morning I was invited by Popitz to a Homer reading in the Staatstheater, done by the actor [Friedrich] Kayssler. The old Homer has made a deep impression on me again.—Love, I am very tired and just randomly telling you things in a jumble. But we may see each other soon. I hope on your end all is now going smoothly. Greetings to the children, and also to Mrs. Schlittgen. Good night for now! Yours, Werner.

Werner to Elisabeth

Berlin, July 21
My love,

Today Wirtz returned from a trip to Cologne and the Ruhr region; what he was reporting from there only confirmed for me that we should, as soon as possible, have our furniture transported to Hechingen. Please send me the address of our Leipzig moving company; I no longer have it here. . . . You can tell—all my thoughts are about the war again, I find it difficult to free my inner self from all the horrors that are happening. I am too depleted to concentrate on scientific work anymore.—Your letter, again, made me very glad, and I am already looking forward to the next one. The fact that you managed to hunt down an axe in Kochel, I think, is a fabulous accomplishment. Perhaps you also would be lucky in finding a carpenter who could make us chairs? (Trading in the maple logs, e.g.!) I have been running around today in various department stores to no avail. Only the utmost junk can be had; but I will keep looking. The days here are passed doing just about any and all pointless things, in the institute or outside of it, it is always the same.— . . .

Say hello to the children, and take care. Yours, Werner.

Werner to Elisabeth

Berlin, July 21 (Wednesday)
Love—

This morning such a bright letter from you arrived—it is a veritable comfort potion in this sad time. Thank you so much, you, it made me very happy. I hope all continues to be so well with you. And if any of you should have the time, do not forget the garden! . . .

Your letter reminds me of something else: that Mayr [hired help] is planning to come up for just one day is regrettable, since he naturally can tackle so much more than the girl can. But please pay some attention so that Mayr does not try to teach the girl things other than just cutting wood. I know my Bavarians; they are, especially with Russian women, completely uninhibited.—The box with the conserved goods will go out today, too much is collecting here. Besides, one needs to discuss the continued harvesting of our fruit; there are many apples already on the ground; the few peaches will be ripe soon, the August apples as well. . . . Otherwise, nothing new, regrettably no new chairs, either.—A good many greetings, also to the little ones! Yours, Werner.

Werner to Elisabeth

Berlin, Monday night [July 26?]

My love—

In the interim, I was in Leipzig with much happening there. . . . This morning then, the news came of Mussolini's stepping down which, of course, was very exciting news. In terms of Urfeld, I worry now, but we can discuss that soon in person. . . . One other thing concerns me too: for about eight days now, my state of health has noticeably become worse, the neuritis and the accompanying rash on my hands have become much more intense. In and of itself this is probably not really worrisome, but it tells me that I am not quite coping with the unpleasant aspects of my work. It may have been a mistake that I have taken on the institute here in the first place. One needs to be much more solidly constructed for it than I am.—

Obviously, I am very excited to come to Urfeld. Say hello to the children, and do not work too much! All my best, Werner.

Werner to Elisabeth

Berlin, August 22

My dear Li—

Today is Sunday, and I have—due to the heat outside—made it a little cozy for myself inside your house. Partly at the piano, partly from the radio, I am attempting to produce good music; so far it went better on the piano. For the afternoon, I am taking with me some good tea, and maybe I can get a piece of cake at the Harnack House; then I want to, possibly together with the other housemate there, Dr. Beil, "indulge" in the style of wartime.

The city of Berlin appears as if in peaceful summer vacation mode: many houses are locked up, the streets and restaurants are empty. A specter, aside from the air-raid dangers, is looming in terms of the evacuation of the inner city out to the surrounding quarters. When the people from the Alexander Platz move into the villas in Dahlem, the status of ownership will change a lot.—

Now, all my best! Greetings to Mrs. Schlittgen, I hope she has satisfactory news from her husband; and say hello to the children. Yours, Werner.

Werner to Elisabeth

Berlin, October 14

My dear Li—

All evening I have been trying to call you, to no avail. I am a bit tired
and feeling stressed and would have liked to chat with you for a few minutes.
Now I want to do it in writing—maybe I can reach you tomorrow. I am
including some bills and such in the letter; maybe you can file them sometime. On Sunday night I will go to Holland after all; I am cautiously looking
forward to meeting the old acquaintances, hoping that it will not be too
politically complicated. These days we have ongoing meetings about the
war-related work. Carl Friedrich v. Weizsäcker is here and we had a long
conversation last night about the same questions you discussed with
Mrs. Westphal at the time. I am fundamentally not agreeing with him; this
tendency to see everything in such extremes, and to want to force the

Werner, his mother, and Barbara on the Urfeld terrace

"ultimate decision," is so totally alien to me. Weizs. can utter sentences such as: he would be quite satisfied with a totally destroyed city, for then one could be certain that this would not recur, and that people would mature into a different way of thinking as a result of experiencing guilt and punishment— which to him means the new faith he himself is beholden to. Then, he says further, that this faith, of course, would be irreconcilably incompatible with that of the old world, that is the Anglo-Saxons', and that Christ, after all, said he had not come to bring peace but the sword—, whereupon one is right back at the starting point, i.e., whoever doesn't believe what I believe must be eliminated. To me, this perpetual circle of belief in a faith that has to defend the holiest matters with fire and sword is completely unbearable; apparently I am quite un-German in this, and during such a discussion I slip—uncharacteristically—into such a ferocious opposition that, ultimately, I end up representing the most boring, commonplace viewpoints. You would have been quite displeased with me again; but it is good that I can pour my heart out to you.—After my return from Holland, I will stay another one or two weeks here, then drive to Hechingen via Urfeld. But tomorrow, I still want to speak to you by telephone. Take care for now! Yours, Werner.

1944

THE EVENTS *of this year again have to be gathered, for the most part, from Werner's letters; only a few letters from Elisabeth are extant.*

The war is nearing its end. One can sense in the letters that the expectation of the impending Allied invasion and the hope invested in "the time afterward" bolster the strength to go on. Hope is needed: the situation in terms of provisions and amenities is becoming ever more desolate. Coal, wood, and potatoes are nearly impossible to obtain by the end of the year. Unofficial purchases of fruits and vegetables are on the increase; although it is forbidden to ship these items, Werner manages to acquire apples and transport them occasionally to Urfeld. Trains are running unreliably and are constantly at risk of being bombed. Packages are plundered or lost, telephone connections are interrupted for days, and letters sometimes take ten days to get from Hechingen to Urfeld. Officials attempt to control the chaos through new and more stringent regulations: not only groceries but also clothing is rationed; household helpers are drafted to serve in the armament divisions, the workweek is increased to sixty hours, vacation time is canceled.

In spite of these constantly deteriorating conditions, Werner travels once more to Copenhagen at the beginning of the year. His old teacher Bohr is no longer there; he escaped to Sweden with his family the year before. But he succeeds in returning to Danish control the Bohr Institute, which had been confiscated by the Germans.

For the first half of the year, Werner is working mostly in Berlin. The city, like all major German cities, is subject to major bombing raids. Days are often spent extinguishing fires and repairing damage wrought by the nightly raids. Werner's letters reflect the destruction he witnesses daily.

Starting in August, however, Werner is living and working mostly in Hechingen, with the exception of a few days in Berlin here and there. Accordingly, the letters take on a different tone: Werner, noticeably rejuvenated and enjoying comfortable housing, reports on excursions into the Swabian Alb, on evenings spent in intense music making, and on being able to focus again on physics and his private, quiet thinking.

For Elisabeth the year is extremely demanding. In March the roof overhang of the Urfeld house collapses under the weight of snow and ice, damaging the living room, bathroom, and kitchen. Only with great difficulty does the couple manage to get permission for repair and the necessary workers to effect it before the next winter.

The house is now very crowded: joining Elisabeth and the five children are Waltraut Krieger, a new nanny, whose mother, a refugee from Dresden, has found temporary shelter in Urfeld; Marianne, a young girl on a one-year obligatory service to learn housekeeping; and the Ukrainian Anna, who does not speak a word of German but is assisting competently with the heavy workload in the house. Later Maria Linder (née Oertel) arrives to help when the whole family comes down with severe cases of influenza and scarlet fever.

Elisabeth's situation becomes really difficult in June, when she is expecting her sixth child and has to leave for the little town of Pähl on the Ammer Lake. Mother Schumacher is unexpectedly not able to come and help, so Maria Linder accompanies Elisabeth to Pähl for the birth. Christine arrives on schedule on June 30.

Fourteen days later, Elisabeth is back in Urfeld, once again the head of a turbulent household. She organizes the twins' private schooling by a teacher who has been evacuated to Urfeld village. Elisabeth also initiates musical studies for the children: they learn to play the recorder, sing together, and even produce a Christmas play.

Werner to Elisabeth

Berlin, Friday night [January]
My love—
Since I do not know whether a telephone connection can happen in the next days, I want to write to you. Thank you so much for the package and the letter. If the departure from Urfeld this time was even harder than usual,

it certainly was not because the time was not good. On the contrary, I am only at home up there anymore, with all of you, and it was not easy to leave it behind. Here we do have the war. Just a while ago, there was alarm, and it was so dark that I did not find the way to the institute for a long time. A wild shooting began and I ran into a tree pretty hard. When I arrived at the institute, the shooting had already lessened. The attack must have been intended for another city. Hopefully we can sleep through the rest of the night.—

So meanwhile, I have drunk a strong cup of tea and, thanks to it, emotional equilibrium will return.

Yesterday I had a visit from Bonhoeffer, who told me much about Leipzig. From our immediate faculty, all of the following have lost their housing: Ruhland, Schaumann, Schmitthenner, Helferich, Hopmann, van der Waerden, Wilmanns, Hoffmann, Döpel, Knoll, and Boehm. Mrs. Knoll supposedly fled in the night of terror to the Johannistal and gave birth to a baby there; but she is doing well, they say. Bonhoeffer had also seen our house and described the destruction on Bozener Weg.— . . . Now do take good care of yourself, say hello to the little ones! Yours, Werner.

Elisabeth to Werner

[Urfeld, January]
My love!

I am lying in bed. Outside the rain is swooshing—the weather is crazy. Snow is a wet mess, and it keeps pouring. One is feeling rather cut off from everything, when rain and the clouds surround you like a wall. I do not mind so much. But I am a little concerned about Waltraut. Maybe it would be better if Mrs. Schlittgen came. It would bring a bit of change to the monotony. I am rather depleted. Today we have begun to transport the coal up here. And it is such a miserable, heavy job. One more week of working as hard as today, then it is all up here. It is pure serfdom. I must say, it is somewhat discouraging. . . .

The children are well. Barbara is infinitely calmer, looking good, and a great joy. She definitely had not been well. Woi showed me the day before yesterday that he is getting a new tooth in his lower jaw. . . . What big children we have already!

I am working a lot. I am doing fine. Only this coal thing is getting too much. Otherwise I am coping well.

That you must go to Copenhagen is not nice. That trip will not come easy to you. But the trip to Leipzig will likely be worse yet. Brace your heart beforehand, and think that here in Urfeld is now the soul that has enlivened that house during these last years—the children, and I too, who wants, above all else, to preserve for you a sense of home.

With love, your Li—may God protect you! Good night!

Werner to Elisabeth

Berlin, January 28
My dear Li—
Yesterday, after our telephone talk, we had to endure another heavy attack; there was fire in many places, but in Dahlem we again fared reasonably well; institute and Harnack House were unharmed. Gradually, I am getting used to this aspect of war. Today I was in Leipzig. On Bozener Weg it looks desolate; it took me a long while before I could recognize our side path and knew which one was our house. I think it is impossible to rebuild. As long as one can see only the devastation, even inside the house, the image stays alien and barely touches you. But in between there may remain some random corner undamaged, such as the window in front of my study with the green roll-up shutters, or the stove in the living room, and that will then cut right through you. The garden is still recognizable, of course the hedge is no more, the red thorn bush is buried somewhere with the rubble. The verandah is gone, one doesn't know where. The houses of Busch [neighbor] and Frels are abandoned but still standing. Otherwise, our side path has become one continuous heap of rubble.

. . . —I have another request that I forgot about on the telephone yesterday. Could you quickly send me the keys to the garage and the car which, I think, are either in my night table or desk drawer? In addition, I am asking for a bar of soap, I am done with my last one (from September!). The car will come to Berlin with me and be used by the institute.

This letter will have coupons included for six pounds of bread; I also will send groceries in tomorrow's package, hoping that it will arrive intact. Now excuse this rather practical matter-of-fact ending of the letter. I am very tired because I have slept way too little; besides, we just now were having another alarm (but no attack). All my best to you and the children! Yours, Werner.

Werner to Elisabeth

Berlin, January 29
My love—
Two very heavy air raids, and all week long too little sleep—that is just too much for any kind of intellectual activity. Since it is now 9 o'clock at night, one is waiting with some anxiety for what is coming. In the city everything is still burning from last night. So I want to chat with you a little, not to burden you with my concerns, I am managing here well enough, but merely to not be alone. The roof of the institute was half torn off last night, windows and doors largely destroyed. This morning I stood for two hours on the roof with my people, in the rain and being wet, and we covered the roof again. Now work can continue. But for how much longer? It is time that I visit you in Urfeld once again; we both could use that, right? Afterward, I want to be in Hechingen for three weeks and relax. . . .

Sunday morning
The weather continues to be horrible, but we were able to sleep through the night, so that everything is looking up today. Pessimists, however, assume that today's date, the 30th of January, will lure the Americans to Berlin in the daytime, due to the expected speeches pertaining to it, but this idea does not worry me too much. Although I will keep my air-raid luggage on the ready. Otherwise I will play a little music today . . . and not work too hard.—

Noontime
In the meantime I have played a little Bach and Schumann, then the alarm started up; the Americans did not want to deprive themselves of

appearing with large companies to the Führer speech. The speech, however, did not take place here at all, but was broadcast on the radio from recordings. So the Americans departed again without much impact. Maybe they will reappear in the afternoon for the other speeches. But I will be having a decent cup of cocoa prepared for me and eat a few cookies, which I had brought with me from Copenhagen; with luck this bachelor idyll will not be disturbed. . . . —

10 o'clock at night

During these last two hours, we again had an attack of unimaginable intensity; the whole inner city seems to be up in flames. We [out here] were treated somewhat more gingerly this time around; if only we would now get a few days of quiet. Now you can see what a Sunday here is like. Good night for now, love. It may be a few days before I can call you again. My best! Yours, Werner.

Elisabeth to Werner

[Urfeld], February 2, in the morning
My love!

Last night I got this telegram from Hiby: "Institute undamaged; your husband is alive." Although I had an inner certainty all the time that you came through, a heavy weight lifted from my soul. How did you manage to notify H.? And how might you have fared? I imagine you, blackened with smoke, somewhere, possibly in the Harnack House, extinguishing flames. My love, I hope you were spared too much horror!—

Here everything is working alright. Anna is back as of Friday night. Mrs. Burckart is a nice woman and very helpful to me, just the children are not as happy with her as with Waltraut. She too is an anthroposophy member and just about as burdened as Marianne [Heisenberg] is. It is weird how anthroposophy is both attractive to me and repellent. It also is weird to see how it shapes people into such uniform creatures. At times it is self-evident to me that anthroposophy is not destined to become a common good, for it leads people back onto themselves to a degree that I believe to be completely outdated. I believe much more that people must bow down under the weight of the demands of life, as they had to in earlier times, and thereby give up self-oriented concerns—not to their detriment. This pondering of self appears to me as a stage of immaturity and hypertrophy.

Forgive this lengthy discussion. Also, Barbara was sitting next to me and interfered a lot; thus the messy writing. . . . But everybody is doing quite well. We enjoy this springlike weather: being outside without a coat for several hours. Hepatica is blooming in between the fallen leaves. It almost is creepy when you think it ought to be winter. . . .

Now may God protect you, dear heart! Yours, Li.

Werner to Elisabeth

Berlin, February 3
My dear Li—
How nice that you called today; it was only one week ago that we spoke, but it seemed to me as if one year had passed. Although it has been quiet since Sunday, the terror of the three nights continues inside the body and I am more anxious than I want to admit to myself. If during this night nothing happens in the morning hours, we should have some peace, since the moon is lighting up the sky for the greater part of the night. . . . In eight days I am supposed to go to Königsberg and give a talk there, and in fourteen days, at the latest, I will be in Urfeld. Let us hope that this program can be kept. My talk in Königsberg is troubling me a little; it is almost impossible to concentrate on any kind of mental activity, so the talk will likely be very bad. If I have to perfect it, I will be able to do it in Hechingen, where I will probably get back to my normal existence.

Friday afternoon
The night was calm but I slept poorly, even got dressed around 5 o'clock because I felt that another alarm would come. In the twilight I lay down again and slept till 9 o'clock. Otherwise nothing new to report; at the institute they are hammering and pounding to replace the doors and windows. For a large number of windows, however, we only have cardboard, so that most

rooms, including mine, must be lit by electric lights nearly all day. Unfortunately, the experiments also are going slower than I thought, and it will not be easy to push them through until the 15th; let us hope that no new interruptions occur.

—Meanwhile, your letter from the day before yesterday came, which improved the whole day. . . . So many thanks for letter and call, and everyone stay well up there; I am looking forward to the days with you all. Yours, Werner.

Werner to Elisabeth

Berlin, February 8

Today your letter came with the car keys; the soap is very nice and the garage keys are not so important. . . .

The previous nights were quiet; today at noon and in the evening we had one harmless alarm each. The moonlit nights seem to give a certain protection; probably next week one will have to count on attacks again. Since Sunday I have been working on my Königsberg talk, it is now essentially done. So I will leave the day after tomorrow for Königsberg and return on Sunday. Then I will have to stay here a few more days to await the result of an experiment, which will, hopefully, be finished by Wednesday; then I could travel to Munich during the night from Wednesday to Thursday. On Wednesday Weizsäcker wants to come here; it might be good if I can talk with him briefly.

Unfortunately, I am battling a flu right now, I hope it is not coming on full force; it would be an extreme nuisance regarding the Königsberg trip. Tomorrow afternoon is Wednesday Society at Sauerbruch's, I am curious to hear something new about the course of the world. . . .

Wednesday evening

Continuing: We were at Sauerbruch's after a brief midday alarm. There was much good food and drink, and besides, the host gave a very pleasant talk about the Vienna surgeon Billroth. About the course of the world, I did not learn anything one could not read in the papers. Do you in Urfeld ever listen to reports on troop movement, or is there too much work all the time?—I was surprised to learn in your letter that the air raids actually are now playing a big role in the imagination of the children; one might have thought that the attacks in Urfeld have been forgotten. I would like to know whether children of Woi's age would be frightened during big attacks. The younger children in our bunker are surprisingly calm; only when the mothers shriek in fear, they become restless. But the mothers are mostly acting in a reasonable manner. Presumably, the children do not comprehend the actual danger, and that is only good.—I am now looking forward a lot to seeing you and the children, hoping to be able to stay on track with my plans. All my best to you all! Yours, Werner.

Werner to Elisabeth

Hechingen, Saturday, February 26
My dear Li—
I ought to have much time here. But I do not know why it is, just that there is so much to do, and I barely have the time now to be writing a letter to you. Actually, I am always hoping you might someday show up here. Unfortunately, ever since the attacks on Stuttgart, there is no more telephone connection, so I don't know whether Mrs. Schlittgen has come. But if she is there, why don't you come here for some time, the sooner the better.

I am very much enjoying the relief from air raids here; my work goes well; besides, I am practicing regularly for one to one and a half hours a day. The philosophy is now finished; maybe in Urfeld, during the summer, you can find the time to type it.—The small apartment here is incredibly cozy; one can become a real mensch here again, compared to the Berlin enterprise. Even though there are often enemy plane formations flying above Hechingen, they do us no harm—fingers crossed. Love, today I am not properly focused on writing letters, because one job is urgent, but tomorrow, Sunday, I will write you a real letter. Hello to the children, and best wishes! Yours, Werner.

Werner to Elisabeth

Hechingen, February 28
My love—

Now I have not heard anything from you in a week. An hour ago I registered for an urgent phone call to Urfeld, but I doubt it will get through tonight. The connections are getting ever worse, trains are canceled too, or they get shot at in transit; at any rate, we are living here cut off. Yesterday afternoon Wirtz arrived here; it had taken him twenty-two hours from Berlin to here; he also brought with him interesting news from there. For instance, there were no more attacks after the 15th. Today I got a postcard from Hund in Leipzig that now the theor.-phys. institute was destroyed by an explosive bomb. Also Döpel's experimental apparatus and his work space are destroyed; I feel so sorry for him.—

. . . Mrs. Wirtz, by the way, suggested she might take care of the twins in winter, so that they could attend school here. The proposal is very kind, but I fear the twins would become very homesick. For when I am not here, they would be all alone. . . .

—It is 10 o'clock by now, the long-distance operator will try again; so now the connection was established after all, I hope you were not taken out of bed too abruptly; how good that you all are doing well. So best wishes, stay healthy, and say hello to the children! Yours, Werner.

Werner to Elisabeth

Hechingen, March 5
My dear Li—

I had always hoped you would one day stand at the door here; it is so nice here, and it would do you so much good to be with me, a little freed up from work. It really is true, one lives here once again, for a few weeks, as in former, better times; you are surrounded again by everything you knew so well: a good living space, nice people. You sit together for music, and talk about the good books somebody just wrote—and the war only seems like a bad dream. It would be too nice if you could come; sadly, I could not get a connection going just now to find out if Mrs. Schlittgen is in Urfeld. But perhaps you are really coming within a few days.

The day before yesterday, I had the Wirtzes, Pahl, and Hiby here with me. Pahl sang a lot of lieder, some even much better than earlier, he really can sing decently. In the end he bellowed the Figaro aria from the *Barber of Seville;* it was truly a pleasure to listen to him. . . .

Tomorrow and the day after I have to be in Tübingen. So all the best to you, my love, I hope you come here soon. Greetings to the children! Yours, Werner.

Elisabeth to Werner

[Urfeld], March 30
My love!

Today I have bad news for you. In reality, we still were lucky, but it is bad enough. To get to the point: at noon the whole roof overhang at the slope side of the house broke off under the weight of snow and ice. We could hear it cracking quite loudly often before. At first we thought the icicles were loosening and falling down. I went out to check what was going on and heard a loud moaning, cracking sound. I assumed, since it was thawing and also snowing heavily, that the patches of ice were coming off the roof. No sooner was I inside the room and we were sitting down for dinner than the whole roof came down with a ferocious noise. It did knock a hole in the wall of the house, and there are cracks in the bathroom and the upper toilet walls. Fortunately, the window, below which the children were seated, was undamaged. My biggest concern was that it would also happen on the other side. Therefore, I called the soldiers at once, got the lieutenant on the phone, and asked for some people to remove the ice. He immediately sent me three people who cleared the whole roof and broke off the large blocks of ice with an axe.

Then we negotiated that on Monday about five men would come to remove the roof rubble. I also called Weitzmann to see if he could send someone to take a look at the condition. A repair is out of the question, since all the big rafters have simply broken off. One has to, at least, create a downspout for the rainwater before it simply runs down the wall, seeps into the house, and rots the walls from the inside. I hope that can be accomplished. We may need your authority to push for it, because Weitzmann said on the phone that only where water is actually running into the house can repairs be done.

The children were, of course, terribly shaken; Woi and Barbara did not get back their equanimity all afternoon. The others collected themselves more quickly. It looks ghastly. We do not need any airplanes—we can do it too. I hope we can get it somewhat back to order before you come, otherwise you will experience the "When it rains, it pours." Now I am dead tired. It is snowing and snowing. It really is dismal. Good night, dear heart! Yours, Li.

Werner to Elisabeth

Berlin, Tuesday night, April 25
My love:
Today I am a little concerned about all of you. I heard that a massive air raid occurred in Munich, and even when I tell myself that you live in the mountains far from there, a trace of danger remains. . . . Unfortunately, I will not be able to call you for a while, since the lines in Munich seem to be destroyed. The foreign office could not make contact in Munich, either. But within a certain time frame, it must also come back in service.—It is now weighing on me that you are so far away. Since my departure, barely ten days have passed, yet it seems like such a long time. I hope to hear from you all soon. All my best! Yours, Werner.

Werner to Elisabeth

Berlin, April 28
My love!
Your letter has reassured me a lot; it arrived even faster than at some other times—also from Mama I had a letter on Thursday, mailed on Tuesday after the attack; it is astonishing how quickly the mail service is back in order. . . .

Here it has been all quiet since I came back from Copenhagen, only the radio is telling us that further west almost incessant attacks and alarms are occurring. From Dortmund, there is talk of one single attack that lasted from 8:30 in the morning till 1:30 past midnight. A lot is pointing in the direction of an imminent invasion; one can only wish that it should happen fast. Today I saw Hund; tomorrow at noon Bonhoeffer comes to the institute, I will serve him a genuine cup of coffee after dinner. I am looking forward to chatting with him at length. . . . All my best! Yours, Werner.

Elisabeth to Werner

[Urfeld, spring]
My love!
Here come the socks. I hope they arrive in time, so that you do not have to run around with holes.—We have had a very strenuous day today. A huge amount of laundry, bedding for five and then some. But all the bedding is in the closet already, all folded. On top of it, our Anna had a badly infected finger. We went with her down to the regiment to see Dr. Pohl. We could not believe it: she sent poor Anna back home with all her pain; she was not in charge of private patients!!!!! This is beyond belief. We should go either to Benediktbeuern or wait until the doctor in Kochel had office hours. The latter was out of the question because the finger looked bad. The first is a completely ridiculous notion when you consider the whole matter is a procedure of two minutes. So I gathered my courage, fired up a razorblade, laid out a sterile bandage, and cut the finger open myself. The dear child could not thank me enough. "You good doctor!" she kept saying, and stroked my hand. But can you believe the gall of this doctor?

Say, how can I actually get a hold of you? Not at all, I fear, since there no longer are advance registrations, and I never can be sure when you are there. So it will be up to you to call me, occasionally. . . .

Good night. May God protect you, my love! Yours, Li.

Werner to Elisabeth

[Berlin], Tuesday afternoon, May 2
My love—

Your letter today was a great comfort to me, even though it too was written on a rainy day. Yes, I also had forgotten about the 29th somewhat, although I thought on that day particularly often of you and of the time seven years ago. But I did not realize it was exactly seven years. The 29th had started so well here; on Saturday morning the sky was a clear blue, and I had the idea I would play tennis again this spring. But then there was this major air raid. That nothing did happen to us I already wrote you on the back of the envelope as a P.S. last time. But yet, this kind of experience always leaves a deep impression on me, and I need a few days to get back in balance. Worst of all is the loneliness afterward. Here I have nobody whom I would consider close, and in such a state you need other people. Therefore I decided to go away somewhere—we had two holidays. At first I thought of Erwin; however, he was not in Wolfen. Fortunately, Bonhoeffer called, who was in Berlin just then. So we decided to try making the journey out of Berlin together, either to his family in the Harz region or to Leipzig. Because all major tracks were interrupted, we only made it circuitously to Potsdam, where thousands tried storming the trains. Only via some obscure ways did we reach a train . . . and eventually arrived in Leipzig, ten hours later, at 2 in the morning. Of course, we had to walk from there to Bonhoeffer's house. We then brewed ourselves some tea, and it was actually quite nice. At 3:30 we went to sleep, and although I was dead tired, I stayed awake a long time and thought about the past and of you all. . . .

At this visit in Leipzig, I have done a lot of thinking and also talking with Bonhoeffer about our plans for the future—as far as they are even plausible. But even if the institute here remains standing, I do not know if I should stay here. What, ultimately, had been appealing to me here was not just the opportunity for a number of experiments at the institute, but equally, perhaps, the garden and the house that appeared as if one could occasionally have time for oneself in quiet. But the Berlin enterprise will make this *"quiet"* impossible anyway, and I have a great fear of suffocating in the enterprise aspect over the next years. If one survives the war, I may have about ten years in which I can hope to participate actively in science. Those I want to keep all to myself, i.e., naturally to us, to you and the children, and then I will gladly take over the duties vis-à-vis the public, which of course include this enterprise aspect. You know, we have all lost so many years to the war, and so one has to really think hard about what to do with the next years. If we were in Munich, I could periodically go to Urfeld for a few days and think by myself, you too could go there for some rest. Also I would have much more vacation time if I did not direct an institute, and that would be better for all of us. But one really does not know yet what is possible after the war. If it is not asking too much of fate, I would want a house without other people looking on and thinking one were not working hard enough; and then I would want much time for work and thinking. I do not know if that would be available in Berlin; but what of anything is available in the ruins of the cities after the war? Besides, it may still be too early to think about all this.— . . .

—On May 25, i.e., the Thursday before Pentecost, I have a talk in Reichenhall. Afterwards I will come to Urfeld. I hope soon you all will have spring and sunshine there. All my best, and say hello to the children! Yours, Werner.

Werner to Elisabeth

Berlin, May 5
My love!
Today was, in many respects, a good day, and before it ends I must talk to you a little. This morning I picked up our car out of Leipzig. I got up at 5:30, took the first train to Leipzig, and arrived there at 10 o'clock. Two of my mechanics had overhauled it, and there it stood again at the station, obedient and cleaned like in olden times. . . . Then we took off, the vehicle running as smoothly as in its best years; through the Düben Heath, past the Eisenhammer, then across the Elbe Bridge, at Sedlin, past the crossing where the road branches off to Ferch, then through Potsdam and across the Glienick Bridge, and finally through the ruins and bomb craters to the institute. This drive

among the young beech forests of the Düben Heath and the blossoming
apple trees was a great joy. I am now sometimes feeling exactly the opposite
of what I felt like in Badenweiler at the time. While back then the threatening
approach of the dangerous storm would, at times, completely discourage me,
I now, suddenly, feel in me here and there a bit of joy of life and spirit of
adventure, without finding a real reason for it. . . . On the other hand, one
then is quickly confronted with the reality that this is not yet the time for joy;
perhaps, though, this awakening does signify an instinctive intuition of better
times ahead. . . . Stay well, and say hello to the children! Yours, Werner.

Werner to Elisabeth

Berlin, May 8
My love—
Since my last letter there have been two more air raids; so one should not
become too exuberant. Both of these took place mostly in the north and east
of the city, so our nerves were less affected. Nevertheless, it would be nice if
we had a few days of rest. . . . —

Today I almost went to the opera, the first time in several years. The
state opera is still standing, and since apparently not all that many people are
in attendance, professors and students received free tickets to *Lohengrin*,
scheduled for tonight. I had a very good seat. Due to yesterday's attack, the
opera did suffer a bit—fire damage I think, but the performance was still on.
When I called today, after that attack, I was told an unexploded bomb was
still in front of the theater, and one could not tell if it would be removed
before the 4 o'clock beginning of the performance; later on it was definitively
canceled. But perhaps we will get to the theater eventually; if not today, then
a few weeks later on. Basically, it is completely crazy that one wants to use
the pause between two air raids, all dressed up, specifically for a visit to the
theater. A theater that is left standing as the only building, only half dam-
aged, among all the ruins. But this is what life has become now. "Keep
smiling," an American would say.

. . . —Tonight I want to take a bath, hopefully without interruption; in
advance I will quickly listen to the reports on conditions in the air, and then

one can dive in the waters, reassured. So, good night for now! Remember to call the county office and apply for wood from the forest department! Be well! Yours, Werner.

Werner to Elisabeth

Berlin, May 19
My love!

Last night you were somewhat subdued on the telephone, and I feel I must comfort you. Truth be told, there was another big air raid here in the meantime, so that I myself also could use comforting. But one just has to keep one's head above water, even when it becomes difficult; and besides, I will be with you in Urfeld in eight days already. If these times of togetherness continue to be a special feast, I will not mind at all; eventually, we will be living together again for good. . . . I hope meanwhile you are getting realistic offers for a compulsory service girl. Today's attack on Berlin must improve the prospects again. That the repairs on the house have now been authorized is a great relief to me. Then I can have another energetic talk with Weitzmann at Pentecost. I hope one can get the tiles before the building begins. Of course, it is also questionable these days whether the factory is still standing. Those worries are, of course, unending.—I hope you can get some rest before Pentecost so that we can enjoy the days. Do not overwork! Say hello to the children. To a good reunion in Urfeld! Yours, Werner.

Werner to Elisabeth

[Berlin], Tuesday, June 13
My dear Li!

During the last few days I kept trying to call you—in vain. So I will now write a letter after all, just so you hear from me. The day after tomorrow, I will travel to Hamburg where, again, I cannot talk with you by telephone.— . . . That I was not well must have been simply the fact that I had slept so little. It subdued me a lot that, even during the invasion, the air raids do not stop. Of course, these disruptive attacks are much slighter than the all-out attacks; nevertheless, there were again six air mines in our vicinity. In the long run, I cannot really withstand this nervous strain, especially when the day is also fully busy with work.

I managed to make the evening today a little more pleasant for the first time in a long while: I had a visit from a fellow youth movement friend who plays the violin exceptionally well, and I asked a cellist from Butenandt's. The first Beethoven trio went quite well, only the cellist is not so especially good. Next Tuesday we will play again.

Well, otherwise, things keep moving along here more poorly than well. I will most likely endure those next five weeks before I can get to the south of Germany for an extended period of time. In Hechingen there is bound to be more to eat still; it has really become very poor here. And how are you doing? I hope you have solved the question of your replacement. Actually, you should be on your way to Pähl in the next few days; is that still realistic? . . . Around the 1st of July, I will be visiting you all—you probably in Pähl, and the children in Urfeld. My very best! Yours, Werner.

Elisabeth to Werner

Pähl, June 23
My love!

Maria just left and I am now alone; I want to tell you at once how it is here, or rather, what I have seen so far. Right now, I find all of it mighty peculiar and cannot quite grasp the whole operation. We were picked up by a sister who led a small horse carriage. Since only one person would fit, I decided to walk on foot together with Maria. The sky was overcast, but the weather not bad. One could sense the sun behind the clouds. Glorious, this wide-open countryside, the uncut fields with their flowers, the luscious green. Gorgeous poppies, so dark red and glowing, as I have never seen them before. And even better, the many hedges of wild red roses. Finally, rather tired, we arrived in Pähl. Had not the very same sister come to greet us,—I would not have believed that this was the house: an old, sturdy house—castle would not fit the exterior appearance—at best a manor. Next to it a wooden house and all of it in a totally unkempt park in which chickens, geese, and turkeys are milling about in great numbers. A fountain in the middle is witness to former grandeur and is now the gathering place for all these creatures. Inside the house, you get more of a sense of nobility; for one, there are all these ancestors on the walls, in each room, in the hallways—everywhere. The furnishings too are old and beautiful for the most part. I have a two-bed room to myself, which I find preferable. It had flowers and was scrubbed clean. A true manor house room, somewhat dark, with old mahogany furniture. They said I would be getting a nicer room over in the other house, but I am very satisfied with this. I look out into green trees and have a room all to myself, so I can do what I want. How one is supposed to give birth here is still beyond me. But it is nice enough for a vacation stay. . . .

Now, however, I am mostly sad that you have had another terror attack. It worries me, because I find the attacks during daytime much more unpleasant than the nighttime ones, since I do not know where to look for you in my thoughts. I tried to call you last night but it did not work out. I have to explore whether it will be possible to do it from here. Tonight I will first have to try calling home, because Nuss [Martin] had to see the doctor. Jochen had hit the tip of his finger with a hammer a few days ago. It turned blue quickly; then it became very swollen and infected, so that I am afraid she will have to remove the whole nail. The poor little unlucky one! I am really immensely glad that Maria is there. . . . For Waltraut all by herself it would have been a huge imposition. On top of it, there are two criminals roaming in the area of the Herzogstand, toward Heimgarten, so it is better to know both of them are together. . . .

I am now very tired. The long trip and all these new impressions were a strain on me, and my head is throbbing. . . .

How good it is that I will be seeing you again soon.

With all my love, yours, Li.

Werner to Elisabeth

Berlin, July 11

My love—

Today I tried once more, unsuccessfully, to reach you by telephone; yesterday there was not enough time, apparently, and today there seem to have been air raids in your vicinity. So I might as well just write, in case the telephone connection is not going to happen. I am counting the days until I can travel south, and am finding the time here really abysmal. On the trip here on Friday, the train was stopped, and we had to flee into the woods; the train, it turns out, was not attacked, though. That same night, there was again a minor attack on Berlin, so I decided to leave on Saturday night for Jassnitz, simply to get two days of rest. There, all I could get was a horrible hotel room with mice, cockroaches, and other vermin, which I had to battle to keep off me. Yesterday morning I returned, and last night we had another minor attack. No decent sleep can be had anymore with all of this. Tomorrow, I am expected to entertain the Wednesday Society; the talk was sort of finished yesterday, the material preparations must be organized early tomorrow morning. Someone in the kitchen had been baking cookies from my rations, and now I am in temptation to eat them all by myself beforehand, but I will be able to postpone my cookie hunger till tomorrow, I think.

. . . When you get this letter, you must already be preparing for your departure to Urfeld. And then, next week, we will have a few good days together up there with the children. I am terribly homesick for you all. From my heart, yours, Werner.

Werner to Elisabeth

Hechingen, July 27

My love!

The days in Urfeld were very nice, and I am still savoring the togetherness we all had. The trip here was, as expected, atrocious: from Munich on, I stood in the center aisle of a completely overfilled train, amid lots of crying children, occasionally I could sit down on my suitcase. Between Ulm and

Plochingen, we were caught in the massive attack on Stuttgart, that is, all around us there was atrocious flak firing going on, like a severe thunderstorm, lasting over an hour; but we were halted fairly safe in a depression. Only toward morning did we arrive in Plochingen; all the way there we had the black smoke clouds from Stuttgart. At 10 o'clock, I finally arrived here. . . .

I got a letter from your parents saying they were no longer allowed to live in Überlingen, unfortunately, so they would like to come to Hechingen now. I was at the county office today, but am very pessimistic regarding an apartment here; at best, I might find them something in a village nearby. But that too is doubtful and not nice for your parents. I will write to tell them about it today.

From Mrs. Wirtz I should pass on greetings; she has a sack with twenty pounds of carrots waiting, but is not yet allowed to send them. Hopefully, transport will soon be opened up again.—I hope to hear from you again soon. I am really doing very well here, strictly speaking in the sense of external circumstances; I hope to get much work done, so you need not worry about me at all. All my very, very best to you! Yours, Werner.

Werner to Elisabeth

Hechingen, August 6
My dear Li—

I came safely back last night from the Freiburg-Strasbourg trip. I was glad to be "home" again, but in some ways the trip was quite nice. I liked Freiburg very much again; it is such a lively city, even the air is different than in other cities. One strolls along the streets and finds everything just as it was earlier: the female students are running about in great numbers, with notebooks or flowers under their arms, vegetables are sold in the street, and on the walls posters of the next concert or theater play. For a moment I imagined the time was ten years ago again—I actually stayed in the same hotel back then—and you, as a student, might come across my way somewhere; I would definitely have fallen in love with you right then and there. But it just is not arranged so simply, is it?

In Strasbourg I gave two talks; I was quite satisfied with the reception. The work of these last years yielded a cogent, coherent unit that can be transmitted well and, apparently, pleased the audience too. At night Weizsäcker and I landed in a music soiree at the Heimpels', where a former St. Thomas Choir member sang Bach arias, and I participated with a Vivaldi concerto; only after 1 o'clock in the morning did it end—at 8:30 the next morning I had to give another talk.

This morning the Häusslers, in honor of Sunday, invited me to an "English breakfast" with ham and eggs, toast with cold cuts or cheese, authentic tea with cream. It was true gluttony to which the good Häusslers had invited me, because they had just received some bacon from a soldier in Denmark. . . . Please write and tell me about the house repair issue. So, stay well—in September all of us will be together once more! Yours, Werner.

Werner to Elisabeth

Hechingen, August 8
My love—

Yesterday your package arrived with watch and bathing suit, and then, at noon, also your letter from the 3rd, which was a great relief to me. That Maria Linder will stay on in Urfeld for some time is certainly a good thing, and I find it nice of her to take such good care of Anna. On the other hand, there are now more than a few people in Urfeld, but when everybody is cooperating and gets along in the tight space, some things will be much easier; hopefully there will not be too much friction. One has to consider that probably in the fall, the means of transportation will come to an end; it will then be good when so many of you are there, so that somebody can always get on the bicycle and bring in foodstuffs.

Your concerns about the events at large are understandable; however, it seems to improve somewhat in the east for now. Unfortunately, the battalion between Riga and Newa has apparently become cut off; one hopes that the troops there will be able to return on ships. Weizsäcker's brother too is serving there as a staff aide. Sadly, Adelheid's husband has been missing for about six weeks; the last news was that he had to take a plane to Minsk and take over the command of a troop, but that was a while back. Perhaps the great disarray at the front there can give one hope that many of those missing in action have ended up, unharmed, as prisoners, and that they are treated humanely. In the west, the situation appears even more unclear; perhaps the war there will transition into a ground war here. When I am with you in September, all of it may already be more clearly apparent.

You probably have received my worried postcard about the repairs on the house. I had learned about new regulations that likely mean that all building projects other than those of highest urgency in the war effort will be stopped so that the crews can be shipped to the eastern front. I cannot tell whether this will be imminent in the next few days, but every day the workers can get a start now will be a win. You write that Biller [a supplier of construction materials] already had brought in the beams, so that now one must motivate Weitzmann and treat the foreman well. Anna should bring up beer for the work crew; perhaps you also can spare some potatoes and such for them. . . . To you and the children all my best! Yours, Werner.

Werner to Elisabeth

Hechingen, August 10
My love—
I am doing better here than I have in a very long time, and I have a very bad conscience when I think about your worries. This afternoon the Häusslers invited me along with Mrs. Wirtz to an afternoon excursion to collect mushrooms. It became a nice walk through the woods from Bodelshausen to Hechingen that yielded us many chanterelles; afterward Mrs. Häussler and Mrs. Wirtz cooked them, and we had good punch as well as new potatoes and salad. . . . Only in the end did we hear on the radio a new missive regarding the total war effort that brought back to mind all the worries.

It also sounded to me as if now Anna, according to these new regulations, would be sent to the armament industry, and we would get a German girl instead. Now, all of it will likely not be happening very soon, but you will have to deal with new worries.— . . .

I was glad about your letters, which sound confident for the most part, telling me that all of you must be doing reasonably well. The military news from the west is causing me concern; in addition, I found the report today on the court proceedings of the assassins [conspirators involved in Stauffenberg's failed attack on Hitler] very depressing. I find it near impossible to also carry the common fate in my own consciousness, and so one withdraws into one's own little world and into those duties that are simple to carry out and always clear; perhaps it is enough when everyone does this also.— . . . Love, midnight is approaching and I have to clean up in the apartment, wash dishes, etc. So good night for now! Yours, Werner.

Werner to Elisabeth

Hechingen, August 18
My dear Li!

That was indeed welcome news today: the repairs have begun! I had already worried so much, written again to Weitzmann, and now all my efforts with the county commissioner, the mayor, and Weitzmann were almost unnecessary. At least these letters may result in a speedy progress with the repairs. Just treat the foreman really well; he is the most important man, also when it comes to the tiles later on.

In the matter of household help, there do not yet seem to be orders on implementation. You might try sending a written request to the Department of Labor that they should draft Anna only once they have given you a suitable German substitute. . . .

Early tomorrow morning (getting up at 3:30!), I am going to Überlingen and stay the weekend; I think it will be really nice. Edith wrote me I would be playing music with Scheck. But I am also very happy to see your parents again.—Last night I had a big gathering here: ten people (the Laues, the Häusslers, the engineer, Genzmer, the Wirtzes, Hiby, Pahl); I assume people enjoyed it (Schubert, Brahms, Wolf, finally Richard Strauss as the "hit"). . . . In a few weeks the Weizsäckers may be moving to Hechingen; unfortunately, their living quarters also are very small, so that they need to take their children elsewhere. How much of their furniture they can salvage is still unclear.—Now all my best, and say hello to the children! Yours, Werner.

Werner to Elisabeth

Hechingen, August 21
My dear Li—

Today I am already very tired, because I got up at 4:30 this morning and then started out from Überlingen on my bicycle—but still you must also get a note. The visit in Überlingen has brought me a great deal of joy. First the trip there: 3:30 rise and shine, at 7 o'clock the train arrived in Sigmaringen, then a trip on bicycle for forty-five kilometers across this glorious region in between Rauhe Alb and Lake Constance. A cloudless sky throughout, just a touch of fog on the meadows, a little early warning sign of fall. From Sigmaringen you first ascend higher ground through a large forest, naturally all deserted at this time of day, then you arrive at the open high plateau, half meadow and agriculture fields like on the Alb, but then also already many fruit trees, loaded with apples and pears, in between a few rocks or a little river run, all this for two hours. Eventually, the street descends, steeply, into a wooded valley, and when you emerge from it at rapid speed, Lake Constance appears in the distance. It was so warm that I was only wearing shirt and pants, and you could imagine yourself being almost young again. Love, if only you could have been there too! I liked Überlingen itself also very much, the old towers and gates and the timbered buildings. Your parents were happy about my visit; Mutti was just arriving by bicycle when I stood in front of the house. Papa has aged, is much thinner, but mentally seemingly unchanged, it worked well between us. . . . Mutti is volunteering some hours a day with ammunitions; it makes it easier for her to bear the collective fate. Both parents are still hoping somehow for a good outcome to the war.— . . .

On Sunday there first came a little morning walk (I lived in a hotel in town), then after lunch we went on foot to Edith's house; the way there is quite strenuous for your father, it leads up a steep hill. On top Edith served us coffee, then at the Rothes' house we met with Scheck to play music. Scheck played beautifully, and I found him nice in general—maybe a little soft—, his wife was too nervous for me. The Rothe house is modern and plutocratic, exactly the environment in which the Schwabing folk feel at home. (The genuine Schwabing person is in contempt of bourgeois wealth, but expects that a bourgeois benefactor has so much artistic understanding that he will offer up this wealth for an appropriate setting.) So it was very nice. Later on an improvised evening meal before I accompanied the parents back to their home and said my good-byes. . . .

So keep well, I must now really catch up on my sleep! Yours, Werner.

Werner to Elisabeth

Hechingen, August 25
My love—
How nice that we could talk on the telephone again yesterday. Today, however, our plans for the future suffered a severe blow with the new edict from Goebbels that blocks all vacations across every business. You must have read it too. (Aside from that, working hours have increased to sixty hours per week. I now have to establish working hours from 8 a.m. to 7 p.m.) Excepted from the vacation regulation is a separate permission to travel a few days every few months to one's family, if one does not live in the same place. I have considered going to Urfeld in about ten days, so that we can talk about everything at length.—The new vacation elimination is once more, of course, a typical punishment for the busy and a reward for the lazy. Those members of the institute who, upon my request, postponed their vacation till later in order for the most important experiments to be finished, and who often, during air raids, would stay on till 2 o'clock in the morning, will not get any vacation, whereas the lazy ones who took their vacations as early as possible have got it made. The new decree will make lots of bad blood in the organization and create unrest. It basically will not in any sense end up increasing output, instead lead to a significant disturbance among the already very insecure people. But the leadership must surely have given that consideration.—So everything concerning our own plans will wait for a good talk when I come to Urfeld very soon. And do not be too sad until then, alright?!

. . . By the way, I now already have here so much organizational stuff to do that scientific work is taking a back seat. The new decree will force me to do for eleven hours a day nothing but unproductive work. Since eating and sleep also require a few hours, there will be just a few hours left for any scientific works.— . . .

Finally, a few requests: do call up Osthelder [coal supplier] again about the coal, and write to [relatives in] Osnabrück once more about potatoes and carrots. Taking care of material things for the winter is now the most important thing. . . . So, until we have a good reunion soon! Yours, Werner.

Werner to Elisabeth

Hechingen, September 1
My love—

Unfortunately, the connection to you is becoming more difficult. I was no longer able to reach you by telephone. In the meantime, the travel prohibition has become more stringent; also they say one cannot travel more than thirty kilometers without a permit. The latter is rather inconvenient, because while I can travel to Munich on business, I have no business in Kochel. Then there is another new prohibition about sending fruit from here to other places. It will not be easy to get apples from here to Urfeld. But I will buy them regardless, and possibly store them here; we will see how it goes. . . . I have now, provisionally, received a travel for business permit for the time from September 5 to 19. So I will get to Kochel most likely on Tuesday night, unless Gerlach tells me he cannot yet use me on that day in Munich. . . . I am very excited about the days in Urfeld, even if it may only be a brief visit. There is so much to talk about.—Did you remember the coal and potatoes?—Greetings to the children and good-bye! Yours, Werner.

Werner to Elisabeth

Hechingen, September 26
My love—

Just now your letter came, a veritable ray of light on such a cold and dreary day. I do not dare to heat yet, because I have very little coal so far; until mid-October it should be fine without heat. Unfortunately, it looks as if my next trip to Urfeld will be a while off. In the meantime, the war here is approaching noticeably. The convoys of army personnel come through the village, not clean lorries but dirt-splattered horse carriages densely covered with straw or leaves, the horses tired, the accompanying soldiers tired and indifferent. One senses that the front is no longer far away. Normal train traffic is rumored to end shortly after Stuttgart already; express trains would then no longer be running at all, ordinary trains only nights, without scheduled timetables or destinations. But I do not know whether these rumors are perhaps exaggerated. In the Rhineland, however, it must look gruesome.

Amid all this, I manage to do a lot of work; I have actually come quite a bit further ahead. It is absurd, in a way, to want to pursue science under these conditions. But I find it nice anyway. I also stay on top with music, in a pedantic, on-time regimen. Yesterday I had brewed myself a decent cup of coffee and was afterward thrilled by the ease of my piano playing. . . . Now stay healthy, I am hoping to see you soon! Yours, Werner.

Werner to Elisabeth

Hechingen, September 27
My love—
The mail from Bavaria to here seems to have gotten much worse yet; I heard that the railroad installations in Munich are largely destroyed. . . .

I am trying to work scientifically, but am prevented by so much practical stuff. The Molières wish I should find a maid for them, three Hechingen families want to see their sons or daughters employed at my institute, the washerwoman wishes a repair of the washing machine done by our shop people, etc. I am trying to keep them at bay.

. . . How about coal, windowpanes, wood, etc.? The coal is really important, because it will be very scarce this winter. Please call Osthelder in case he has not yet delivered. Possibly he should just deliver Penzberg coal to us; everything else may already be hopeless.—Otherwise not much new here. Tomorrow morning my piano should be getting tuned!! At night we will play trios. So all my best to you all! Yours, Werner.

Werner to Elisabeth

Hechingen, September 30
My love—

I have just played music for two hours with so much enjoyment: in the large library room of the old town hall there are two grand pianos, one Steinway from Wettstein and a Bechstein from Mrs. Belar. Now, I had heard that the daughter of the local choir director supposedly played the piano really well, and I had asked her to play pieces for two pianos with me. Although she looks like a somewhat simple peasant girl, she actually plays exceptionally well, and we have played one Mozart sonata, one Bach concerto, Schumann and Brahms variations. It went just as well as with Jacobi and Bücking. In between there was a warning alarm, but we did not let it disturb us.

This morning was peculiar anyway: first there was ongoing alarm for three hours straight without any action, and then there came the all clear. One minute later there appeared seven airplanes above Hechingen. . . . When we looked outside, we saw plumes of smoke shooting up above the Bissingen airport, and two airplanes that must have come down to the airfield in a nosedive rose steeply high up again to escape the antiaircraft guns. The poor mayor must have been so shaken that he only gave the alarm ten minutes later, but by then everything was long done with and nothing else happened before the second all clear. It seems to have become a habit here that there will be an alarm twice a day. . . . In contrast to Berlin, it does not worry me one bit so far.

— . . . All my best love! Yours, Werner.

Werner to Elisabeth

Hechingen, October 3
My love!

Now fourteen days have already gone by since I left Urfeld. Not much has changed, strictly speaking, one just must be patient. . . . There is much airplane alarm; this morning we again saw hundreds of planes flying overhead, but it does not worry us here.

—This morning I sent you a twenty-pound package. It almost is not worth sending such small amounts. One has to stand in line before 8 o'clock at the railroad post office, then wait, standing, an hour, and finally risk that the quota has been reached. That all shipments of fruit from Württemberg are forbidden I must have written you already. I want to keep buying large amounts of apples anyhow, and have already gotten some half promises. If you were here like last year, you would be savvier in shopping matters than I am.

The most important and difficult, by the way, is the coal supply. You have to keep working on Osthelder and beg him to deliver coal from Upper Bavaria if he cannot get any other. For weeks not a single train wagon has made it to Hechingen anymore. It seems to be related to the fact that traffic in the Rhine area has practically stalled, and that in the Ruhr area traffic is so hindered that nothing gets through to southern Germany any longer.

. . . Helmut Becker was here with me yesterday as were both the Weizsäckers. Just like we have in Leipzig, they too lost several of their neighbors in the attack.—Helmut Becker still is fond of theorizing a lot, but it is quite pleasant to talk with him. He had just been in Sigmaringen, where Pétain and all of the French "government" is now located. Pétain, apparently, views himself a prisoner of war, does not participate in any kind of public events anymore, but takes walks through the little town for a few hours a day, much to the delight of the people in Sigmaringen. H.B., however, witnessed the French military marching to the castle and a French official giving a speech to his people. Aside from the few military boys, only the good people of Sigmaringen, with gaping mouths, seem to have been present at this rousing demonstration, which ended with the shouts "Vive la France, vive le maréchal!"— . . .

What you wrote about the children and your industrious sewing activity made me very happy. Just also keep up the recorder for Woi and make sure he does his homework properly. About me you really need not worry, by the way; I have plenty to eat. Last Sunday I even splurged with an egg for breakfast and some coffee; if that is not a debauched feast! I'm not doing that always, though! By the way, I asked you to send me my old coupons; I hope I can still get a few eggs; I also am urgently in need of shaving soap.—In a few weeks I have to come to Urfeld in any case, to pick up my winter suits. . . . —Stay healthy and do not succumb. Greetings to everyone in Urfeld! Yours, Werner.

Elisabeth to Werner

[Urfeld], October 5
My love!

I forgot to send along the shaving soap. So I will send it promptly today, together with the egg coupon and a postcard from Buchheit. . . .

Things are bad in terms of wood and coal, love. They sawed apart the remaining wood, have not yet brought it up, but placed it down on the slope for now. . . . The coals are even more of a problem, since I simply cannot get hold of Osthelder. . . .

Last night I was listening to Schubert's B-major trio on the radio. I became indescribably nostalgic, love. I saw your trio playing it together, saw the festive, beautiful room, smelled the warm air, redolent of good things, and remembered that once one could live happily and have plenty. All I want is to live together with you again. The work, the worries, and the hard times—I do not care if they remain, unless they become much, much worse. I am not made such that living for the children is enough fulfillment. Women differ in this. Some continue to live for the husband as they did during their honeymoon phase, and some forget all that and become consumed by their children. I do not belong to these; although you know how much the children mean to me. But I see them growing up, and consider them like ships that are pointed to leave the harbor eventually. I will do everything and sacrifice all to make them "fit for life" as much as my strength will let me; but my soul belongs to you and not to them. Say, how much longer will it take? . . .

I should see a doctor and a dentist, urgently. . . . I must wait for that too until the end of the war; I hope it won't be too late by then, and I end up a ruin. But it will have to do.

Now stay safe, my dear heart. That you must go to Berlin is not good. From there you cannot come by bicycle! In love, yours, Li.

1944

Werner to Elisabeth

Hechingen, October 10
My dear Li!

Today your lovely letter arrived with all its concerns and wishes, and I would just want to be with you to be able to talk it all through. But soon I am going to be with you all, and as far as the future goes, I am optimistic regardless. That your health is not great gives me concern. Is Dr. Otto not in a position to suggest a few health management ideas and prescribe medication? One simply must be healthy right now because during the next months, our strength certainly will be needed in the utmost. Often, when I think of you all, I am very troubled to be sitting around here so passively, instead of helping you solve practical matters. One simply must provide for coal and wood and potatoes, and here I cannot do anything. Only with apples I can help; so far I have packed a large crate full of almost one and a half zentner, unfortunately not actually the winter apples that will keep, but some merely picked off the ground. Whether I can still get more and better ones I do not know, but am hoping. Are you at all still getting some fruit from Berlin?—Then I learned the catastrophic news that, until next June, only two zentner potatoes per person are allocated, that means we could only have eighteen zentner in storage. That would be very bad. . . .

Otherwise, all is fine here, except for my slight intestinal flu, which will get better too.—The young pianist with whom I played a while ago is drafted to serve in the air defense unit.—Today they announced on the radio that 70 percent of all sixteen-year-olds had volunteered for military service. How lucky for us that our children are still little.— . . .

—I hope to reach you by telephone again, eventually; I have tried a few times already. My very, very best! Yours, Werner.

Werner to Elisabeth

Hechingen, October 12
My dear Li—

I have such a need to chat with you and tell you things from here, even when nothing much of importance has happened; it is a pity that the telephone connection is apparently completely gone, so I wait for the mail all the time, hoping to get a letter with good news. The little mishap with the shaving soap, by the way, is already resolved. When I told the Häusslers that the soap had been stolen out of your letter, they presented me with a new piece. How nice of them! The post office, however, wrote that they only cover the total loss of a piece of mail, not the contents. So one always has to send food coupons in a sealed, insured letter. My attempts to buy apples are progressing only very slowly. In the stores, apples do require food stamps. There the ration is limited to about ten pounds per person. That just won't do. I will keep on looking for other fruit until I find it. . . .

Here we all are in good shape. I am starting on new scientific work that makes me very happy, although at this time it is kind of crazy to want to still engage in science. Outside it was warm and sunny today, however, there was almost always alarm; the constant switching between the siren signals has become so normal that one doesn't always remember if there is alarm off or on. The Americans are often flying very close above, but will attack mostly just the railroads. Any travel at this time is something very unpleasant.— Last night I was invited by Mr. Grotz [owner of a former textile factory, to which the whole Berlin institute was relocated], and I do not dare tell you the menu so that you will not become envious.—Love, I hope you don't get too burdened. Once the moving van to Kochel has left, I will also be coming to you. To you and the children my best! Yours, Werner. . . .

Werner to Elisabeth

Hechingen, October 22
My dear Li—
I was glad that I spoke with you today before your telegram arrived. Now I am not quite so worried. . . .

Here everything continues to go unbelievably well; yesterday, in a three-hour battle, I managed to acquire another zentner of apples in Boll. There I will also still be getting one-half zentner of pears, but then my sources will likely dry up.—I want to make the trip to Urfeld during bad weather, if possible, because in good weather the trains are targeted all too often. Two nights ago we twice had an unbelievable number of planes above Hechingen; once it was the attack on Stuttgart, then on Nuremberg. Even from far away, the attack was so horrible that one gets frightened at the thought of entering again into these grinding mills. But when the night ends, one sees the golden leaves of the trees up on the Zollern, and life begins once again, like usual. . . . Weizsäcker has come back from Berlin, everything there is still the same; I run into his children once in while in the street. So, soon we will meet again; everything will turn out alright! Yours, Werner.

Werner to Elisabeth

Hechingen, November 27
My dear Li!
How good that I was able to get in touch with you again yesterday. These constant attacks on Munich worry me a bit, ever since the bombs were dropped on Urfeld the other day. I hope it is not getting too unsettling in Urfeld. . . . Life overall is as calm as ever except, on such clear days, there is almost constant alarm. Toward evening there usually is a warning alarm, provisionally, so to speak, and throughout the night no all clear; thus the mayor is removed from any responsibility, and whoever is sleeping is doing it at his own peril. . . . During midday dinner, a low-flying plane whisked by close to the roof of our restaurant. But nobody gets excited over it. Yesterday a rumor coursed through Hechingen that in Singen, on Lake Constance, air units had landed, and that enemy tanks were standing near Horb. Toward nighttime one could confirm that it all was nonsense. All the various noises that cannot be distinguished yet, bombs, artillery, or antiaircraft fire, must be the cause.

. . . Last night Wirtz suddenly showed up from Berlin, he must have been worried to be too far away from his wife. Besides, he wanted to know how things with the People's Defense League here were developing. The danger that individual people will be sent to the front,—with some Hechingen people it did happen—is, I believe, not currently an issue for the institute. But right here, on location, we do have to participate energetically.—I have no coal yet, am heating with the little electric heater for now. It is very cold outside, so I am quite afraid that the apples will arrive frozen. . . .

Stay healthy and say hello to the children! Yours, Werner.

Werner to Elisabeth

Hechingen, December 2
My dear Li—

Today I wanted to call you, but unfortunately no calls to Kochel are handled today. . . . Overall, I am doing so well here that one simply is left with a bad conscience. . . . This is, after all, just a seventy-kilometer distance to the front! The work at the institute is also progressing nicely right now, as is my own work. For scientific work you need the absolute precondition of a certain unpressured state of mind; with so-called industriousness, namely, hasty puttering along, nothing is gained. Of course, nobody knows for how much longer this peaceful island here will remain. In Freiburg, sadly, it is all over. Helmut Becker was there shortly after the attack and reported about it: the inner city is largely destroyed; only the cathedral is still standing. Wirtz and Pahl have not come back from there yet; hopefully nothing has happened to their relatives.— . . .

I would like so much to know what is going on where you are: whether the wood is ready, the lignite coal brought up, how the children and you and Maria Linder are doing. I will try again tomorrow to get a telephone call through.—Besides, I am looking forward to Christmas already, it will certainly be nice. All my best! Yours, Werner.

Werner to Elisabeth

Hechingen, December 8
My dear Li—

Since I spoke with you on [my] birthday, a few days have passed, and I will tell you a few things in writing; maybe I can also talk to you again tomorrow or the day after. The birthday was quite cozy, but lonely. . . .

Yesterday Mrs. v. Weizsäcker returned from an excursion to Radolfzell and recounted what she had heard through Helmut Becker about the Heimpels and Hubers: Heimpel was serving in Strasbourg with the People's Defense League and was leading a company of 20 Germans and 230 Alsatians. The curator had scheduled a meeting for Wednesday evening and forbidden any departures. Mrs. Heimpel came Wednesday evening to Strasbourg to visit her husband, the children were in Falkau. When she went shopping on Thursday morning, she encountered American tanks. Since her husband was in the barracks, she ran to Huber, all terrified. He was sitting at his desk, working. So the three of them (Mr. and Mrs. Huber and Mrs. Heimpel) quickly gathered up the most important things and rode on their bicycles to the Rhine. The bridges were already closed off. Eventually, they located a half-broken boat, stuffed its hole, and set off into high-water conditions on the Rhine. There they reportedly almost sank, but at any rate they made it to the other side, although with just one of the bikes, but without any shooting. They continued on for twenty-four hours to the house where the Huber children were staying. Mrs. Heimpel was frantic about her husband, whom she envisioned fighting on the last barricades. When she came to Falkau two days later, however, she found her husband there unharmed and cheerful. He had, because the Alsatians had decided to join the opposite side, taken his 20 Germans and made it somehow across the Rhine Bridge, which is now blown up. One can see, once more, that a quick takeover is a relatively harmless affair. Although: the Alsatians, supposedly, went on a rather gruesome killing spree afterward.

By the way, at this time the Rhine valley between Lörrach and Waldshut is being evacuated because they are expecting an attack by the French. But before Christmas nothing is likely going to happen. Carl Friedrich is expected back from Switzerland tomorrow; I am curious what he has to tell from there.

Tomorrow night I will play trios once more, but then prepare for my departure. . . . To you and the children all my best! Yours, Werner.

1945

HUNGER, *frequent exercises with the People's Defense League, incessant air raids with low-flying bombers aiming at anything that moves—the dire conditions Werner endures before the end of the war make professional work impossible. In Hechingen people band together tightly, connecting and attempting to support each other with music, lectures, and excursions. Werner is feeling torn: he must carry on his professional duties as head of the institute, but he is desperately concerned about his family. Letters, if they get through at all, take many days to arrive; telephone lines are, for the most part, interrupted. Each partner is essentially on his or her own. Thus the surprise is stunning when Werner arrives in Urfeld, coming up the mountain on his bicycle. It is April 21, 1945. He left Hechingen three days earlier as the foreign troops were marching in, determined to assist his family.*

He finds a full house: Elisabeth, Maria Linder, the Ukrainian helper Anna, the nanny Waltraut, and seven children (added to the group is Maria's little son). In subsequent days, Lieutenant Schuster, an old acquaintance, joins the household. His military unit disbanded, he is in hiding, glad to have found a place of sanctuary. One small bathroom has been converted into a chicken coop, due to dire need. Under these circumstances, it is out of the question that "little Omi," Werner's mother, can also live in the house. She is brought from Mittenwald to live in a different house close by.

On May 2, an American advance troop under Colonel Pash arrives to arrest Werner. The next day, after the Americans help the family get food supplies, Werner is transported to Heidelberg, then to several intermediary stops, and ultimately to the manor Farm Hall near Cambridge. Thereafter the correspondence stops.

We now know in some detail what these last days of the war were like for the family, thanks to the diary Werner kept from April 15 to May 3. It is included here to show the events of these days more clearly.

Only from the months of July, August, and November do we have a few letters the couple exchanged. While Werner and the other scientists at Farm Hall are leading a relatively uniform but materially carefree life, Elisabeth has to muster all her strength to get the family through. In July her mother-in-law dies, and a few days later Maria Linder, friend and housemate, also dies.

Since there is not enough food to go around, Elisabeth takes the twins to a children's home near Weilheim, where they also have access to regular schooling. In November she travels to Frankfurt to the American Headquarters because money is running out and she does not know what to do or when her husband will be returning. This travel is possible because she has found capable help through intermediaries, a young woman who can lead the household independently. Hopes that Werner might be released at Christmas are not fulfilled, but letters point to the possibility that the separation of the family will not last much longer.

Elisabeth to Werner

[Urfeld], January 8
My dear heart!

Today we missed you especially much, you, my love! We have celebrated a very lovely birthday. Maria got one "ball of wonder wool" and knitting needles. Inside the ball of wonder is a tiny game of dominos. In addition, she got a mosaic, three school writing tablets, and a pencil. Woi got a wooden cannon (from Lieutenant Schneider [a soldier stationed with his unit in the Hotel Fischer in Urfeld]) and also some writing tablets with the pencil; and together they got their schoolbag. They were very happy. We then cooked a fancy Sunday dinner, toasted each other with raspberry juice, and sang: "Three cheers to her and him." That was a great success, and the twins were ecstatic. Particularly the fact that they could eat meat till they were really full was a treat. . . . Only Mama is gripped by a sheer endless agitation, because

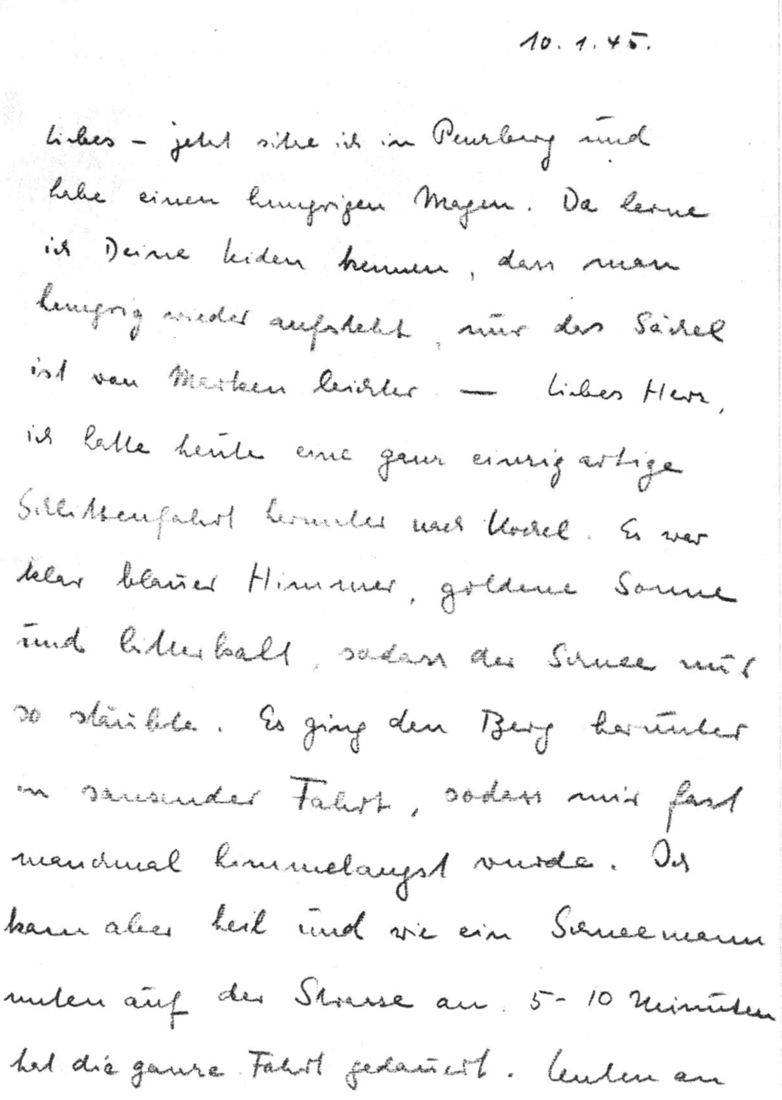

10. 1. 45.

[handwritten letter in German]

Letter from Elisabeth to Werner, January 10, 1945

she cannot yet leave. Today it was impossible to call her due to the incredible attack on Munich. The planes were flying almost continuously from 8 till 11 o'clock. It was pretty horrific. Up from the mountain, one could probably have seen Munich in flames, since the night was so clear and studded with stars. We kept the windows covered almost all the time and were sitting by the light of one candle. . . .

Love, being alone is almost unbearable for me. I think I will soon have to start the children on music again. Maybe then I might become a little happier.

So much for now. Stay safe, my dear heart! Be well! Yours, Li.

Letter from Werner to Elisabeth, March 1, 1945

Elisabeth to Werner

[Urfeld], January 10
—Dear Heart,

. . . I was on an extraordinary sledding trip down to Kochel today.
The sky was of a clear blue, the sun golden, and it was so bitterly cold that
the snow spewed about behind me. Down the mountain I went, at break-
neck speed, so that I got almost scared to death sometimes. I arrived,
nevertheless, safely down at the road, looking like a snowman: five to ten
minutes for the whole trip. Down at the road there was a thick, dark fog;
but during the long way into Kochel, the sun and the fog were battling, so
that the sun and I arrived in Kochel at the same time. You know, there is
nothing more beautiful in nature than this battle between fog and sun. And
when the sun breaks forth victorious, it has a glow, so splendidly golden
and inspiring, that one becomes practically a bit turned inside out, ready to
feel the joy of the world again, as one did earlier, when life first opened up
to you . . . .

Be well, dear heart. And do call us, whenever you can.

May God protect you! Yours, Li.

Werner to Elisabeth

Hechingen, January 11
My dear Li—

Today it is late again; I ate dinner at Weizsäckers' and then played chess
with Karl-Friedrich. Thus an otherwise somewhat miserable day ended on
a halfway decent note. Since Christmas I have been having trouble getting
used to the separation from you all; besides I am also troubled by the whole
atmosphere so close to the front, which is more tangible each day. I find it
very good that we did not move to Hechingen.—The cold these last days has
been barbaric, this morning about −20 [Celsius]; it has warmed up a bit now.
Of course, the little heater cannot get the room warm, so I have done a little
actual heating. But if I do not get any coal at all, I will be able to afford this
luxury only rarely.

—Sadly, I have no news at all from you, mail must be unpredictably slow; maybe I can get through tomorrow on the air force phone lines, although the last attack on Munich appears to have destroyed a few things in that respect too.—Sunday morning is duty at the People's Defense League again, so we will have to get up early and freeze for a half day. Last night we had two hours' worth of duty and have learned the songs "Die Wacht am Rhein" [The Guard on the Rhine] and "Deutschland Hoch in Ehren" [Germany High in Honors]. In the end it even worked polyphonically. About its use during action, I was a little unclear.

—Wirtz went back to Berlin. Pahl and Miss Troll want to come over tomorrow to sing. In early February there will be a public concert in Hechingen in which those two are also participating as singers. The accompaniment (opera duets from *Figaro*, *Magic Flute*, and Verdi) was handed to me. Mr. Bausch also wanted me to play solo, but I have—partly upon considering the probably impossible piano—declined.—Deep down, I do not like the whole thing here, and want to be with you all. Since that is not possible, I am consoling myself with memories of Christmas, especially the pageant. Do make lots of music with the children, and give them all my love! Don't worry about me; I will get back on track again. So, my very, very best! Yours, Werner.

Werner to Elisabeth

[Hechingen], Sunday, January 14
My dear Li!

Now it has really become difficult to get in touch with you. Mail will take very long because since last Sunday, apparently, many connections have been destroyed, and even the people from the air force tell me that their Kochel line is still affected. Today I will just try again via the phone company, but am skeptical about the success.—Here everything is going along sort of normal. This morning I had to get up at 7 a.m. to make it in time for practice at the People's Defense League. The gain out of such multiple hours' worth of freezing in open air is really very negligible. I have held a rifle for about three minutes and fired one shot. The rest meant standing around and freezing. Fortunately, I was suddenly, unexpectedly, visited by some high-ranking officers who came in a fancy car and picked me up for a meeting; thus I was home at about 11 already and drank a few glasses of sherry from the last Speer package with the gentlemen. Besides, such an event impresses the good people in Hechingen no end, which does no harm. . . . Now all my best, love; do not worry if you hear little from me. Greetings to the children. Yours, Werner.

Werner to Elisabeth

Hechingen, January 21
My dear Li,

Due to the events of the past weeks, the way from Urfeld to here has now become very far. Since I have left you, I have no news anymore, except the one telephone call. . . . In the meantime, the war in the east has developed in such a way that very sudden and unexpected turns might result. Should the Russians advance through Czechoslovakia to the Bavarian border, I would attempt to come to you—although it would not be easy to be granted the necessary furlough from the People's Defense League. But one has to see how everything develops. Here we have had much airplane activity during the last weeks. . . . One more thing: buy everything that you can get on the stamps: bread, flour, butter, etc.; also salt, which may soon be in very short supply! . . . Now stay healthy all of you, and keep up your courage! Yours, Werner.

Werner to Elisabeth

Hechingen, January 28
My dear Li—

As of yesterday, supposedly, one has permission to write letters again; I want to take this opportunity quickly before any new barriers will interfere again. Things here are going along so-so; I gave up on the hope of acquiring coal; I manage with my little electric heater, as long as I may still run it. I am wearing two layers of vests, two pairs of underpants,—a sweater and my winter coat over everything——, then it is bearable. Also, the institutes cannot be heated anymore as of next Monday. At the same time, electricity for all businesses is off; ten days ago in all of Württemberg factories stopped work and this will continue for now. I am trying to keep the institute functioning on the smallest scale; under all circumstances, one must avoid having it be shut down and then having the people taken away. Now I will not, even during the day, be sitting anyplace warm, which will diminish the overall well-being a little,——some coughing as well as rheumatism in the joints has affected me for several weeks already——, but much more awful worries are out there. . . .

News from the east is really very alarming, and one cannot yet quite imagine how the war will continue if Berlin were to be occupied. But one just has to hope for the best.——This morning we had duty with the People's Defense League again, we were led on a little walk through the fields. Weapons we do not yet have.—— . . . Please write more often, so that I hear from you often. Maybe in the not too distant future, I can get to all of you again. So all the best! Yours, Werner.

Werner to Elisabeth

Hechingen, February 1
My dear Li——

Since yesterday it's been warm here and almost springlike; so my vital spirits are perking up anew, after a recent period of less than good health. Mostly I am still bothered by my finger joints; the front joints were——, perhaps due to the playing on the cold piano or something else—so affected by the cold that they are still swelling up a lot during the night and hurt. But that will probably disappear now too. At any rate, I am feeling well and ready to take up the battle for one's existence again. In our nuclear physics group, the internal battle (Diebner vs. K.W.I.) [Kaiser Wilhelm Institute] has broken out anew, probably as a result of the new wave of conscriptions and the threatening danger in the east. Maybe I will have to travel in the next days to Thuringia (Stadtilm) on account of this; I do not really like it, but perhaps it is necessary, and besides, I might, on the way back, travel via

Munich. As long as I am healthy, I will cope with the problems, and the fact
that things are showing movement is only giving me new courage.

If I do worry, then it is actually only about you all. . . . Following your
wish, I have bought some medications and will continue to do so; of course I
cannot send them, but maybe bring them along next time. You have to take
care in Urfeld that any groceries we are eligible for with our stamps are
bought at once, so that there are supplies. Then you might talk with Miss
Penzberger, she ought to call the farmer Oswald and tell him that, when the
need arises, he has to supply us with milk. . . . I hope there will be some mail
again soon. All the best! Yours, Werner.

Werner to Elisabeth

Hechingen, February 15
My dear Li—

Today we had a real spring day outside, completely cloudless and warm,
and the sky a steely blue. After lunch I went a bit up the hills west of the city
and found it all very enjoyable. I did not want to take a trip farther away,
partly because of the many planes, which are a nuisance in this kind of
weather, even for solitary people in the fields, partly because yesterday I
already was outside on duty for half a day with the People's Defense League,
albeit in terrible weather. That duty, by the way, was again very comical: it
was not slated as an exercise but as a "mission," that is, we were supposed to
comb the woods and fields for runaways. Since we had no weapons, it was
difficult to imagine how we should arrest armed people. And since it would
be, even with a military company in disarray, already next to impossible to
lead them through the woods without losing half of them, I was prepared for
anything. It then played like this: we marched with our troop, in the pouring
rain, to the Hauser farm (near Sindich); since we were drenched, the farmer's
wife came out with a large tray of schnapps glasses and poured us each as
much as we wanted. Thus the stay there took almost two hours and the mood
became very jolly. Then we realized that the connection to the parallel troop
was hopelessly lost, and we gleefully went home in little groups without
sighting a single enemy.—

. . . There is nothing else new here.—In clear weather you have to watch out even in Urfeld, so that the children will not suddenly be targeted by low-flying aircraft! I hope you do not have inordinate household worries. My best to you and the children!

Yours, Werner.

Werner to Elisabeth

Hechingen, February 18
My dear Li—
Now it is Sunday again; a week has passed since my visit with you all. Generally, I have now adjusted to being here; I am working a lot, also on real science, and besides, I am enjoying the beginnings of early spring, which awaken life's spirits and make the future, overall, appear full of hope. I was outside a few times these past days, always in bright sunshine; today the sky has clouded over again for the first time. In turn, there is less alarm today than usual. In the evenings we are preparing for the concert, scheduled for Thursday. . . .

Pahl and Miss Troll will perform the lieder, in the second half mostly Pahl; the violinist will be a musician who once had studied it and then played gigs in coffeehouses, with a decent technique; the cello part will be taken by a professional cellist. I will be featured incessantly at the piano. It may, perhaps, be crazy to undertake such a thing in these times, but at least for a few evenings one then does not talk about politics.—Are you too busily playing music with the children? Someday, later, when we are all living together again, there definitely will be lots of music. I hope you all have an enjoyable Sunday! All my love! Yours, Werner.

Werner to Elisabeth

Hechingen, February 23 (fifth letter since Urfeld visit)
My dear Li—
Do you hear anything from me at all? Since my return, I have only gotten letters that were written even before my Urfeld visit. One arrived yesterday from January 18. But you will most likely be fine; a blessing, that

Urfeld is not near a railroad. The plane traffic here has become rather enormous. Nevertheless, these last few days in Hechingen were really beautiful; fantastic warm spring weather, and then, every evening, rehearsal for the concert. Yesterday, after nearly incessant all-out alarm from 10 a.m. to 6 p.m., we kept rehearsing diligently in spite of the planes; the concert itself went on splendidly from 8 p.m. till 10:30 p.m. without alarm and with about five hundred people in the audience. . . . Pahl easily filled the large hall with his voice and was singing better than ever before. The audience went wild with enthusiasm, especially after the "Zueignung" [Dedication] by Richard Strauss which, of course, was a wonderful closing piece. He then had to give an encore and sang in the end the "Heimweh" [Homesickness], naturally to incredible effect. Yours truly was given assorted compliments and two books; when in passing I overheard the remark: "like Raucheisen," I, naturally, was lapping it up. And I really did play well. Oh, if you could have been there! Many have inquired after you, whether you might not be here once in a while. If there were not the difficulties and dangers of travel, you should come by; for you it would also be a change and a boost. . . .

—I myself am feeling very well, knock on wood, both physically and emotionally. Except on the bicycle trip to Haigerloch I did notice that the reserves of body strength are less than I would have thought. Whether they would be sufficient for a bicycle trip from here to Urfeld, I am not quite sure. But I am feeling alive and active and am forging plans for our togetherness after the war. That will be very nice, I think, in spite of everything else.

Love, I hope all of you in Urfeld are getting by. Make sure that you can get a replacement for the Russian girl with a capable German one, maybe from the east. The timing for this is right just now.

All my best to you and the children! Yours, Werner.

Werner to Elisabeth

Hechingen, March 1 (seventh letter since Urfeld)
My dear Li!
These days you will be quite worried about me, and I am quite worried about you. The air offensive that has swept over Germany in the last eight

days will probably be the most horrific thing a people had to endure in Europe since the Thirty Years' War. Based on the experience of the last days, I would like to mention to you some safety measures that I consider necessary for you in Urfeld, particularly once the front moves closer to your area. The biggest danger for such a tiny village are attacks from low-flying planes. However, these are possible in Urfeld only during clear weather; they will likely occur from the lake, so that the planes then fly off through the Kesselberg notch. Thereby our house and the meadow below are very much in danger. . . . Now I am asking you to take the following safety measures: on clear days, the children should never go down to the road. The best would be if on those days one of you would always sit outside and watch the situation in the sky. As soon as one sees or hears attack planes, everybody should go to the basement. But that is probably not feasible. Just this: if down on the road some larger convoys are driving, or if some units are doing exercises on the slopes and have set up their MGs, and if then, in clear weather, attack planes show up, you *all must immediately move into the basement*. On such days, the children should only play on the terrace. When on such a day suddenly a plane comes darting in, then the best thing is for everybody to throw themselves down inside the terrace wall, closely pressed against the ground. I would just practice this with the children. I think one could get the children used to needing cover from any airplane without them getting very anxious. . . . But you will do the right thing; just do not take the dangers too lightly. Overall, Urfeld should be a relatively safe place due to the mountains and because there is no railroad.

I doubt very much that I can come back to Urfeld in the foreseeable future. Trips by train are too risky; by bicycle it is a rather long way, and besides the smaller roads are dangerous too. In any case, do not worry, if I do not come soon and if you don't hear from me for quite a while. I will do everything that is best for us, and that can only be determined at the moment.

Otherwise, things here are basically alright, a letter from you took only eight days from Urfeld to get here; that was very nice. At mealtime outside in front of the house, you must really watch out for airplanes!

All my best! Yours, Werner.

Werner to Elisabeth

Hechingen, March 4 (eighth letter since Urfeld)
My dear Li!

You have probably received my last letter on security measures against attacks by low-flying planes. On clear days, please be very careful, because your life and that of the children depends on it. Since we had bad weather here for the last three days, it was quieter, for which I was very grateful. The days right before were awful, but now the emotional balance is more or less restored.

Yesterday morning, with chief architect Genzmer as my guide, I was on the Hohenzollern and saw a number of beautiful paintings from the Wallraff-Richarz Museum: the *Madonna* by Stephan Lochner, a large portrait by Rembrandt, French impressionists (Renoir and others), the famous bridge over the canal by van Gogh, and several very good paintings by Leibl. It was a great treat, particularly since one could just hold the paintings in one's hands and study them thoroughly. A very small picture by Caspar David Friedrich: a tree before the darkening evening sky and in the background the thin crescent moon has also made a big impression on me.

. . . Good night for now, and all the best! Yours, Werner.

Elisabeth to Werner

[Urfeld], early Monday [March 5]
My love!

Today Maria will drive to Staltach to return with Stofferle [her son] on Wednesday. In terms of food, this becomes an issue, particularly if there were no more potatoes available to us. However, I am firmly convinced that this is the only right thing to do. I hope all is going well and without trouble. . . .

I am longing for mail from you. But probably in vain. How should mail get through anymore with all these raids! So one just has to accept total separation. We are now making our own yeast. It works fine. The only question is if we will still get our total allotment of flour. It would amount to forty pounds, since white bread is no longer available. . . .

Now be well, my love! When shall we see each other again? Even official trips are out of the question with these extreme attacks. Do you know that tomorrow will be my father's birthday? He will turn seventy-seven. Will I ever see him again? Be well and stay safe! Yours, Li.

Werner to Elisabeth

Hechingen, March 9 (ninth letter since Urfeld)
My dear Li!

The other day a letter arrived from you, only five days old, but since then, no news has come. I think you must be alright; in this bad weather the danger from airplanes is less; instead, you probably have snow again. My biggest concern is the question of how you are supposed to get something to eat later on. I am asking you to do anything and everything possible in this regard. . . . I do not know whether I can come to Urfeld anytime soon; I think a lot about this question, but right now I have a feeling it would be better for the future if I stayed here. But then all this depends on details, which one cannot predict; I hope I will eventually arrive at the right decision.

During the last days it was quiet here due to the bad weather, an enjoyable reprieve. Now it looks as if it will clear up, then one has to go back to living like the deer in the woods, who listen to every sound, ready to get to safety with a quick jump. You should not worry too much about me; this is still a very advantageous patch here on earth to be living on. So I do have more worries about you than for myself. Also, I will not starve here; there are many friends who can help me in need. . . . Well, when we meet the next time, everything will look very different; let us hope it will look better then, right? To you, the children, and all of you, my best! Yours, Werner.

Elisabeth to Werner

[Urfeld], March 12
My love!

Yesterday, finally, we had news from you. . . . It was really nice to hear from you again, finally. You mention the safety precautions with the low-flying airplanes that you had written to me. So far I have not gotten anything. Maybe you could write it again. Although I believe you should not worry too much about it, because here in the mountains they cannot so easily go low. So far we have not had anything like it here; but we are very careful, regardless, and I have also stressed utter caution to the children.

The Rhine has been crossed, although in an impractical place, all of Pomerania is in Russian hands. That is the picture we have, as of now.

You will no longer be able to come, beloved heart, you! What will be ahead of us? Here in Urfeld, the mood is excellent. The people firmly believe in the turnaround of events. Such steadfastness is truly shocking, isn't it?

But despite all the chaotic events, we are, for now, just living our peaceful existence. All the children were vaccinated, Tinchen [Christine] against smallpox, the others against diphtheria. Today they were mightily grumpy, although we have perfect weather; in particular Barbara and Woi, who were quite strongly impacted. . . . Now farewell, my dear heart! May God protect you and us! Yours, Li.

Werner to Elisabeth

Hechingen, March 13 (tenth letter since Urfeld)
My dear Li!

No more news from you has come for a long time. A soldier was telling us that the Danube Bridge at Ulm was destroyed; it makes sense then, if mail can no longer pass through; so I am trying not to be worried.

This afternoon I bicycled under a cloudless sky and in the warm sunshine to Haigerloch, where a part of my institute work is now taking place. This early spring can be incredibly beautiful. Especially on the way home, when the sun was already low, the colors of the mountains became so very delicate, as if submerged in a bluish tint, the way the French impressionists were able to paint it. This type of employment that allows you to be alone outside in nature belongs to the best that the war has brought with it. The fact that occasionally one has to also play the mouse and hawk game with the airplanes infringes only a little on the enjoyment; for you are actually always at an advantage, given the many places for cover, if you keep your eyes and ears open.

. . . Overnight I shall have to stand watch on a bridge for the People's Defense unit. Originally I was supposed to show up at the guard station at 7, but through a lucky confusion, we managed to have my duty start at 11, so I can still write this letter. In a way, it is a little strenuous when you were gone during the day by bicycle to then add a night vigil, and the next day have to be at the institute again for work. But somehow it can be done.—

In your last letter you wrote about Woi's music. I am curious what the little guy will be able to do at my next visit. It is very nice that you are keeping both of the twins so interested in music. Skill and knowledge are, ultimately, the only permanent possessions; and music is probably the most important part of Germany's past that can still be passed on to the next generation.—I hope to hear soon from you once again. I feel quite deprived when it seems that I no longer have any contact at all. . . . So, I am off to guard duty; good night for now! Yours, Werner.

Werner to Elisabeth

Hechingen, March 16
My dear Li—

I just received your letter from March 1, the first sign of life in a long time. You report important news: that Mrs. Linder's child is going to come to us and that Mrs. Krieger is in Urfeld. . . . With Hans-Christoph [Maria's child], the nutrition problem is, of course, the most difficult aspect. One can hope that you can at least get potatoes for him. Other than that, I would think that Maria Linder will perk up if she has him back with her, and that this will make many things easier. On the other hand, Waltraut should not be saddled with extra work on his account; and the problem of his father must not be discussed. But you will have considered all this. I think it is important that you should visit the Schmidts in Starnberg in the near future (but *definitely not* by train in good weather; preferably by bicycle in a two-day trip). Because with respect to food, it is now becoming virtually a matter of life and death. Even here in Hechingen, I am far from getting enough to eat. The packages from Speer are used up; only the apples from the Häusslers make a small difference. I am becoming thin and thinner, and less physically able. On your end it will, in the long run, be much worse, though. In a couple of weeks or months you will be getting practically nothing anymore with food coupons. So you must negotiate how to get something for money. One cannot take this problem seriously enough. . . . So, love, now begins the fight for survival in real terms, and I am terribly distressed that I cannot help you now. . . . —So, love, best wishes, I hope that in your "refugee camp," Urfeld, it is relatively harmonious. . . . Give the children my best, and do take care of little Ria! Yours, Werner.

Elisabeth to Werner

[Urfeld], April 6
My dear heart,

Yesterday your dear, sad letter from Good Friday and Easter Sunday arrived. Dear you! Do not worry too much. I am coping quite well and am confident I will act appropriately when danger is near. . . . —School for the children has still not begun. I will step up more energetically and demand that something be done. For the children it just is not healthy to have nothing to challenge them. Woi may be passionately playing the recorder and is advancing on the alto quite nicely. But it is just not the right thing.

I am quite sad that I did not write more often last week. The trip to Staltach and the chasing after the chickens, which at first always escaped, were really strenuous for me. I am now also feeling the effect of the poor food. Although at the moment, we are still doing quite well. Once we no longer have potatoes, it will be grim. Of the allotted nine zentner, we have gotten five. The other four were promised us. The whole batch of flour we received is almost used up already. One needs horrible quantities for the many people. I am so glad that you got some supplements. In the morning the children eat flour soup: simply stir salt and dry flour into boiling water. There will be clumps, but those are especially desirable. The children get milk with it. One can eat it without, though, and still one feels full. It is exceptionally delicious when, instead of the water, you take some meat broth. It becomes something special for evenings. And if you then want to do something extra, you combine the milk with an egg and stir it in the soup. It tastes delicious and even has a noble name: "Königinsuppe" [queen's soup].

We suddenly have deep winter again as of today. There is a lot of snow, and it keeps on snowing steadily. Good thing that I have not yet started getting the garden going. The radishes that I had sown out into a box are coming up in great numbers despite the weather. The lettuce too is germinating. . . . Be well, my dear, dear heart. I am glad that you have the occasional nice time in Hechingen too. Hopefully you will be spared the bad. "Es vergeht kein Stund in der Nacht, wo nicht mein Herze wacht und an Dich gedenkt" [Not an hour passes in the night when my heart is not awake and thinking of you]. It has always been my favorite song and has come true for real. May God protect you! Yours, Li.

Werner to Elisabeth

Hechingen, April 11
My dear Li—

I have not written you for a while, partly thinking that letters would no longer get through, partly that I might soon come to see you all. The prospects for driving over to you have now become better again, because there is a new decree by the Führer that possibly might make it happen. Naturally, I would then only be able to leave here at the last minute, and there are some further "taboos."

Generally speaking, things here are fine, and I am confident about the near future. . . . There are only two major malaises spoiling this time here (aside from the separation and the human problems): hunger and the airplanes. Although I am getting something to eat from time to time as a gift, it remains, overall, too little. Who would have thought ten years ago that one would someday be grateful for every piece of bread someone gives you? And then the planes are there all the time and disturb any quiet work. They come so fast that one has barely the time to, let's say, run from the living room into the safer kitchen, then they shoot, mostly at cars and trains, throw a few bombs (smallish calibers) and off they go again. . . .

For two days, endless fighter units came by here and threw their ballast into the woods about twenty kilometers east of Hechingen. I heard there are large depots of ammunition buried underground. Formations of planes carpeted the area with bombs again and again until eventually a portion of the depot exploded. Then, after the indescribable thunder of the explosions, there developed an actual mushroom cloud, which then drifted westward above us for an hour as the only white cloud in the dark blue sky. Although we understood after a little while that all this did not amount to any danger for us, the emotional aftermath of such elemental events is very great. The force of the waves of pressure was strong enough, despite the twenty kilometers, that a window in my kitchen shattered;—toward evening then, one becomes tired and lethargic without having worked or accomplished anything. Yes, it certainly is a strange life! When I have time, I often simply go into the woods, bring my work along, and enjoy there the calm of being out of danger. This is also what I did this afternoon, in order to prepare a talk for a local Coronella [a subgroup of the Corona Werner had joined in Leipzig] here tonight. The topic: interpretation of the *Chromatic Fantasy and Fugue* by Bach. My stay in the woods also was combined with sunbathing. By the way, today was a little bit better with the airplanes; but sometimes you think of the old saying of soldiers: "Dear God, let evening begin—morning will then follow on its own."

Love, stay well and prepare for the more difficult times. Make sure that there are provisions for food; and give my best to the children! Yours, Werner.

Werner's Diary, April 15 to May 3, 1945

Sunday, April 15
In the morning on duty with the People's Defense League at the rifle depot. All three companies are to watch the use of the antitank weapons. A

large sheet-metal sign, simulating the tank, is set up in a hollow. Of the three devices number one doesn't work at all, number two is shot too short, and so is the third that had been aimed from a short distance. Two new devices must be brought in, and two people are charged with fetching them from the depot. With some excuse I follow them, so that I know where the ammunition is stored. But the people have to drive into Hechingen. Meanwhile, I stand close to the NS [Nazi] notabilities: Weidle, Holzheuer, Kirner, and listen to their talk about the situation. Only Kirner still believes in new weapons, tells tales of the supposedly existing two thousand German jetfighter planes; Holzheuer replies: "Die Botschaft hör ich wohl" ["I can hear the message, yet I am lacking belief," from the first part of Goethe's *Faust*]. General impression: when needed, the People's Defense League is not going to do anything. After arrival of the two new devices, the first shot goes too far to the right, the last one, shot by Kirner after lengthy preparations, goes too far by a good thirty meters. Roaring laughter. On the way back C.F. [von Weizsäcker] and I take some blooming hawthorn branches home.—After the meal, sunbathing at the Säuweiherle to get away from the low-flying fighter planes. Battle noise from the direction of Horb and Freudenstadt. In the evening, the planned trip of the Weizsäckers to Radolf-zell falls through. Glare of fire at the horizon; Freudenstadt and Nagold are probably burning.

April 16

Immediately after my arrival in the institute low-flying planes attack a train at the station. Miss Pletz has not come in, call to Tailfingen where Miss Pletz fortunately had not yet left. Various walks to the Säuweiherle to study the battle lines. At noon there are soldiers at Fecker's [an inn or restaurant in Hechingen] coming from Wildbad; they were suddenly attacked, and their commander was killed; now they are trying to get to Ulm to reassemble. In the evening large retreat activities on every street. Vehement thunder of canons fired near Horb. Later that night lightning flashes all around but no detonations; we discover only gradually that this is a natural lightning storm. I work until midnight, then attempt, unsuccessfully, to call Urfeld over the lines of the air force. At 1 a.m. alarm from the institute, caused by a moot report from Sauerwein. I stay at the institute until 3 a.m., then I finally go to bed.

April 17

In the morning trip with Wirtz, Bopp and Fischer to Haigerloch, to determine the place for the U-metal. At the Seehof a division troop is staying, bound for the Alb during the night. In the distance smoke clouds of burning villages; at the horizon for the first time detonations of grenades. The defeated German artillery has passed through Haigerloch during the night and went on in the direction of Balingen. Horb is said to have been occupied in the morning. Haigerloch itself quiet, only low-flying planes. Return around noon; after the meal meeting at Laue's with Hahn, Götte, and Wirtz. Trip of C.F. to Reutlingen and Tübingen is necessary for twofold certification as indispensable; C.F. is to leave the next day. For 7 p.m. a complete staff meeting at the institute is scheduled. Much interruption from low-flying planes. At 5 p.m. Pahl comes up to me on the street: can you be my witness, I am marrying Miss Wolfram in half an hour. Wedding at the town hall from 5:30 p.m. to 6:30 p.m., accompanied by low-flying planes. 7 p.m. institute meeting: start of evacuation of the facilities, secrecy, I myself will be leaving. After 8 p.m. departure of the technical staff for Haigerloch, the uranium metal will be buried in the night. In the evening visit from Miss Reinbeck's father in my apartment, who most graciously brings me wine, cigarettes, and chocolate.

April 18

At early dawn a walk to the Pheasant Woods to get some flowering branches, stopped at Pahls' to congratulate them. Trip of C.F. to Tübingen and Reutlingen. The walks to the Säuweiherle let me see fighting near Rottenburg. Haigerloch, however, is not occupied yet. On my way back, I am at Wirtz's for a brief moment. Air raid by some fighter planes, which we endure in W.'s basement. Preparations for my departure, which I am scheduling for the next morning. Around 6 p.m. final visit at v. Laue's. Inquiries at the train station: stretch from Hechingen to Jungingen destroyed. So I will have to use the bicycle just to get to Jungingen even. 9 p.m. to 11 p.m. visit from Mrs. v. W. [Gundalena von Weizsäcker] and Wirtz; last conversations and planning, I am very tired, but finished with the preparations. The bicycle had a last checkup. By 11 p.m. C.F has not yet returned from Reutlingen; farewell to Wirtz and G. v. W., then to bed. Around midnight C.F. comes by and reports the successful result of his trip, thus I can leave reassured. 12:30 a.m. farewell to C.F., I sleep poorly and restlessly. The alarm goes off at 2:30 a.m.

April 19

Quick breakfast, departure by bicycle at 3:30 a.m. Streets pretty empty, clear, starry night, but very cold. 4:15 a.m. arrival in Jungingen, the train at the station ready to leave, the conductor urging to hurry up. Ticket to Hettingen. Since the sun is already up when we arrive in Gammertingen, I decide to get off there and not risk attacks by low-flying aircraft. From there bicycle ride across the Alb, many destroyed cars by the side of the road; some twenty-five kilometers to Riedlingen on the Danube, where I arrive around 8 a.m. Clear blue sky, east wind, which is somewhat bothersome on the bicycle. On in the direction of Biberach, before that a branch-off to Kleintissen. At a roadside crucifix, some kilometers before Kleintissen, breakfast in the warm sunshine, lovely view across fields and woods. Around 10 a.m. in Kleintissen. There I meet Erwin, who came home from Bitterfeld after an adventuresome six-day journey. His whole family is there too. Breakfast again, walk to Schmied about a vehicle, after lunch a long, deep sleep. Around 7 p.m. departure by bicycle to Aulendorf, nice stretch of road through the hills past Saulgau. Here I can see the mountains of Oberstdorf, finally. Arrival in Aulendorf at about 8:30 p.m. I want to take the train for a bit; but the train for Leutkirch-Memmingen doesn't leave until 12:40 a.m. Actual departure finally around 1:30 a.m. The train only goes a few kilometers, engine trouble. We get another engine—that one does not really work either. Only at around 6 a.m. in Waldsee, eight kilometers away from Aulendorf. So I decide to keep going by bicycle.

April 20

First a long and rather arduous trip by bicycle from Waldsee to Diepoldshofen; there a Frenchman points me to the Grosse Mühle, the residence of Miss Reinbeck and her mother. It is only 8:15 a.m., both have not yet had breakfast. I partake of a good breakfast and leave around 9:30

a.m. toward Leutkirch, where high party officials in cars cross my way. Shortly behind Leutkirch, there appear large convoys of American bomber planes accompanied by fighter planes up above. From a sheltered spot near a little chapel I watch the destruction of Memmingen. Huge plumes of smoke and waves of detonation; thus I am glad not to have gone via Memmingen. In Krugzell in the Iller Valley a decent meal in a diner, then a long nap under trees on a glacial hill, about nine kilometers north of Kempten. From there, one can see all of the Allgäu Alps, especially the mountains surrounding Sonthofen, where I had been in boot camp seven years ago with the mountain troops. 5 p.m. departure in the direction of Kaufbeuren. Cloudless skies all the time. Since I have been going for fifty kilometers already this day, I have trouble ascending from the Illertal. Around 8 p.m. arrival in Kaufbeuren, fight for a glass of tea in the overcrowded waiting room at the station, I am hungry and am now feeling the exertion of the last days. 10 p.m. the train leaves for Schongau, there pacing from 1 a.m. to 5 a.m. in the waiting room, filled with a horde of half-grown boys in SS uniforms, probably from the Balkans. I don't dare sleep, fearing for bicycle and luggage. At 5 a.m. departure of the train for Weilheim.

April 21

In Weilheim, we arrive at about 6:30 a.m. near the station, which had been destroyed a few days ago. There I wait next to our train for the connection to Garmisch. Several hundred people are with me on the tracks, when suddenly a low-flying aircraft comes by at twenty meters, everybody diving for cover! People roll down the embankment with baggage and kids. But it was only a German plane having fun. Since the sky is now covered with low-hanging clouds, I will risk the train trip till Ohlstadt. The mountains in Garmisch, only visible in the distance a day ago from Krugzell, now lie south immediately in front of us, but only the lower contours are recognizable. Around 9 a.m. we come to Ohlstadt at the foot of the Heimgarten Mountain. From there bicycle trip via Grossweil, Schlehdorf, through the moor to Kochel. In front of the wooden bridge in the moor, there are SS cars whose passengers are hiding weapons under mounds of hay and are eyeing me suspiciously. But they let me go on my way. I call Urfeld from the post office in Kochel to announce my arrival. There is yet the long ascent over the Kesselberg to manage, I am very tired. Finally, around 11:30 a.m., I am on top of the pass, the blue Walchensee lies below and behind it the Soiern Peak, half hidden in fog. Now this part of the battle is won, I am soon up at the house, Elisabeth and the children are well.—In the afternoon a bicycle trip to Sachenbach to get milk. The house has a few changes I will slowly have to get used to. The chickens on the lower floor bother me a little, though their usefulness makes sense to me in every way.

Sunday, April 22

After a long sleep a real day of rest. Elisabeth and Mrs. Linder have baked a cake, the children are playing out on the terrace in the sunshine, and thus we are celebrating the Sunday as if it were total peacetime. According to the news from the radio, it is possible that Hechingen is occupied by now, and apparently fighting has started around Ulm. There seem to be no low-flying aircraft in Urfeld. Below us, in the hotel Fischer-am See, are the headquarters for a regional elite training group. What a real NS hotbed Urfeld is. But secretly many are scheming where to escape to.

April 23

Morning flyover by bomber squadrons over Urfeld heading east. Work in the vegetable garden, the last beds are planted. Then by bicycle to Sachenbach to get milk. The ball bearings break, I will have to use the other bicycle from now on. Deliberations about further measures to weather the war; paramount: to manage getting food. Unfortunately, I am unable to get a telephone connection to Mittenwald to let Mama know of my arrival, due to the destruction of the telephone office in Weilheim. In the afternoon a crate of food is buried. Radio: fighting in Ulm, Regensburg. Berlin is surrounded, the Führer in Berlin.

April 24

Trip to Kochel. Shopping at Demharter, but fruitless negotiating for potatoes with Helmer [shopkeeper], who wants to engage me as an observer of aircraft traffic. Food rationing stamps for myself, return home for lunch. In Urfeld it turns out that overnight the garden was trampled by deer. So I continue working in the afternoon to get the garden back in order. Radio: traversing of the Danube in Dillingen; the Americans are near Augsburg.

April 25

Cleanup work in the house. Deliberations about living quarters for Mama, telephone conversation with Dr. Hermann and Miss Penzberger. Return of Waltraut from Garmisch.

April 26

Trip to Kochel, shopping for fabric and food. Everything still calm there. Rumors that the Americans have pushed past Augsburg to the area around Weilheim. Thus I have to get Mama as soon as possible from Mittenwald. Preparation of the room at Leonhardt's [a house owner in Urfeld].

April 27

Bicycle trip to Mittenwald. Many soldiers on the road near Krün; generals who are walking in the sunshine and who have apparently given up on the war. 11:30 a.m. in Mittenwald, I find Mama at a diner eating lunch. Mama's departure in Dr. Hermann's car around 3:30 p.m. The room turned out quite cozy and comfortable, so we are hoping that Mama will be feeling good there. I myself return to Urfeld around 5 p.m.

April 28

Trip to Kochel to buy powdered milk and food. I have to stand in line at Demharter for some time but get a whole backpack full of provisions. At Schermer too I am in line, there are huge amounts of cheese available. On my return, I learn that the Munich broadcast station has announced the "Bavarian Liberation Movement." Singer is ecstatic; but at noon the broadcast has ceased again. In the afternoon I get some firewood for Mama, splitting it and stacking it at Singer's. On my way to Sachenbach for milk I run into Colin Ross and his wife near the beach area. They are pushing a suitcase in a wheelbarrow; appear to be on their return from Sachenbach. I jump off and happily greet them: from now on we will probably see each other more often. Colin Ross replies that he is very happy that I have managed to get back to Urfeld after all. Otherwise, however, they both appear somewhat curt and quickly say good-bye. I did not think of the possibility that this might be our last meeting. Toward evening the Munich broadcast station announces that the Bavarian Liberation Movement was quashed. Gauleiter Giessler and Mayor Fiehler are talking on the radio of victorious endurance, and so on. . . . A telephone call to Miss Penzberger indicates that apparently Weilheim has been occupied by the Americans.

Sunday, April 29

The 29th was supposed to be our anniversary, and I had hoped for some peace and quiet to celebrate. But I have to go to Kochel to get provisions at Demharter; despite it being Sunday, the store is going to be open from 10 a.m. to 3 p.m. Once down there, I find out I will have to be in line till late afternoon. I am a bit unhappy about it, call Elisabeth on the phone. Later Elisabeth comes by bicycle with some food so we can take turns standing. Kochel is an anthill. Soldiers, SS, foreign laborers. In the train station a cargo train is standing with prisoners from Dachau who look terribly starved and pale. During the time that Elisabeth is standing in line at Demharter I go to the hill behind the station to lie down in the sunshine. From there I now can also detect the first grenade hits in our area, apparently in the stretch Murnau-Ohlstadt. Around noon Elisabeth and I are walking together through Kochel; suddenly First Lieutenant Schuster stands in front of me. He has stayed overnight in Schongau with the remainder of his troop, nearly witnessed the occupation, and is now with a car and driver in Kochel. He gets an invitation to Urfeld for the evening. Later I go once more to our hill to try to get a picture of the current battle and am assuming, based on the plumes of smoke, that the offensive is taking place in the valley along Weilheim, Garmisch, and Murnau.—

Elisabeth has learned, suddenly, that Colin Ross and his wife have shot themselves during the night. People are talking a lot about this; Colin Ross was popular, his action is considered decent. "The decent Nazis are taking the consequences, the scoundrels are left behind." Around 4:30 p.m. we get our purchases at Demharter, upon our return trip the old road up the Kesselberg is already blocked off, we have to push the bicycle up the long new road. When we arrive in Urfeld, around 6 p.m., we are asked by Brackenhofer's daughter to go immediately to the funeral of the Ross couple.

So we attend, as dressed, with lederhosen and backpack. The bodies are laid out in the living room in which we had visited occasionally with them; shrouded in tent cloth, only the faces uncovered. The face of Colin Ross looks very striking, yet calm and at peace. This face makes a rather profound impression on me, but generally speaking, this time is so fraught with tension and events that even death no longer moves me a whole lot. Elisabeth feels similarly. Soldiers carry the dead to their graves, dug a few meters above the house. Lieutenant Schneider reads a last letter by Colin Ross: "He did not want to survive the demise of Germany and the new idea. His wife, companion on so many hikes, also wanted to accompany him on this hike." For the last time we use the Hitler salute. Around 7 p.m. we arrive home, tired. After dinner, Schuster visits us. We decide that he should await the occupation together with us, and thus live with us for the time being.—According to the news, the advance is apparently coming along the line Murnau-Mittenwald-Innsbruck. It is therefore possible that we will be occupied from either the north or the south. Simultaneously, the ring around Berlin is closing more tightly, the Führer is going to disappear one of these days, besides it is rumored that Himmler has offered surrender to the western Allies. Now there is a race on between four scenarios that would be able to end the war for us. But what will this end look like in Urfeld?

April 30

Car trip with Schuster to Kochel. Unfortunately, no success either at Schermer or Demharter, I only get some meat at Pfleger. The train with the prisoners from Dachau is no longer in Kochel. In the town there are foreign SS people loitering, young fellows who seem to make ends meet by plundering. Organizing a resistance is not on their agenda either. Since Schuster's car is defective, we cannot go to Benediktbeuern, therefore no more bread. Around noon we are back in Urfeld. Preparation of the cellar, trip to Sachenbach. Soldiers have taken up residence in our hay barn to sleep or hide out. It is getting colder and beginning to snow.

On the trip to Sachenbach I see antitank weapons aimed at our road from the beach area. In Sachenbach too there are antitank cannons. Near evening, I climb with Schuster up to the huts below the summit of the

Herzogstand to find a place of refuge when things become serious. Up there, however, a complete unit of mountain troops is stationed. Battle line at 995 meters altitude, up above antitank cannons; in the hut below the Herzogstand cliff, which I had considered at first, there are soldiers cooking. All the huts are occupied, not usable for us. The other Urfeld inhabitants have long since fled to the other shore across the lake, but even there in Altlach SS are reportedly in place. Besides, the heavy snows would hardly allow us to cross the lake with our small children. When it clears up temporarily, we can see fire down in Grossweil and Schlehdorf. Suddenly the whole gravity of the situation hits me; resolution: ready the cellar and stay put.

On the road still a lot of car traffic. Miss Penzberger tells us on the phone that Kochel was under fire, Blessing's daughter a casualty. The American tanks had advanced to the bridge Schlehdorf-Kochel, but turned around there, since the bridge is destroyed. Mittenwald is occupied, so it is possible for the Americans to come from the south too.—As Schuster and I descended from the ridge to the house there was another very critical moment of danger: the commander of the mountain troops stops Schuster and me and asks what we were up to up there, did we want to investigate ways to cross to the enemy. Schuster is very clever in his reply; his identification papers suffice to legitimate him. During the night, still a lot of car traffic, this time from south to north. Sent away Schuster's car and driver.

May 1

Car traffic on the road almost ceasing now, Krün supposedly occupied. I place calls to Walchensee and Einsiedeln, but no tanks have shown up there yet. Bicycle trip to Sachenbach much more difficult due to the snow. Conversation there with the soldiers about the imminent end of the war. The convalescence unit in Urfeld is disbanded. The youth in the elite training school are burning their song books, Hitler pictures, and so on down below in the big meadow. All morning long we listen to the heavy detonations, bridges and roads are being destroyed. We have open windows, shutters closed.—Wolfgang is a little sick; he looks pale and scared and is brought to bed. Elisabeth thinks it is merely the turmoil of all the blasting and the sense of danger; he more than anybody is in tune with the emotional situation of the adults, even though they hide it well. In the early afternoon a call from Miss Penzberger in Pessenbach: "Now the tanks are rolling in, we can hear them in the street." Two hours later she reports that the tanks have gone through Pessenbach and have occupied Kochel. Apparently, only tanks and trucks. Black people are among them too, but we still do not know whether it is the French or the Americans. The German troops in Kochel are said to have surrendered, probably the SS has retreated to our region or into the Jachenau. The weather is turning worse and worse, you can make out only the immediate area around the house. Near evening Wolfgang has a high fever, is vomiting, pain in his right side. We are afraid it might be an acute appendicitis. There is no doctor left in Urfeld; Dr. Otto has fled to Altlach and the field hospital in the youth hostel has moved on. There is no alternative than to go to Walchensee. Since we cannot get through by telephone, I start out just by myself, despite the snowstorm, by bicycle. For a stretch of two hundred meters the road is blocked with blasting debris off of the mountain, I have to carry the bicycle across. The military doctor, a surgeon, advises that Wolfgang be brought in at once, no matter what. I return as fast as I can, it has now turned completely dark. Wolfgang is wrapped in blankets, placed in the hand buggy, Elisabeth and Schuster take him in the snowstorm to the barricade, carry him across, on the other side, he is picked up by the military ambulance car. In the meantime I go down to Mama to give her comfort. Schuster returns, strangely without the buggy. Around 11 p.m. I come back up, Mrs. Linder calls out to me from the door: Hitler is dead!—Just maybe now we will get around having a battle here in Urfeld.

—I cannot get a connection to Walchensee. Around midnight, calls from the street below. Elisabeth is returning with Wolfgang. The doctor does not think an operation is necessary, but wanted to keep Wolfgang there. This Elisabeth did not agree to, so they are both returning. Wolfgang is even feeling a little better. Finally, Schuster and I go once more to the barricade, a two-kilometer round trip, to fetch the buggy. Around 1 a.m. we conclude the day with hopes and fears for the next day. Since it is completely quiet, we forego the planned night watch.

May 2

Deep snow. The attempt to get to Sachenbach by bicycle fails. So I go on foot. At the hotel Jäger Am See I meet Brackenhofer in the bicycle repair workshop. He has hoisted the white flag and tells me with every indication of terror that during the night sixteen soldiers from the convalescence unit were stopped by the SS on their retreat and hanged. The SS were loitering in the woods near Sachenbach and Jachenau, he says. Thus I go on to Sachenbach with some mixed feelings. There I come upon soldiers, but the antitank weapons have moved on. The news of Hitler's death is new to them, but even to that the soldiers react with total indifference. The name von Dönitz [the admiral who took over the government after Hitler's suicide] was familiar only to some of them. The farmer's wife relates that the SS are in the woods and have plundered in the Jachenau and set houses on fire that had the white flag up. Nobody dares utter an opinion whether that was right or wrong. It appears that, deep down, everyone is hoping for a quick arrival of the Americans. Upon my return, I hear from Miss Penzberger that now several hundred Americans have arrived in Kochel. Still plenty of battle noise from the south. The fisherman Lexer comes to me and tells me I have to go for duty at the barricade by order of the local unit. Having negotiated surrender, they now have to clear the roadway. I cautiously decline, and chop firewood for Mama's room with Schuster. Around noon, gunfire on the way to Sachenbach; Schuster and I try to identify the shooters with binoculars; we have no idea what is going on. Mrs. Linder is in an elevated mood, "just like before Christmas." In the afternoon I go to Mama with Ria. While up in the house Elisabeth and Schuster are sitting in their armchairs in the dining area, there suddenly appear three armed men on the terrace who push open the door and come up to Schuster and Elisabeth with their automatic weapons drawn. Both at first think they must be SS, but the Americans at once ask for me. I am told by phone to come back up. Colonel Pash, the leader of the group, wants to speak to me alone. As we sit in the armchairs together, a wild shooting erupts outside. Colonel Pash jumps up, the automatic rifle on the ready, goes out to the terrace. I myself am still too caught up in the fact that now, finally, everything had come to pass that I had for many years expected, feared, and hoped. Thus I watch this little skirmish in total calm and in the best of moods. Only the rest of the household, especially the children, are quickly sent to the cellar. After about ten minutes of shooting with automatic rifles and guns, it turns silent. One major general reports to the colonel that one SS man is dead, two wounded and arrested, the rest had escaped. Then the talk with Pash continues: he is under orders to arrest me, but will continue to take care of the family and me in every possible way. The departure is scheduled for the next day or so, until then I can take care of the family and make preparations. We talk mostly about the difficult situation with food: we have not been able to buy bread in four days, the nearest place to get bread is twenty kilometers away, and some of the roads there are destroyed. Pash thinks the bridge across the gorge on the Kesselberg road will probably be repaired by the Americans overnight. He himself, in the interim, has been able to come only with ten men and on foot. The situation in Urfeld from a military point is now quite weird: in Urfeld there are ten Americans; five hundred meters above on the ridge on the Herzogstand there is a complete unit of German mountain troops that probably wants to surrender; in pockets in the woods, there are SS. Pash is negotiating with the commander of the unit, which is supposed to surrender its weapons at 10 a.m. the next morning. Until then, he too is hoping for reinforcements. My house is supposed to be highly guarded, at night nobody is allowed to leave it. That night we have a little celebration for peace with the last remnants of alcohol, we are in bed around 11 p.m. Everybody is in the best mood, especially Mrs. Linder, only Elisabeth is very tired. Wolfgang is doing slightly better, but the little guy still looks not well; he keeps asking me why I was again going to leave; didn't I promise that in peacetime I would always stay with him.—During the night I lie awake for a long time. Around 1 a.m. I hear steps near the house, do not know whether it is SS or Americans. Fortunately, we have Schuster's pistols nearby; I do not wake anybody up and eventually go back to sleep.

May 3

Around 4 a.m. another huge explosion. The children are crying; most likely the Americans have blasted another target. At 7 a.m. the American night watch comes in demanding breakfast: two eggs. Elisabeth is in despair, since for us this represents a fortune. Later Colonel Pash comes. He offers I could ride in an American military vehicle to Benediktbeuern. The bridge is repaired, and I could go buy bread. Meanwhile, trucks and small tanks have arrived in Urfeld, the military situation is now clear. Pash mentions that the SS had been in Urfeld during the night; the unit from the Herzogstand had not appeared at the weapons handover, had apparently been prohibited by the SS from doing so. Pash thinks he has so much in troops and material in Urfeld now that nothing could go wrong anymore. Trip to Benediktbeuern, result: twenty pounds of bread, fifteen pounds of flour, one pound of butter, seven pounds of cheese. The whole region full of tanks, trucks, troops. The huge advantage in resources is in plain view for everyone. On the return trip Pash gives me another crate of provisions for Elisabeth. In addition, we receive a protection order for the house and a weapons permit for Schuster. Waltraut goes on foot to Sachenbach for milk; upon her return she relates that in Sachenbach there are still German troops and SS. I reproach myself in retrospect for exposing her to danger.—The weather is gradually improving; it is clearing up, but stays very cold. Final visit at Mama's, around 4 p.m. departure for Heidelberg. The trek creates quite a stir in Urfeld: a tank in front, then two military vehicles with automatic rifles. Dinner in Augsburg; for the first time in many months I am so full that I wouldn't want to eat more. Around 2:30 a.m. we arrive in Heidelberg, completely stiff from the cold. I take a warm bath and then rapidly fall asleep.

Werner to Elisabeth

Heidelberg, May 4
My dear Li,

Today just these few short lines, which I hope I can pass to an American officer. Yesterday we drove here, a car ride incredibly beautiful in terms of the landscape but very cold in the open vehicle. At about 3 in the morning we arrived. In my feelings, the calamity of the past and the view of the endless destruction are intermingled with the intense happiness about being able to start anew and to rebuild. For our little circle too life is beginning anew.— From the outside I am doing extremely well, I am staying in the nicest room in the fanciest villa in Heidelberg, a view of the Neckar and the castle, am getting plenty to eat and am being treated very nicely; albeit as a captive, for I am not allowed to go out. But that is alright, is obvious in light of the situation. There is talk that I may be off to America, perhaps San Francisco (that is what Diebner, who is also here, heard). In that case, I will try to take you along. I for my part am feeling that for the first time in twelve years I can do something for Germany and am so fresh and alive as I have not been in years. May fate grant me that I am up to my task.—Stay safe, I will soon come, I think, to visit you and to discuss all this. I am sending along the food stamps, since I do not need them here. A thousand greetings!

Yours, Werner.

Werner to Elisabeth

Heidelberg, May 7
My dear Li,

I am writing to you on the typewriter so that the censor can read the letter more easily. As of today, I know a little more about the plans for the future. First something sad: it will take a little longer until I can return. Prof. Goudsmith, who is here, assumes it could be eight days or equally four weeks. Most likely I will be brought for a short while to the Paris area. But, otherwise, all the prospects for the future are positive. The wishes of the committee here with respect to our scientific work later on largely overlap with my own. We talked about the issue whether or not I should go to America, but concluded that one ought to try anew here. Whether in Berlin or in Hechingen would need exploration, it also depends on how much of the Berlin institute remains standing and on whether Debye wants to return, which Goudsmith deems possible, strangely enough. At any rate, I now have the distinct hope that already this summer we will move together into our eventual place, and since everybody is helping, I think we will settle in nicely.

My main worry for these coming weeks is whether you in Urfeld will go hungry. It may be best if Schuster discusses the difficulties that arise with the officer in charge. The issue is, primarily, the bread transports from Lugauer and delivery of butter and milk from Schermer, which are hampered by the destruction of the bridge in Schlehdorf. The American agencies themselves have the utmost interest in getting these things back to order, and besides, the Urfeld population will be just as happy too. I am going to ask the officer who will kindly deliver this letter to you to inquire after your concerns and if possible be of help. In light of the great kindness we have been shown here, I have no doubt that help will be given whenever feasible.

The conversations with Goudsmith and Kemble were so amicable, as if the last six years had not happened, and I myself am doing so well within and without, better than in many years. I am filled with hope and an enterprising spirit for the future. Naturally, there will be some setbacks, but that must not deter us.

So, love, during this year already we will actually start from scratch; whether there will be a house with a garden full of roses right away I do not know, but it will be better than before. So do not be too sad if I am gone a little longer still, the worst is now behind us.

To you and the children all my best, yours, Werner.

Why don't you hand the officer a few lines for me?

Werner to Elisabeth

[Farm Hall, July 12]
My dear Li!

The external circumstances of our lives have, after a much less pleasant interim, changed back into the most pleasant forms, and if it were not for the separation from you and the worries about you, I could not imagine a better existence. We, that is, the eight most important members of our work group, are staying in a little castle. A section of the park is accessible to us, and so we are for large amounts of time amid the most glorious early summer. From the festive dining room one steps out onto a terrace, below which begins a scruffy lawn with ornamental bushes, not trimmed for ages. To the right corner a gorgeous climbing rose reaches up to the balcony, the blossoms all large and filled, much more beautiful than at the corner of the Bozener Weg, and of the finest fragrance I have known in roses. On the first floor I have a room of my own with a ceiling-height window, of which the lower portion is protected by an artfully crafted iron grid, so that it might be almost a kind of balcony. Here I can work by myself and sleep. Our circle is guided and guarded by an unusually nice British major, with whom we take the meals in the dining hall. This way we are also getting the officers' rations, which in every respect are equal to the fare on a large Atlantic steamer. You see that it hardly could be any better physically, and the temporary loss of freedom is no bother either, after having gotten used to that during the last years. The most important remaining wish is that negotiations and deliberations should begin more quickly. Apparently, for now, we are to be safeguarded, and even if in the interim a report on the first consultations has reached America, it will take some time until it results in decisions about our future activity.

Farm Hall manor in England, where Werner and other German nuclear physicists were interned after the war

If I knew that you all are well, and that you can make it without my labor in Urfeld, I would not be too anxious about my time of waiting here. But this way the waiting is harder. We must console ourselves that the coming weeks will be decisive for the whole future life of our family, that we are now beginning anew, but with much bigger hopes than before. We just must have patience in this. I hope to receive also some news from you soon. Greetings to Mama and the children, and stay healthy and brave. Yours, Werner.

Werner to Elisabeth

[Farm Hall], August [6]
My dear Li!

After a long time we are, finally, allowed to write home again. But I do hope that you were informed occasionally by the American officers that I am well, and that my silence does not mean anything bad. If there were not the separation from you all, I would be doing quite excellently here. The fact that we are completely sealed off from the world at large does not bother me, and I am using the time for scientific work as well as exercising a lot. So you need not worry about me in the least. Even though nothing can be said about the date of my return, I am still optimistic on all counts regarding plans for the future.

The only thing really weighing on me a lot is the worry about you all. I have a very bad conscience that I am not with you in this most awful time, but I really cannot change that. So I am asking you to write to me, in great detail, what the conditions are like for you, if you have food, if you have help for the work, where Mama is living, and if you are healthy. So far I have only received a letter from May 17 from you. The officer who will bring you this letter will also send back your answer, and since it is possible that he himself will come here again, it would be good if you gave him a verbal account of what the conditions in Urfeld are like.

Greetings to Mama and the children, especially to little Martin, whose birthday is tomorrow. I hope the separation will not last too much longer now. All the best! Yours, Werner.

Elisabeth to Werner

[Urfeld], August 20

My dear Werner!

How glad I am to hear from you again, finally! Since May 7 I have not
had any news from you. Here a lot of sad things have happened in the
meantime. These have been difficult months. Brace your heart for what I am
about to write to you.

At the end of June, Mama fell in her room. I had the impression that it
was a minor stroke. She complained about pain in her leg. We took her up
to us and nursed her day and night. But it was impossible. Her mind went
downhill more and more. Someone needed to be there all the time, or else
the worst things happened. Then she started to scream, so that I needed to
take her to the hospital in Schlehdorf. There they found out that she had
fractured her femur. They put her in a brace bandage—against my objec-
tion, for I did not want to torture her further. So I decided to take her to
Tölz. I contacted Professor Lange for consultation, who advised to bring her
to the evacuated [from Munich] Schwabing Hospital in Tölz. There would be
an excellent doctor. I managed to find a single room for her there. But eight
days later, the doctor told me he could no longer keep her there; she needed
to be transferred to Munich to an insane asylum. Fortunately, I met Wolf
Jaeger in Tölz, who advised me to get a second opinion from a psychiatrist in
Tegernsee. That took a few days. When I next came to Tölz, pneumonia had
set in, and she was close to death. She died that same day, July 17, in the
afternoon at 2:30. I was there. But she never regained consciousness. Any
transfer to Munich was impossible; therefore we buried her in the Waldfried-
hof there. Wolf Jaeger and friends played a Beethoven string quartet. And I
had come by bicycle to Tölz with all our roses and the twins. I am glad that
she was spared the worst, a transfer to Munich. But I wish I could spare you
and say she did not suffer, not so much physically—everything possible was
done in that respect—but mentally. Her illness took about three weeks.

That was the first severe blow. On the day Mama died, I brought Maria
Linder to the hospital. She had a case of tonsillitis and a strange stiffness in
the back of her neck that nobody could make sense of. Eight days later I saw

her again and was devastated by her condition. She had tetanus. Diagnosed too late. She was brought to Tegernsee and died there five days ago. Father Exner [hospital chaplain?] was there. He is the one who told me. But I could not get there. In her delirious state she had always talked of me and Stoffer. That makes it the more painful that I could not be there.—I have not told the children, because Stoffer should first forget his mother a little.

Now on to something lighter. The children all are healthy and I am too. Herr Schuster moved, after Mama's death, into her room, and has pretty much ignored us. Overall, he has been quite a failure. But we continue to live on in friendship. Today he wants to leave Urfeld and go to Sonthofen. Thus, for too many weeks already, everything now has been resting on my shoulders. Fortunately, on August 15—Maria's death date—Fritz showed up. He introduced me to the commandant in Walchensee. This may open a way to get some vegetables. Otherwise, the provisions for winter are pretty poor, naturally. We have not begun to preserve anything and are still using previous provisions against the hunger. But I am counting on getting something extra now. The deer have again pretty much destroyed our garden, so that it is not much use to us.

We still have enough here to live for seven or eight months. What will happen then? Are you coming back by then? I could not find out anything about the fate of our Hechingen belongings. My parents are doing relatively well. It would be good if you came before the winter. But we will get through it, as is; Waltraut is faithful, more attached and indefatigable than ever. The children all are very healthy, even without enough vegetables. I have become very thin. But I am now calmer and look toward the immediate future with more confidence again.

Now be well. It would be nice if some news came through again. But that is not in your own hands.

With warm greetings, yours, Li.

Elisabeth to Werner

Frankfurt, November 14
Dear Werner!

I am sitting in Frankfurt with Hilde Pape, hoping that Professor H. P. Robertson will forward this letter to you, and to find out what they are planning for you and us. Winter is here, and we are waiting almost day by day for you. We have neither fruit nor vegetables for the winter. Wood too is scarce, since we had to cut it ourselves. The supplies are used up. The only bright spot is a very appealing young woman, Marlene, who is with us to take over the household. . . .

From here I want to go to Überlingen to see my parents. Papa must be quite weakened. Then I want to go to Hechingen. There I will probably encounter difficulties, which I may not resolve to your satisfaction. Firstly, I am asking for your authorization for the Hechingen bank account. If I do not get any money there, and have no success here in Frankfurt either, I only have the means for two, at most three months of living expenses. I have sent the twins away, due to schooling and also due to better eating opportunities, not, as first planned, to Edith, but a children's home near Weilheim, Oberhausen. It is very nice, there is an engaging teacher, naturally they are a little homesick, but on the whole they are cheerful. I visited them the other day and was really pleased how nicely they have come along in these few weeks. At least there they are now also getting fruit and vegetables. It is not cheap, however, almost 300 marks for both, then the pay for the helpers at home; this already comes to a firm expenditure of 500 marks every month without food and the other expenses, etc. I do need almost 1,000 marks a month, and have only 2,000 marks in the account in Kochel. Maybe I will have some success here as well as in Hechingen. . . .

Something else: you have a chair offer from Heidelberg and an unofficial one as Sommerfeld's successor—how to proceed with that?

You! Be well! . . . Stay healthy! Yours, Li.

Elisabeth to Werner

Frankfurt, November 15
Dear Werner!

Only last night I wrote you a letter full of worries and distress and tonight everything is resolved. You cannot imagine how uncannily my luck turned for the better. At the end of October, Professor Zwicki came by, and he fully understood my concerns: the uncertainty about you and the terribly difficult circumstances. Zwicki advised me to go to Frankfurt and speak to Professor Robertson. So I set out with many blessings on November 11. Waltraut and her mother are with the children. Newly added is a truly lovely young woman, Marlene, an acquaintance of Wolf Jaeger, who was prompted by the most unusual circumstances to come to us and deal with the household. She is a treasure of a person with whom I get along exceptionally well, who has life experience and energy.—

Now I first traveled to Munich, stayed with the Sommerfelds, who spoiled me most kindly. There I also met Mrs. Gerlach, who was rather overworked but unbelievably nice. The preparations for the trip went splendidly, so that I arrived here the night before last. After many dead ends, I finally found lodging at Professor Madlung's house, whose daughter was generous enough to turn her bed over to me. The next morning I started out and, helped by a secretary from the headquarters, whom I knew from Urfeld, I easily found the way to Professor Robertson, who immediately turned all his attention to my concerns. But today fortune was even more generous with me. Professor Robertson, attempting to do something for me, ran into Officer—his name is not clear to me yet—who had just arrived to take care of me. He told me that you are well, and that soon some decisions will be made, that we will receive food and money and can remain in Urfeld. Love—this is more than I could have dreamed. And even now all this still seems like a dream. He also made it possible for me to travel to my parents and to Hechingen, spoiling me in every other way possible. The day after tomorrow, I will go on to my parents and stay a few days. Next I will try to take care of some things in Hechingen and see what can be done for my parents. And then home I go. There your letter will await me—what joy!

The twins have been in a very nice children's home near Weilheim since October 1. They are well taken care of there and are relatively happy. . . . While writing this, it becomes clearer to me that I will keep them with me after Christmas. A teacher will be found, I am certain!—The other children are well and give me no trouble. Jochen also needs to go to school. It is quite urgent!

As far as Stoffer is concerned, I do have word from the Jacobis. Their circumstances are marginal. The news of Maria's death has deeply shaken them, and as soon as they have permission, they want to come across the border [from the Soviet sector] to pick him up and adopt him. I am glad for the dear little fellow, just afraid that he will suffer hunger over there.

Little Tini [Christine] has grown a lot and runs swiftly like a weasel.—I also think that with the cigarettes from the good officer today, we can get enough wood cut, so that we can heat at least two rooms.

Everything is so much, much easier now that we have fewer deficits all around. I could never get any helping hand here because the saying went: "One cannot work for the Heisenbergs because they live only off the rations"!

Now farewell! Perhaps the separation will indeed not last all that much longer now! How lovely that would be!

Yours, Li.

1946

THE FAMILY'S *separation is nearing an end. At the beginning of the year, Werner is released from internment and moved to the British occupation zone, at first to the little town of Alswede near Osnabrück and then to Göttingen, which was essentially spared bombing. In the buildings of the Aerodynamic Testing Institute (AVA) the scientists, in the opinion of the Allies, should find a suitable temporary space to begin working again. The couple's reunion takes place at the end of January in Alswede. Elisabeth must undertake the complications of travel because Werner is not yet allowed to leave the British occupation zone.*

The family's new beginning turns out to be more difficult than expected. Life in three different occupational zones—Göttingen in the British, Urfeld in the American, and Hechingen in the French—carries with it unexpected complications and delays. Communication between the couple is difficult: letters get lost or take many days in transit, and telephone connections are not functioning yet. Added to these troubles are the dire nutritional situation and the uncertainty where in Göttingen the family might be housed; additional problems arise over how to manage a move from Hechingen and Urfeld, and what to do about the house in Urfeld. But eventually, in mid-January, the situation is resolved: the French release the Hechingen institute, with its inventory, for transport; a house in Göttingen is ready to receive the family; and a renter for the Urfeld house is found. Now, finally, the family can move to Göttingen and start a new life together.

Werner to Elisabeth

Alswede, near Minden, January 3
My dear Li!

This is the first evening back in Germany since the end of the war. Whether and when this letter will get on its way, I don't know yet, but I do want to chat with you right away. It was a beautiful flight from England over here, clouds and blue sky in succession, the sea below us with little waves, much like in a calm voyage. Now I may perhaps, finally, be permitted to tell you where I have been and where I am now. We got around quite a bit in Europe. First from Heidelberg to Versailles, then we stayed for a few weeks in a small suburb of Paris, even saw the city occasionally; in early June we arrived at a manor in Belgium near Liège, and finally, in early July—by plane—to England, where we stayed in a little village near Cambridge at a small country estate. That is where we remained these last six months, completely closed off from the world outside. I saw just a few colleagues and friends: Blackett, above all, has attended to us. Twice I saw Fritz, as recently as last night at a meeting of the Royal Institution in London. . . . Aside from these few exceptions we were prisoners; we were treated decently, were cared for excellently in material terms, it is true, but the fact that we were told nothing about our future fate and that of our families—the secrecy in this seemed to us totally absurd—made our life actually quite difficult.

This long time of captivity seemed bearable only through the scientific work, which we did partly together, partly each on our own, about anything that came to mind. Books were graciously supplied. What it will be like here, we do not know yet. It looks as if we will be much freer. But one has to wait and see. The purpose of our stay is the following: the highest ranks have determined that all of us should have our future workplaces in the British occupation zone; why, we do not know. Perhaps because it is easiest here to have our work supervised for the long term. We have been told by many sources that the conditions in the British zone are the most favorable. Thus we have no reason to be dissatisfied. But no matter: we are now supposed to find the future location for our institute here. I get the impression that we will eventually either be brought to Hamburg or to Göttingen. Both of these locations have many positive aspects. The British will be providing for the institute and living spaces. So the next weeks will be spent making plans and arriving at agreements. Once we are a little clearer, Blackett will come here and discuss the situation with us. Before then, a very nice British chemist is taking care of us. So I cannot say anything yet about the positions in Heidelberg and Munich; as far as I can tell, I will not be allowed to take them—which is bitter as far as Munich goes, for one because of Urfeld and because of Sommerfeld. But this decision seems to be forged by the mightiest gentlemen in this world, so it will therefore not be easily changed. Besides, both in Hamburg and in Göttingen, I can imagine quite a pleasant life.

Whether I can come to Urfeld before the eventual move, sort of on a vacation, I do not know yet. It would probably be easier for you to visit me here than the other way around. But that too will only be decided in a few days. I am hoping that beginning next week, something will really start to happen with regard to our future. . . .

We are staying in a small storefront house in the village of Alswede near Minden. From my south-facing room the view extends over some five kilometers of solidly frozen farmland and behind it to the hilly range of the Weser-Bergland. I am pleased to see mountains again, finally. Any excursions further afar, however, are already canceled out by the cold; we only have summer suits and summer coats with us.

Sunday night

In the interim I have had a conference with two men of the science advisory board at the British Headquarters. Next week the first trip to Göttingen is scheduled; then we will see about institute and living spaces. Harteck is going back to Hamburg in a few days; he can explore the conditions in Hamburg. We are now permitted to run around totally free and write letters to our heart's content. You too can now write me via standard mail at my address: Alswede at Lübbeke, Minden County, Westphalia, c/o Albersmaier. If my stay here lasts much longer, then you could come visit me someday; but for now there is hope that it will progress more quickly, so that I can come to you all in the not too distant future. At any rate, I will keep you posted. I am curious as to when I will get your first letters here. . . .

So now I want to send this letter off as a first dove, who will return, I hope, with an olive branch. . . . Here is hoping for a reunion soon! Greetings to the children! Yours, Werner.

Werner to Elisabeth

Alswede, January 9
My dear Li!

Since my first letter from here not too much else has happened; but I want to use my writing to you as an opportunity to be with you again for a short hour with my every thought. Today we had another, rather long, negotiation with one of the British officers, who is a physicist and also in charge of setting our relocation in motion. Once you get to the practical issues and realities, only then do you see the incredible difficulties that need resolving before we can again live together reasonably and do work. On Saturday, Hahn and I will drive to Göttingen to investigate the possibilities there. My sense right now, however, is that we might eventually end up in Hamburg; for I do not see how we can obtain living space in Göttingen, whereas in Hamburg, with its greater supply, it is possibly easier. Also there still need to be negotiations with the French as to whether they will let the institutes leave Hechingen. The strangest thing is that the Americans do not want to let us into the American zone; and this order comes from the highest ranks. The only reason I can come up with so far is that there they do not have enough control—the Americans have left behind very few troops—, and the main concern of the political entities seems to be that we should not be suddenly abducted by the Russians; of course, I would not be the least bit interested in that myself, but one is astonished that the Americans, apparently, do not believe they are safe from the Russians in their own sector. Eventually, for the move, the Americans will undoubtedly have to allow me into Hechingen and Urfeld once. The transport will, of course, be an incredible task once again. But we are coming from England, healthy and well nourished, and are full of energy for the reconstruction of the institute. If on top of that I get letters from you—and this is my great hope as of next week—then the occasional emotional setbacks will be surmounted more quickly too.—Since you have probably been asked often whether I am connected with the "atomic bomb," I am sending along a copy of a section of a letter of v. Weizsäcker to his wife that describes this problem exactly right. I know many of the British and American colleagues who have worked on it, some of them are my pupils, and they have my sympathy, because their names are now tied to this atrocity. That the physicists did not want this use of their knowledge goes completely without saying, and there may be, behind the scenes of American politics, some complications on account of it. But this has now happened already; and perhaps when people have calmed down a little again, then this new threat awakens the sense of community of all people in such a dangerous world.

—If you still have pictures of the children, why don't you send a few along; and do tell me lots about them, of Christmas and of school. Give them my heartfelt greetings!

Yours, Werner.

C. F. von Weizsäcker to his wife, Farm Hall, August 1945

P.S.

You have probably often been asked about our supposed work on the atomic bomb. You do know what I have thought about these questions in general, but you will not mind if I tell you, in particular, something about the main points.

As far as our work during the war is concerned: we were spared the difficult moral decision whether we should build an atomic bomb. The technical and organizational means available to us in Germany would not have permitted at all the effort America had to put forth in regard to the problem. We confined ourselves to the preliminary work on the lesser effort of building a machine capable of producing heat, along the same paths that America apparently used as well in its pursuit. At the end of the war, we were close to a success. Thus we have done everything in our power to secure for our country a share of an inevitable technical development.

Elisabeth to Werner

[Urfeld, January]
My love,

Initially this morning I held your letter in my hands for a long time before comprehending that it was really from you—my dear heart! And this evening it's the same thing: somehow I cannot yet grasp that I can write to you to my heart's delight after this long, long period. Most of all, I would love to come right to you, but a few circumstances are preventing me. First, Waltraut is on leave right now, so that Marlene and I are alone. Although Marlene says, and I believe it, seeing how capable she is, I could really go, she would manage by herself; but for other reasons, it also might not be all that feasible, because I am not quite well enough health-wise, am terribly thin, even with the best care from Marlene am not getting any fatter, have a cold all the time, and lots of little ailments that could use a proper time to get cured. So I better not undergo any extra stressors unless they are necessary. And if you were coming very soon after all, we would possibly drive by each other—that would be bad luck! We are now leaving the light on in front of the house every evening, because the radio reported a few days ago that Hahn is released to Germany. "Just you wait, your husband will come via the mail bus," Marlene always says, and so we light the little lamp between 7:30 and 8 every night. Marlene is an absolute gem. There is not another one like her in terms of niceness and capability. I thank God every day that M. is here. She said to me the other day: "I have a really peculiar relationship to your husband. For one, I can imagine him so well, and second, I always have the feeling that I am accountable to him for your welfare." Isn't that nice? . . . All the children are here. Woi is visibly gaining weight on account of our food nowadays and he is practically going crazy with his pugnacious energy and exuberance. In good weather he is outside on skis for hours, and then when he comes in, he sits down at the piano practicing Clementi sonatas—or rather the first one—or he fights. We have very structured days with firm music and practice sessions. . . . We all are getting great enjoyment from it, and it is only possible due to Marlene's capability.—Ria has become a regular big daughter. She is in the process of knitting herself some socks with great enthusiasm.

Wolfgang and Jochen skiing

She sings and plays the piano and loves it. Jochen is totally delighted with school. The teacher who is teaching our three and Helga Strauss [the daughter of the owner of the hotel Fischer am See] is quite thrilled with him; she is drawing with them a lot, and Jochen seems to do that best of all. Nüsslein is not quite well. He has a persistent low-grade fever. And he has been in bed for some time now. . . . The little girls are mostly back to normal after sick time during Christmas. Barbara, the worrisome child, with a kidney infection, and Tinchen with bronchitis. But by now it is on the mend. Tinchen has become a big little girl already, very clear in what she wants, and quite energetic, sweet, and happy, when she has slept enough. Otherwise, however, she can act immensely serious and reproachful, so that one always has to stifle one's laughter.

Love, can't you come soon? How wonderful that would be! Unbelievable. We left the Christmas tree up until the 12th, always thinking deep down that you might come yet and see it. . . . Now I must end for today. How wonderful that not everything has to be crammed into this letter. Be well, my heart! Come soon! Yours, Li.

Werner to Elisabeth

Alswede, January 14
My dear Li!
A few letters of mine should have reached you, I think, since the time we came back to Germany. Now that one of the fellows who previously was looking after us in captivity is traveling to Bavaria, I want to send him to Urfeld—his name is Scholz—he can also bring your answer back here. Take care of him a little, that is, give him something to eat or someplace overnight, if he needs it. Unfortunately, I cannot send along any packages, since he cannot carry much. I have here a whole suitcase of children's things that Fritz gave to me in London; in addition some treasures like tea, coffee, and cocoa. Maybe you could visit me here sometime and take the things—; otherwise it will have to wait till I come to Urfeld, which will probably still be some time off. I know that travel is now very difficult and so I do not want to impose on you anything that is not absolutely necessary. In any case, here we would be at liberty to receive visitors—, and that I would love to see you again, I do not have to go into; but why don't you write first what you think about this possibility.

I just spent three days in Göttingen together with an unusually nice British officer and have deliberated on the future of my institute. There are many indications that we all will come to Göttingen not too far down the line. They have huge empty institute rooms there, so that the external givens are not bad. Difficulty: proximity of the Russians and lack of housing. . . . Before this plan gets activated, however, some more time will pass; for the decisions about us appear to be actually made by

Mr. Truman himself. Atomic physicists are regarded as very suspicious people. . . .

Overall, I am very optimistic after my visit to Göttingen, in spite of all the difficulties still ahead. Sadly, Walter Weigmann appears to have been let go from the university due to party membership; I did not learn anything else about him. I also do not know where he is now staying and living. Almost nothing in Göttingen is destroyed. That too would be, particularly with regard to the children, a big plus for Göttingen.

If you see Sommerfeld, then please tell him the following: the Americans have at this time given orders that we should be in the British zone; a reconstruction of the University of Munich does not seem to get much support at all. I learned from Jensen that Sommerfeld's professorship would be offered to Mr. Ganz as acting substitute, for now; I think that is a rather good plan, since definitely for now—that is, in the next few years, I will not be allowed to go to Munich. . . .

So I now have to end, because I have to hand the letter over. I am so happy in anticipation of an answer from you; maybe the mail will bring something in the next few days already. Many greetings to the children, also to Waltraut and the others in Urfeld! Yours, Werner.

Elisabeth to Werner

[Urfeld, January 18?]
My love!
Now I will always use the half hour in the morning to write to you while I have to wait from 7:30 to 8 o'clock until the room next door is free for me to get dressed. Slowly I comprehend, even when I am not outright thinking of it, that you are near. And a great warm joy is in me. Slowly too the thoughts begin to create some kind of image of the future. Göttingen would be my favorite. You know that I have always had a fondness for Göttingen. . . . But Hamburg also is nice, as long as one does not have to live in the ruins. Göttingen would be nicer, where you do not always have this hopeless misery in front of your eyes. That may, ultimately, be the most difficult part these days: the horrible, gruesome misery everywhere washing over you.

I wonder whether you had any choice at all. From Leipzig I got mail (Jacobi) saying you had a choice and that you all had decided in favor of Germany. Jacobi wrote this already at the end of December. But rumors existed like sand at the beach. For a long time I assumed you were in America. Somehow—I now realize this—I must have hoped that over in the more fortunate America, we could avoid this encroaching misery here. And yet I am content to stay here in Germany. And someday our children may well decide for themselves if they want to get out or not. By the time they are grown up, this hatred and disgust vis-à-vis the Germans might have subsided somewhat.

Over in the living room, Woi is practicing piano. He is doing quite well. Our daily routine is very firmly organized. From 8 to 8:30 Ria and Woi practice, alternating every two days. Then breakfast at 8:30 sharp. At 9 o'clock the three older ones have to be in school, i.e., at the Strausses', who have a very nice teacher. Then the children come home at around 12 noon. At 12:30 is mealtime. If the weather is good, the older ones go skiing, if it is bad, they are allowed to read in bed. If they have homework, which is quite rare, they have to do it from 3 to 3:30. At 3:30 begin the music lessons: twice a week singing for all four, twice recorder for Jochen, twice recorder for Woi. Then we have coffee time until 5 o'clock, after which there is one hour of piano lessons for whoever did not have practice that morning. Such one day follows the other, and I am happy if nothing interferes, so that everything can be strictly adhered to. We do have unbelievably nice days right now. And the nights in moonshine are even nicer. I am concerned that you have no warm coat!— . . . Be well, love! If only you could come soon! Yours, Li.

Werner to Elisabeth

Alswede, January 20
My dear Li!
This morning Hahn and I went on a long excursion with Major Blount from here to the crest of the Weser Mountains and back. Of course, there was lengthy talk about our plans for the future. The general plan is as follows: first the politicians in Washington have to decide that we go to

Göttingen, and the French have to agree to release the institute from there. All this is supposed to happen in the next weeks, but of course takes much longer than one would like. Then we would likely relocate to Göttingen very soon, would oversee the refurbishing of the (probably not too ample) living space, and then the move of the families could ensue. It does not look as if we would get permission to go to, say, Hechingen or Bavaria, before the move or during. Somehow, technically, the move for the families will be facilitated, but the execution would rest with the women. Only men from Hechingen can be utilized for the work, in particular our own mechanics. We can confer by letter about the details; also you could come visit me anytime, but nowadays one will travel—especially if it is as cold as right now—only if it is unavoidably necessary; so let us wait and see first how it develops.

During the last week we have had many visitors here and thus learned a few things about Germany. We had to fill out questionnaires that resembled to a T those of the Third Reich—except for the premise. I was reminded of the stupid joke of many years ago that posited that the questionnaires of the Fourth Reich would contain the question: Have you ever been in a concentration camp? If not, why not? The first question is actually in the questionnaire, just slightly different; only the second one is omitted. Among the more problematic joys here we count the visiting colleagues who have very actively, and some of them plain awfully, participated in the NS ideology and who are now seeking our friendship. But all of this is not essential.

Overall, I am doing fine here because I have the feeling I am working toward the future, not just for that of our small circle but for that of our extended cultural community. I would be glad if in the future that extended cultural community were not only called Germany, but Europe; however, unfortunately, politics do not always run the course one would wish. Weizsäcker and I have written a few papers on hydrodynamics, a field that I have never dealt with earlier, except for my dissertation. I believe that these papers turned out quite well. Of course, for the time being one can't publish anything in Germany, but that will soon change.

Greetings to the children, Waltraut too, and all the other housemates! Yours, Werner.

Elisabeth to Werner

[Urfeld, January 23]
My dear,

Do you know what day it is today? We have known each other for nine years today. And how long have we lived together? It must be barely half of the time. But I am full of hope now that soon it will change. Waiting is now getting hard for me. With each incoming mail, I expect news from you, and evenings, when the mail bus arrives, I think you might be on it. We turn on the light at the front door, and I go out to listen if perhaps you are whistling. My God, how different the world and life appeared when we met. Surely one must forget that kind of bourgeois life altogether. The new life will surely be much more primitive and proletarian; somehow one must attempt to live daily with a purpose, create a lifestyle similar to your youth movement and to the one we have here in Urfeld. I assume we will keep this lifestyle here in Urfeld, be it voluntary or by necessity, however you want to look at it. But I am content, have accepted it, and thank God every day that we still have it so good. If only there will not be another war. There is so much talk about it. Generally speaking, humanity is so overly endowed with horrific aspects that I get gripped with a fear, the kind of which I only had when the enemy planes came, or much worse even—not for myself but the children who are flourishing all around me, and you do not know into what kind of life. I need you a lot, love. I keep thinking that you men, as well as those of other nations, like Blackett, Bohr, and so forth, you ought to find ways and means to prevent these catastrophes of mankind.

But what is happening in the east is so monstrous that there too revenge will once again be coming back to strike the innocent. Maybe all this is weighing on you anyhow, and it is not right for me to add my darkest thoughts. I really believe that only faith in God can help in these times. Good for those who have it. I have a bit of it, and it protects me. For you cannot actually count on human reason and understanding. Up to now, I had thought that only here people were incapable of reasonable thought, honesty, and humanity. But it is no different in the rest of the world. And it must not ever have been different.

Here in Urfeld, the only nice human is Mr. Gatz. And when I am totally downcast and hunger for male conversation, I invite the Gatzes up, and I immediately feel much better. He is currently studying your essays and said you definitely ought to study Thomas Aquinas sometime. He deems him the greatest mind of the Middle Ages. I know that many people are now resorting to Thomas Aquinas, being moved deeply by how relevant he is for the present time.

But this will not be of much interest to you right now, because you will probably be occupied with work and plans. It is quite incomprehensible to me that they will not let you come here. For a few days, at least. But maybe you will show up here, suddenly, after all. That is the only thing keeping me from coming to you: the chance we should miss each other en route, or that you are not in Alswede but in Göttingen or Hamburg. Otherwise, I am so very anxious, and as soon as Waltraut is back from her break, it will become mighty difficult to stay put. Right now it is not feasible, for it would be altogether too much for Marlene alone.

I am terribly happy to have the children here now, even if at times it becomes too much. The rations for children have again been reduced, and they could not live on what they have been allotted. But here we are now doing quite well, and we are not starving. Marlene even goes above and beyond in feeding me, thinking you would be shocked if you saw me like the night owl I am. But I believe it will improve with time. . . .

Now it has become a long letter conversation, and all it says is that we all wish you could come here. Be well, my love! Yours, Li.

Werner to Elisabeth

[Alswede], January 25
My dear Li!

Today came your first letter since my stay here; it was such a great joy. Your letter was dated the 18th, apparently, you had written me once before but that one has not arrived yet. What you write about the children was really exciting for me; basically, among everything the children can learn at this time, music and skiing are most important, in my opinion. Both of which, it seems, get plenty of practice time, and your letter makes it sound as if they are also making real progress. That they can already read in bed after dinner! That must indicate that they no longer have any difficulty reading. You write nothing about food and money issues; I conclude that you must not have all too many worries, but you should report more in detail sometime. . . .

You ask whether we had any choice about staying in Germany or going to America. I do not believe that they wanted our entire group over there; but Hahn and I were asked semiofficially: Goudsmith asked me right at the first "interrogation" in Heidelberg whether I wanted to go to America, and Blackett, in England, reiterated the question later on. I had already pondered it very thoroughly before and arrived at the following position: it is completely clear to me that in the next decades America will be the center of scientific life, and that working conditions for me in Germany will be much worse than over there. Exactly because of this, on the other hand, I am not needed there as much: many excellent, competent physicists are there. Here, however, it matters a great deal that an intellectual life should again become viable. Since 1933 it has been clear to me that here a terrible tragedy for Germany was in progress, only I could not have imagined the extent and the ending; and I stayed here at the time so that I might also be here afterward and help. This was exactly what I also told my American friends in the summer of 1939, and the best among them could understand it; this intention remains firm and will not be betrayed. Goudsmith understood it and thought it also quite correct. The war, from an American point of view, would actually have been totally senseless if we did not succeed in connecting central Europe again with the intellectual tradition of the last two thousand years; had it only been about destruction, one could easily have left that to Hitler. At any rate, no American could seriously claim that Germany had been a threat to America, or that a Hitler Europe was more dangerous, in terms of power, than a Eurasian continent under the political leadership of Russia. So the deeper reason for the war was surely the danger of a break with Western culture, and in this sense, the Americans also must prefer that there are still people who want to foster this kind of thinking in Germany, instead of everyone leaving Europe to emigrate to the west. I believe I know that a man like Roosevelt quite understood these kinds of deliberations, but

Werner and Elisabeth in Göttingen after the war

the current American politics are opaque for me, and some of the things I hear from the American sector appear unsure and contradictory. Occasionally, I hear voices now that the Americans intend to leave Europe again and, what almost amounts to the same thing, to let it become part of the Russian

Empire. If that is so, then of course the question whether one should stay here appears in a whole new light. But I cannot imagine at this moment that American politics will actually develop in that direction.—Our children, naturally, should have the opportunity later on to go out into the world and find a home where they think is best. We must, through our work, endeavor to create this free choice for them later on. The children also should learn many foreign languages. I myself am, at any rate, going to try to help here in the reconstruction, and if the partisanship of politicians does not interfere too much, it should be possible to reawaken some of the active intellectual life of the 1920s. . . . One must simply accept that, in many ways, it would be nicer and more comfortable to live in America. . . .

So I am now very tired, it is late, and I took a long walk this morning. Thank you again so very, very much for your letter. It was wonderful that you wrote and told me so much about the children.

All my best, and say hello to the children! Yours, Werner.

Werner to Elisabeth

Göttingen, February 15
My dear Li,
Even though only a day has passed since your departure, I will write to you so that you do not have to wait so long for a letter. The time in Alswede was so especially nice, a good beginning for our future life together, and I am so grateful that they let us have these fourteen days. Hopefully, it will not take too long before I get your report on the children.

Here in Göttingen, I relish the "being busy" part. I have lived so much all for myself ever since the end of the war that it is good to see new people again, make plans, and participate in the battle of life through negotiations and conversations. Our relocation to the AVA will take place in about ten days, until then I shall relish the full pots of meat on Nikolausberger Way. Tonight I will participate in the first colloquium, and it will not take all too long before I start with lectures and talks again. I have always believed that I am lazy by nature, but am finding out now that after such a long break, work is giving me pleasure.— . . .

Just now, I hear that I have to go down to the British. So be well, and write soon! Yours, Werner.

Werner to Elisabeth

Göttingen, February 22
My dear Li!

The startup into Göttingen daily life has been more difficult than I thought at first; for one, being alone after your departure was naturally more difficult than before your visit—and second, I have been quite horribly sick from a first vaccination against typhoid fever; on Tuesday and Wednesday I had a rather high fever and toward Wednesday night could move some limbs only with great effort. Since one knew that the thing would correct itself, one could keep oneself calm, to a point, but I do hope that the follow-up vaccinations will not have the same effect. . . . Last night Hahn and I went to the theater together; *The Abduction from the Seraglio* was on the program. That was, of course, a great pleasure; the theater now is much better than before the war, since actors and singers from much bigger opera houses have fled to Göttingen. I deem the *Abduction* not yet quite as good as *Figaro* and *Don Giovanni,* but it simply is wonderful music, all the same, from beginning to end. A small section of the theater is reserved for the British military, but there also are many Germans at the invitation of the British. And the British are always tactfully reserved. I only was surprised when, in accordance with British custom, they played the anthem "God Save the King" before the performance, with everybody getting up. I did not find it unusual at all, but unconsciously waited after the last measure for the ensuing "Die Fahne Hoch" [Raise the Flag], etc. I would like to know how my good Göttingen compatriots are feeling about it; a few would probably welcome it if they could count themselves as subjects of the British king, who would then, like a good Führer, take care of them. But maybe it is not all that bad when the world appears so simple to people.— . . . Overall, my impression now, over and over, is that everything is going very slowly, but eventually it will turn out quite well. Both of us will just have to have patience. And you must take care of your health, right? Do not overwork yourself! Greetings to the children, I will soon write to them again. Yours, Werner.

Werner to Elisabeth

Göttingen, February 28
My dear Li!

In my thoughts I am so much with you; I do not know if you can sense it, and I am longing for your first letter from Urfeld. Not that I have real concerns, at least not consciously; but when I heard today that Irmgard Schumacher wanted to talk to me urgently, it really scared me at first, and I was relieved to find out on the phone that it was about some harmless matters. Apparently, in the unconscious mind, a certain latent uneasiness has remained, caused by the events of last summer and the difficulties of keeping contact via the mail service. . . .

Well, here in Göttingen things are limping along, more or less. Our rooms in the AVA, at this point, are ugly, some basic office space devoid of any hint of warmth, but useful enough as temporary campsites in the crusade of life. I also am almost never losing my courage, although the troubles appear bigger the closer they come. What our future will look like in all its reality, I cannot yet tell at all. In spite of it, I have the clear sense that it will not really be all that bad, if only we are patient. What happens here, on a small scale, is simply one segment of that grand game that has been played for several thousands of years: The battle between mind and brutal force. And everywhere in the world, the purely human powers are getting stronger, and I sometimes almost can sense it viscerally that the fury of the demons is losing strength. These are such general sentences, which may simply mean that an undefinable place within me believes firmly in the future. You too must do that, and stay patient, and then we must firmly unite. . . .

All my best, my love, stay healthy and say hello to the children! Yours, Werner.

Werner to Elisabeth

Göttingen, March 10
My dear Li!

Today was a rather nice day. I was invited on a ski tour to the Harz by our commanding officer. I borrowed some pants from Becker, a colleague, the sweater from Hahn, the skis from British officers. So we left by car at 9 o'clock for Altenau, located some twelve kilometers west of the Brocken at an altitude of five hundred meters. The Russian border runs straight along this side of the Brocken summit from north to south.

There was much snow in Altenau, and it was foggy and warm. We then ascended the Bruchberg, not quite as high as the Brocken; shortly before the summit, we broke through the fog, everything above was clear and there was even a bit of sunshine. And then one could see all the places we have known so well from earlier times: The summit of the Brocken, which looked like a medieval fortress with all its towers and houses, the angled top of the Achtermann, which I had climbed back then with Ernst, and below the *Oderteich*, so familiar to me from ski excursions twenty-five years ago. But the most beautiful were actually the snow-covered trees and the whole snowy mountain expanse. It is truly astounding how deeply the environment in which you have grown up matters; this first ski tour in the new life has touched me very poignantly; a few times I became so homesick for my Bavarian mountains that I was very close to tears and barely could talk with my nice companion. I have pondered again whether we should go to Munich or Göttingen. Perhaps both of these might be options, obtainable with great efforts. If I decline Munich definitively, it would probably mean that I will never again live in my real home. But do I have the right to wish it, when your own home is further north, and you would probably be happier here? . . .

I have also been fighting courageously for your rations; there seem to be people who are supposed to use the curbing of rations as leverage to move you out of Urfeld as soon as possible, most likely here into something "provisional"; in other words, more like a refugee camp. I am now quite optimistic, though. The day after tomorrow the decisive negotiations about it will be taking place in Frankfurt, and I believe that you will still keep getting extra rations for some time. . . . Greetings to the children and stay healthy! Yours, Werner.

Werner to Elisabeth

[Göttingen], March 20
My dear Li!

Today I will answer your worried letter from the 10th at great length. . . . As expected, on March 12 an officer was in Frankfurt and succeeded in keeping your improved rations coming. I hope that this order has penetrated to the lower levels, so that you are now getting more again. . . . No sooner did I think this worry was resolved when a second one cropped up: my place in Hechingen was emptied out on official orders, my grand piano taken. . . . There too I have begun taking several decisive steps but, especially in the French zone, everything is very complicated. You can imagine that this hit me hard. I am still hoping that we can retrieve the bulk. The third hit was the imminent reduction in pay; initially, it appeared as if I would only get half of the previous sum. Meanwhile it appears somewhat more favorable, except it means a great deal of aggravation and doing battle in the matter. So these were the bad Jobian news of the day, and I was actually rather "down" while this was ongoing. At least, I think I have done everything possible now. . . .

I only know about the father v. Weizsäcker that he is living in Rome and that the pope is apparently safeguarding him with his protection. I do not believe that much will happen to him, especially with Henderson having praised him so much. It is kind of sad to see how many decent people are now thrown together in the same lot as the worst Nazi criminals; my opinion in this is that foreign countries are likely subject to misidentifying people, whereas from the German side there is ill will involved sometimes. In Berlin every Pg [Nazi Party member] supposedly is allowed to enter the KPD [Communist Party of East Germany], thereby getting "cleansed in character." It probably is not exactly like this, but also not completely different,

either. "Wanderer, against such malady you be a struggler—whirling wind
and excrement—let those turn and sputter" as the author of the *Götz v.
Berlichingen* so aptly put it.—

What you write about the health of the children and your own makes me
very concerned. But I am unable to help at all from here, unfortunately. . . .
Here, by the way, I am getting a "heavy-duty worker's" supplement and am
sufficiently nourished; do not worry!—Have you found a possible renter for
the Urfeld house yet? Now I will end, the letter is so full of factual things
that I am appalled.

Sometime in two or three weeks I will be with you all! Yours, Werner.

Elisabeth to Werner

[Urfeld], March 30
My love!

This will be the last letter before you come! And I will mail it express so
that you will get it at all.

I have thought a great deal about your long letter, particularly since the
new tax regulation has come out. One knew already that it would be incredibly tight, and we will have to discuss everything very carefully. Our
greatest luxury is Waltraut. And her contribution is not equal to what she is
getting. If we knew that Marlene will be staying on with us, we would have
to make some kind of change. It would mean 100 marks savings per month.
That does make a difference.

Yes, it is a very sad story about our furniture. I cannot really imagine
that we should not get it back, though. If it actually were to work out with
the Sommerfeld house, you, that would be truly wonderful. Then everything
might probably happen very fast. But have you really decided now what you
want? To me it seems quite reasonable to start in Göttingen for now, and
decide more later on. I believe if you could now see life in Munich for
yourself, you would also think so. . . .

How will it be, I wonder, when we live together again? I am pondering
that a lot. And I think I will probably have to pull myself together quite a bit,

for I have not had to be accountable to anyone for my being. And I am now as nervous and labile as I was as a young girl. You will not be impatient with me, right? But now I have to quickly get up. . . .

See you soon! We all are full of anticipation and joy. Yours, Li.

Werner to Elisabeth

Göttingen, May 17

My dear Li,

Today I am in bed and am playing a little at being sick. I must have a slight case of the flu, but I think I can work again tomorrow, so no grounds for worry at all. On the contrary, I relish the quiet of being alone and not having to negotiate things, and therefore I can write you a long letter. Your letter from the 12th just arrived, how nice that the mail is now faster. I have a bad conscience that I have disturbed you with my letter, and that you now are under the impression that we would move here suddenly. I myself have succumbed to the pressure of the high officials who give orders intermittently that the Hechingen transport and the move had to take place within a few weeks. In reality, the things they command are plain impossible, but soldiers never want to acknowledge this. At any rate, the impossibility was fortunately never our own fault, so far. The permission from the French to let the transport out of Hechingen has not been given. Only when it is given can the order to "crank up" everything be given; you then will receive a telegram to go to Hechingen, where you will have to pack up, and eventually arrive here. Then we will furnish the house we do not have as of yet, and only then can your relocation be organized. In other words, I think it is impossible that the relocation will take place before early July, and it would not surprise me if it turns out to be at the end of August or September. Even the decision which of the Urfeld things will come along can only be made when we have our furniture here in the house: for then we know what is needed.

In terms of our housing, in about eight to fourteen days the state of affairs may be ripe for the military to realize how enormous the difficulties are. For soldiers it always suffices to get an order, then they will have a house, empty or furnished, depending on one's wishes. How often a few people take their own lives in the process is of no interest. The soldier only looks at how easy it is to get a house and how comfortable the inside is. To me such a procedure is unacceptable; I can only take the house as long as the owners or renters agree. From this point of view the house of Sommerfeld is a singularly suitable prospect. In the meantime, some other houses have been proposed, so that I must, as soon as possible, go to the expelled German families and talk with them. At Nikolausbergerweg 20 it went, as expected, awry; next will be Rohnsweg 21 where, earlier, Walter Weigmann was living. Where his wife and children are now living, I will have to find out first. That I would, via the armed powers, take away the housing for this family in their utter need is, of course, out of the question anyway. It would be different if I could help out the Weigmanns this way. In spite of all these complications, which will probably persist for a long time, you must not become pessimistic and think that we would not get anything suitable here. In the end, I will manage a good outcome. . . .

I am most concerned about food; the British zone is apparently the most drastically affected area in Germany, due to its industrial concentration. In this respect, we have been very unlucky; but I am trying to get help through Uncle Karl and the Bohrs. There also is a certain hope that we may get our car back, which would, of course, make things easier in many respects. . . .

For the day after tomorrow, I have a ticket to the opera *Martha*. I will enjoy hearing it, since I never heard the hit parade numbers from Grand-father's days. Hahn would often sing: "Martha, Martha, you have vanished— and with you my wallet!" But perhaps the opera is better than its "velvet upholstery reputation." The book Erich Kuby had lent me, an American novel, was rather awful, in my opinion. That kind of tired, pessimistic attitude of the modern intellectual toward life is so totally alien to me. Basically, I always come back to being happy about this life, particularly ever since you have belonged with me, and the children too; and even the sur-rounding immense tragedy, as I am finding in myself, did not change anything in this harmonious core. I am glad that you have read my "philoso-phy" and that it has meaning for you. It really does no harm to keep it between us, for the time being.

Love, be calm in Urfeld and do not worry too much about the future. The Hechingen transport will bring you here, alright? Be well, and say hello to the children. Yours, Werner.

Elisabeth to Werner

[Urfeld, May 26?]
My love,
Just before Sunday comes to an end, you should get a note. I have written so many letters, reduced the mountain of letters I owe, but now I will just indulge in the joy of chatting with you a little.

Tomorrow will be a good day: I am looking forward to it because there is bound to be a letter from you. The last one was dated ten days ago, that is a long while. Perhaps you are up again and pretty much feeling fine? Love, can you come here this summer? But you yourself will not know all this and be faced with a huge mountain you must scrape at with a teaspoon. Oh, it is altogether dreadful.

. . . Woi and I are now playing the trio sonatas by Corelli quite decently. But he is terribly unmotivated and unhappy. It really is time to get to Göttingen. Jochen also is so unmotivated and lazy. He simply does not want to play the recorder, and I want to ask you if I should just give it up or force him? . . . Perhaps one should not torture him anymore until he can begin with the cello, but let him now sing and tumble and spend time with a carpenter. It just does not work anymore.

Love, this morning I found something, you surely know it—that would lend itself perfectly to be the maxim for your "philosophy": "Im Namen dessen, der sich selbst erschuf von Ewigkeit in schaffendem Beruf" [In the name of Him who—being the creator—from eternity also created Himself]. I think it touches so much on what you are after, and—do not laugh, now—I find the idea that God has created himself is very much related to Einstein's idea of eternity always returning into itself—do not think me ridiculous, love! It moved me all day long, and I thought I ought to just write it to you.

Faithful little Ria must have written you another letter. She is a dear little chap and by no means my great concern anymore. She is developing so dearly that she is becoming almost the closest to me of all the children. Now farewell and good night. It is past midnight. May God protect you. Yours, Li.

Werner to Elisabeth

[Göttingen], Pentecost Sunday evening
My dear Li!

Before the day ends, I want to chat with you a little. Outside we have a real, warm summer night.

I have just been walking home from an invitation at the other end of Göttingen, between all the gardens and in the moonlight. Well, love, things with me are not quite right, I am very displeased with myself, but really do not know anymore what to do about it. . . . Why that is I do not know, I am likely completely healthy, but always tired to the point of exhaustion. Hunger must be a big part of it; but with the gifts from Fritz I am better off now, and it surely is not merely the hunger; I just cannot quite cope anymore with the constant organizational buzz and the many disappointments. I tell myself every day that it just has to be done, because so much of what I am doing determines our future and, actually, during negotiations, I seem to be still quite energetic. But inside, I cannot quite keep going anymore. When you get here, it will likely improve, because then at least you can encourage me and bring with you hopes and desires. It would be essential now not to be always totally by oneself, but as of yet Göttingen is completely dead to me. I have a bad conscience to write you all this because it will worry you. But when I pretend that everything is fine, you will be alert to what is said between the lines, and you will think I am distanced from you. But all in all, I will just have to wait for you to come here, and it is, in practical terms, right to first go to Hechingen and then come here. Until then I will do what I can within my power.

I have begun a little with the scientific work at the institute, at least with respect to organizing colloquia. In addition, we continue getting the building ready and to acquire machinery and apparatuses.— . . .

So, love, do not be too unhappy with me when I am tired out; it will certainly be better when you are here, and when I get more to eat again. . . .

Be well, and say hello to the children for me! Yours, Werner.

Elisabeth to Werner

[Urfeld], May 29

My love!

It has become all quiet around me; only outside the wind is rustling in the trees. I have been playing piano until now, and am sitting at the open window now, thinking a lot about you—full of dread and concern, my love. When your letters come only so sporadically and are then so tired and distant, I want to be near you in all the peace and quiet you need, and then I want to build a containing wall around you from all the love I have in my heart. You should see me now, and know me, as I am so calm, secure, and feeling rich and strong. But I am not like this with you as of yet—I can only hope from the bottom of my heart that I learn to be this way when we are together—to your benefit and mine.

I am not impatient about the house, love. Just that I am thinking of you with concern, how you are struggling and have no joy. I relish every day I have here. And on a beautiful day the magnificence of the mountains, the fragrance of blossoms and the earth, this sun-drenched wind, appear like a gift from heaven, and I realize that I will probably never again have it so good. I have no problems, and my heart has also returned to being calm and peaceful. When I leave here, it will be as if I were leaving firm ground and were to venture onto the vast ocean. And yet I want to be with you in hopes that you will find happiness also with your wife—not only the children. And then I want to calm down my heart and tell myself: it is enough that you are now back home with me—anything beyond that is good fortune—but in and of itself this is so much that one can be calm and contented.—Well, this cricket-chirping summer night is awakening a lot of thoughts!

Today Mr. Steiniger was here, sent by Ilse Roth. He is an actor in the Kammerspiele [theater] and searching for a house for his parents, his sister, and her two children. He made a very nice impression, and I referred him to you. He will get in touch with you. It would be good and convenient if something came of it. . . .

Be well. And do not let it get you down!—Yours, Li.

Werner to Elisabeth

Göttingen, May 31

My dear Li,

Today two of your letters arrived, one took eight days, the other four; how nice that the mail is now faster.— . . . I often reflect here in my emotional outpost on the future condition of our family life; what strikes me is that in this one respect, I am always optimistic, which is a really good sign. Woi and I will always get along very well, precisely because he is so much like you, and with Jochen probably also. That you are now getting so friendly with Maria makes me especially glad. In the meantime, our prospects for a house are rapidly increasing; but I will only tell you more once I am completely certain which one it will be. . . . I was also very happy about your increasing attachment to Urfeld. Then you also will ensure that we can keep it and, down the road, spend our summers there too. It will most likely be possible.—I am very much looking forward to your arrival, although it means that at first you too will bear some of the burdensome concerns

The postwar home at Merkelstrasse 18 in Göttingen

here; but perhaps you will then also enjoy all that we will establish here together. All my best, and say hello to the children! Yours, Werner.

Werner to Elisabeth

Göttingen, June 5
My dear Li!

So that you may get a better impression of my Göttingen plans, I am enclosing a picture of the house we are probably getting. The owners gave it to me today, it was probably taken ten years ago; by now the house does not look quite as whitewashed as back then. The yard reaches down to the lower of the two rows of hedges; it is now much more densely grown in, also the upper hedge is now so high that it almost completely separates the garden. In the lower half you find the vegetables and the berries; we are getting half of this year's fruit harvest. On the ground floor there are, aside from the kitchen, three larger rooms and a nice, spacious verandah; on the first floor five small rooms, very useful for "dividing" the children, and above, under the eaves, two or three more rooms.

The main entrance to the house is on the right, not quite visible in the picture, behind it is the garage. The rent will be 250 marks; it will not be easy to come up with that, since the taxes on our relatively high income are enormous. But finances can be discussed later on in greater detail. . . .

Wednesday evening

In the meantime I have been out walking, along the Leine River to a large gravel pit, filled with water and used by swimmers and boats nowadays. You know, somehow I will get used to Göttingen and make my peace here. I see that this fertile land is in some ways more alive than our rocks, and the people are much less self-centered and obstinate than our Bavarian farmers. But I have the occasional bout of homesickness. I think of the immaculate beauty of the view from our terrace, and I would have loved to live up there through all the seasons of spring, summer, and autumn. You know the kind of October day when behind the pass a fog is rising up, and the lake shimmers in all the marvelous colors so common to the Italian lakes.

But one cannot have everything; I must, after all, do my work, and in Göttingen too we will be better off than most other people. And possibly we can get Urfeld back for ourselves in a few years. By the way, you can deal with Mr. Steiniger completely on your own, knowing everything as well as I do. . . . So, we soon will have a good reunion here! Yours, Werner.

Elisabeth to Werner

On the train, June 11
My love!

Today I got your letter with the picture of the house. It is really extremely promising! It surpasses all expectations. The Sommerfeld house cannot possibly be any nicer. Will I soon get the notice that I should set out? Ever since your letter came today, I have calmed down a little and no longer feel that I am missing something. . . . Is this house a definite deal? You have not written anything about the owners. I have a terrible fear that it will yet come to naught, not so much that we will not get it—it is to me still too good to be true—but because you would be so awfully disappointed. But I want to be totally optimistic and start taking the house wholly in possession within myself. Have you already considered how you want to allocate the rooms? And that garden, that fruit! It really is unbelievable! And you are bound to become fond of it later on. You know, I am gradually getting used to the thought that eventually we will end up in Munich, but now you yourself would not be happy there. Our house is confiscated, and Munich is dead and desolate, especially if one has loved it like you have. But later on—I kind of know that we will get there and then you will have your mountains back again also. Perhaps our little house will not be lost to us for all that long. And my heart's desire would be that you will come with me from Göttingen back to Urfeld and stay with us for about four weeks up there before we take on the relocation together. Is that not a possibility? . . . But now, be well, my dear heart. I am looking forward to you and I hope this is now the last letter.

Yours, Li.

New and better times have begun: Maria, Jochen, Barbara,
Christine, Martin, and Wolfgang

TIMELINE

1901 Werner Heisenberg born in Würzburg on December 5

1904 Elisabeth Schumacher born in Berlin on July 4

1920 Werner begins his studies with Arnold Sommerfeld at the Ludwig Maximilian University in Munich

1922 Werner first meets Niels Bohr during a lecture series in Göttingen; in the fall, continues his studies with Max Born in Göttingen

1923 Werner earns PhD from Ludwig Maximilian University

1924 Werner earns his habilitation (*venia legendi*, a qualification for teaching at universities) in Göttingen

1924–26 Werner receives Rockefeller stipend; assistant to Niels Bohr in Copenhagen

1925 Werner formulates quantum (matrix) mechanics while on Heligoland

1927 Werner formulates the uncertainty principle.

1927 Werner becomes professor of theoretical physics at University of Leipzig

1933 Werner wins Nobel Prize for Physics, retroactive for 1932

1937 Werner and Elisabeth first meet and wed

1938 Wolfgang and Maria born in Leipzig

1939 Jochen born in Leipzig; Werner travels to the United States

1940 Martin born in Munich

1941 Werner travels to Copenhagen and has conversations with Niels Bohr

1942 Barbara born in Leipzig; Werner becomes director of the Kaiser Wilhelm Institute of Physics in Berlin and continues as professor at the University of Leipzig

1943 Part of the Berlin institute moves to Hechingen/Haigerloch in the Swabian Alb; Heisenbergs move from Leipzig to Urfeld

1944 Christine born in Pähl at the Ammersee; Werner travels to Copenhagen

1945 Werner interned in England

1946 The institute in Göttingen is rebuilt, named Max Planck Institute

1950 Verena born in Göttingen

1953 Werner becomes president of the reestablished Alexander von Humboldt Foundation

1958 Werner becomes director of the Max Planck Institute in Munich; the family moves to Munich

1970 Werner retires

1976 Werner dies on February 1 in Munich

1998 Elisabeth dies on February 27 in Göttingen

NAME INDEX

HESS, RUDOLF, deputy of Adolf Hitler since 1933,   145

HETZER, THEODOR, professor of art history at Leipzig University,   131

HIBY, JUSTUS WALTER, physicist, W.H.'s coworker at the "Uranium Club" in
    Hechingen,   201, 206, 219

HIRSCHBERG, gynecologist in Leipzig,   106, 107

HOFFMANN, GERHARD, professor of experimental physics at Leipzig Univer-
    sity,   184, 198

HÖRHAGEN, DR., surgeon in Leipzig,   59, 60

HUBER, colleague of Heimpel at Strasbourg University,   231

HUND, FRIEDRICH, professor of mathematical physics at Leipzig University and
    close colleague of W.H.,   205, 208

JACOBI, ERWIN, professor of public law, canonical law, and workers' rights law at
    Leipzig University, also musician friend (violin) of W.H.,   4, 49, 60, 69,
    70, 171, 173, 179, 224, 282

JAEGER, WOLFGANG, professor of ophthalmology in Heidelberg and family
    friend,   156, 187, 268, 271

JENSEN, J. HANS D., professor of physics at Heidelberg University, member of
    the "Uranium club," Nobel Laureate,   140, 281

KEMBLE, EDWIN, American physicist and member of the Alsos Mission,   265

KIENLE, HANS, professor of astrophysics at Berlin University, later at Heidelberg
    University,   114, 170

KNOLL, JOSEF, professor of agriculture and plant propagation at Leipzig
    University,   198

KRESS, HILDEGARD, painter,   53

KRIEGER, WALTRAUT, the Heisenbergs' nanny,   197, 198, 201, 214, 232, 247,
    256, 263, 269, 271, 278, 281, 283, 285, 293

KUBY, ERICH, journalist, married to Edith, E.H.'s older sister,   31, 103, 295

LAUE, MAX VON, physicist and Nobel Laureate,   219, 252

LENARD, PHILIPP, physicist and Nobel Laureate, proponent of "German
    physics,"   3, 175

LEY, ROBERT, high-ranking Nazi politician,   188